Third Edition
Solutions

Elementary

Student's Book

Falla   Paul A Davies

OXFORD
UNIVERSITY PRESS

I

Introduction

Personal information

I can exchange basic personal information.

1 Complete the questions in the dialogue with the phrases below.

are you from   do you spell   old are you   your name

Woman	Hello. Welcome to Europa Language School!
Kadir	Thank you!
Woman	What's ¹_____?
Kadir	Kadir Demir.
Woman	How ²_____ that?
Kadir	K-A-D-I-R, Kadir. D-E-M-I-R, Demir.
Woman	Thank you. Where ³_____?
Kadir	I'm from Turkey.
Woman	And how ⁴_____, Kadir?
Kadir	I'm eighteen.
Woman	Great! Thank you. You're in room 53.
Kadir	Thanks. See you later!

2 🎧 **1.02** Listen and check your answers. Then listen and repeat the dialogue.

3 🎧 **1.03** Listen and repeat the alphabet. What sound do the blue letters share?

abcdefghijklmnopqrstuvwxyz

4 Now put the red letters into the correct category below, depending on the sound they share.

1 b, c, …
2 f, l, …

5 SPEAKING Work in groups or as a class. Think of a famous person and start spelling his or her name. Who can guess the person first?

T-A-Y-...   Taylor Swift!

6 🎧 **1.04** VOCABULARY Listen and repeat the numbers (1–50). Then say the numbers backwards (50–1) around the class.

50   49   48   47

➡ **Vocabulary Builder** Numbers and ordinals: page 117

7 🎧 **1.05** Listen to two dialogues. Complete the table with the names and ages of the four speakers.

Name	Age
1 Antoine	
2	
3	
4	

8 🎧 **1.05** VOCABULARY Which country are the students in exercise 7 from? Listen again and match them with countries from the list below.

Countries Argentina Australia Brazil Canada China Croatia the Czech Republic Egypt France Germany Greece Hungary India Italy Japan Mexico Poland Russia Slovakia Spain Turkey the UK Ukraine the US

Antoine is from France.

9 SPEAKING Work in pairs. Test your partner's spelling of the countries in exercise 8.

How do you spell 'Spain'?   S-P-A-I-N. How do you spell … ?

10 Answer the questions about the countries in exercise 8.
1 Which are in Europe?
2 Which are in Asia?
3 Which are in North and South America?
4 Which are English-speaking countries?
5 Which are near your own country?

11 Work in pairs. Invent a new identity for yourself. Choose a new name, a new nationality and a different age.

12 SPEAKING Work in pairs. Find out your partner's information. Ask and answer questions from the dialogue exercise 1.

What's your name?   It's …

How do you spell that?

be and *have got*

I can use be *and* have got.

1 🎧 **1.06** Read and listen to the dialogue. How old is Joanna's sister?

Max Have you got a brother?

Joanna No, I haven't. But I've got a sister. Here's a photo of us. I'm on the right.

Max Are you twins?

Joanna Yes, we are, but we aren't identical. Emma's got black hair, like me, but she hasn't got brown eyes.

Max Is that your dog in the photo?

Joanna Yes, it is. She's called Rosie. Rosie is Emma's dog, really.

Max How old is she?

Joanna She's sixteen, of course.

Max That's very old for a dog!

Joanna No, Emma's sixteen. Rosie is six.

2 Find all the examples of *be* in the dialogue in exercise 1. Complete the Learn this! box. Use short forms.

> **LEARN THIS!** *be*
>
> | **Affirmative** | **Negative** |
> |---|---|
> | I ¹_____ | I'm not |
> | he / she / it ²_____ | he / she / it isn't |
> | you / we / they are | you / we / they ³_____ |
> | **Interrogative** | **Short answers** |
> | am I? | Yes, I am. / No, I'm not. |
> | ⁴_____ he / she / it? | Yes, he / she / it ⁶_____. |
> | | No, he / she / it isn't. |
> | ⁵_____ you / we / they? | Yes, you / we / they ⁷_____. |
> | | No, you / we / they aren't. |

3 Write two sentences with the verb *be*, one affirmative and one negative. Which is true for you? Which is false? Write T or F.

1 We _____ at school.
  We are at school. T   We aren't at school. F
2 My teacher _____ very tall.
3 I _____ 16 years old.
4 My friends _____ all girls.
5 It _____ very cold today.
6 My friends and I _____ in an English lesson.

4 **SPEAKING** Complete the questions with the correct form of the verb *be*. Then ask and answer the questions in pairs.

1 _____ you hungry?
2 _____ our teacher male?
3 _____ we at school?
4 _____ your friends all at this school?
5 _____ you eighteen years old?
6 _____ I from the UK?

> Are you hungry?   Yes, I am. / No, I'm not.

➡ Grammar Builder 1B page 122

5 Complete the Learn this! box. Use short forms. Use the dialogue in exercise 1 to help you. What are the long forms?

> **LEARN THIS!** *have got*
>
> We use *have got* to talk about possessions and family members.
>
> **Affirmative**
> I / you / we / they ¹_____ got
> he / she / it ²_____ got
>
> **Negative**
> I / you / we / they haven't got
> he / she / it ³_____ got
>
> **Interrogative**
> ⁴_____ I / you / we / they got?
> Has he / she / it got?
>
> **Short answers**
> Yes, I have. / No, I ⁵_____ .
> Yes, he / she / it has. No, he / she / it hasn't.
> Yes, you / we / they have. No, you / we / they haven't.

6 Complete the sentences with the correct form of *have got*, affirmative or negative. Make them true for you.

1 I _____ two brothers.
2 We _____ a maths lesson next.
3 Our teacher _____ short hair.
4 I _____ blue eyes.
5 Our teachers _____ a big teachers' room.

7 🎧 **1.07** Listen. Tick the things that Joe and Amy have got.

	Joe	Amy	You	Your partner
a pet				
a skateboard				
a bike				
a smartphone				
a laptop				
a watch				

8 Write sentences about Joe using the information in the table in exercise 7. Use the correct form of *have got*.

Joe's got … .   He hasn't got … .

9 **SPEAKING** Complete the column for you in exercise 7. Then ask and answer in pairs and complete the column for your partner.

> Have you got … ?

10 **SPEAKING** Tell the class about your partner.

> Marianne hasn't got a pet.

➡ Grammar Builder 1B page 122

Talking about ability and asking for permission

I can talk about ability and ask for permission.

1 🎧 **1.08** Read and listen to the dialogue. What is Alfie's opinion of the girl in the photo? What is Rose's opinion?

Alfie Let's stop and listen. This is a great song.
Rose Hmm. She isn't very good. She can't sing.
Alfie She can play the guitar really well. And her voice isn't bad.
Rose I can't hear the words.
Alfie But she's really young. She's only fourteen or fifteen. Can you play the guitar like that?
Rose No, I can't. But I can play the piano. Come on, let's go.
Alfie No, wait.
Rose What's the problem?
Alfie I can't find my money. Can I borrow £1, please?
Rose For her? Really? Oh, OK.

2 Read the Learn this! box. Find an affirmative, negative and interrogative form of *can* in the dialogue in exercise 1.

LEARN THIS! *can*

a We use *can* to talk about ability.
b The form of *can* is the same for all persons (*I, you, he, she, we*, etc.).

  Affirmative: *I can play football.*
  Negative: *They can't hear you.*
  Interrogative: *Can you dance? Yes, I can. / No, I can't.*
c We also use *can* to ask for permission.
  Can I use your phone? Yes, you can. / No, you can't.
---

3 Complete the sentences about the dialogue in exercise 1. Use the affirmative or negative form of *can*.

1 The girl _____ play the guitar well.
2 Rose _____ hear the words of the song.
3 Rose _____ play the guitar.
4 Rose _____ play the piano.
5 Alfie _____ find his money.

4 **SPEAKING** Work in pairs. Ask permission to do the things below. Use *Can I ... ?*

borrow your pencil   use your dictionary   ask a question
share your book   copy your answer

> Can I borrow ... ?   Yes, you can. / No, you can't.

➠ Grammar Builder IC page 122

5 **VOCABULARY** Complete the list of musical instruments. The missing words are in the dialogue in exercise 1. Then check the meaning of all the words.

Instruments clarinet drums flute g_____
keyboard   p_____   saxophone trumpet violin

6 🎧 **1.09** Listen and identify the instruments.

1 clarinet
2 _____
3 _____
4 _____
5 _____
6 _____
7 _____

➠ Vocabulary Builder Musical instruments: page 117

7 **VOCABULARY** Check the meaning of the verbs below. Match four of them with pictures 1–4.

Action verbs dance   play basketball / football / tennis
play the drums / clarinet   ride a bike / a horse   skate
skateboard   sing   ski   speak Chinese / French / Spanish
swim

8 Write a questionnaire about ability for your partner. Write six questions with *can*. Choose verbs from exercise 7 and include one musical instrument from exercise 5.

1 *Can you play the violin?*
2 *Can you ... ?*

9 **SPEAKING** Work in pairs. Do your questionnaires. Make a note of your partner's answers.

> Can you play the violin?   No, I can't.

10 **SPEAKING** Tell the class about your partner.

> Mina can't play the violin. She can ...

Articles: *the*, *a / an*, *some*; *this / that / these / those*

I can use articles and this, that, these *and* those *correctly.*

1 VOCABULARY Match the pictures with eight of the words below. Check the meaning of all the words.

In the classroom bin blackboard calculator chair computer cupboard desk eraser exercise book interactive whiteboard pen pencil pencil case pencil sharpener ruler schoolbag shelf

2 🎧 1.10 Read and listen to the dialogue. Where is Olivia's pencil case?

Charlie Have you got a pencil and an eraser?

Olivia I've got a pencil, but I haven't got an eraser. The pencil is on my desk.

Charlie Thanks. Have you got a coloured pen?

Olivia No, but I've got some coloured pencils.

Charlie What colours?

Olivia Red, blue, green, brown – lots of colours. They're in my pencil case.

Charlie Is that your pencil case?

Olivia No. That's Jemma's. My pencil case is in my schoolbag. Hang on. ... Oh, no! It's at home. Sorry.

3 Read the Learn this! box. Underline all the examples of *a / an*, *some* and *the* in the dialogue in exercise 2.

LEARN THIS! Articles

a The definite article is *the*. We can use it with singular and plural nouns.
the chair   the books

b The indefinite article is *a*, or *an* if the noun begins with a vowel sound. We only use it with singular nouns.
a pen   an exam

c We can use *some* with plural nouns when we don't know, or we don't want to say, exactly how many.
I've got a pen and some pencils.

d We use *a / an* and *some* when we mention things for the first time.
I've got a skateboard and some rollerblades.

e We use *the* when we mention them again.
I've got a skateboard and some rollerblades. The skateboard is red and the rollerblades are blue.

4 SPEAKING Work in pairs. Ask and answer questions about the things in exercise 1. Use *a* or *an*.

> Have you got a pen in your schoolbag?

> Yes, I have. / No, I haven't.

> Have we got an interactive whiteboard in our classroom?

> Yes, we have. / No, we haven't.

➡ **Grammar Builder ID** page 122

5 Put *a*, *an* or *some* in front of the nouns.

1 _____ address
2 _____ pens
3 _____ old car
4 _____ dogs
5 _____ eye
6 _____ blue pencils
7 _____ rollerblades
8 _____ teachers
9 _____ cat
10 _____ photos
11 _____ watch
12 _____ skateboard

6 Complete the sentences with *a*, *an*, *some* or *the*.

1 I've got _____ red pen and _____ green pen. _____ red pen is on my desk. _____ green pen is in my pencil case.

2 We've got _____ exams next week. _____ first exam is maths, _____ second is history and _____ third is science.

3 My mum's got _____ orange Fiat and my dad's got _____ blue Renault. _____ Fiat is new, but _____ Renault is very old.

4 I've got _____ CDs and _____ DVDs, but I can't play _____ DVDs because my DVD player is broken.

5 We've got _____ cat, _____ dog and _____ mice. _____ cat's name is Sooty and _____ dog's name is Freddy.

LEARN THIS! *this / that / these / those*

We use *this* (singular) and *these* (plural) for things that are close to us, and *that* (singular) and *those* (plural) for things that are further away.

this chair   these books   that cat   those dogs

7 Read the Learn this! box. Find an example of *this*, *that*, *these* or *those* in the dialogue in exercise 2.

8 SPEAKING Work in pairs. Take turns to ask and answer questions about the pictures.

> Are these your coloured pencils?

> Yes, they are. Is this your ... ?

➡ **Grammar Builder ID** page 122

1

Family and friends

Unit map

● **Vocabulary**
Family members
Adjectives and prepositions
Housework
Describing people
Personality adjectives

● **Word Skills**
Singular and plural nouns

● **Grammar**
Present simple (affirmative)
Present simple (negative and interrogative)

● **Listening** Spelling and pronunciation

● **Reading** Sibling rivalry

● **Speaking** Describing people

● **Writing** A personal profile

● **Culture 1** The Royal Family

● **Vocabulary Builder** page 117
● **Grammar Builder** page 124
● **Grammar Reference** page 125

1A Vocabulary

Family
I can talk about family members.

1 🎧 **1.11** **VOCABULARY** Work in pairs. Put the family members below into three groups: a) female b) male c) male or female. Then listen and check.

Family members aunt brother child / children cousin daughter father (dad) grandchild / grandchildren granddaughter grandfather (grandad) grandmother (grandma) grandparent grandson husband mother (mum) nephew niece parent sister son uncle wife

---

LEARN THIS! Possessive 's

a We add 's to a name or noun to show possession or a family relationship.
my cousin's husband

b We just add an apostrophe (') to plural nouns ending in -s.
my parents' friends   (but his children's school)

---

2 Read the Learn this! box. Then complete the sentences, adding possessive 's and the correct family member.

1 Harry is Tom's son.
2 Martin is Tom _____.
3 Nathan and Rosie are Sophie _____.
4 Harry is Liz _____.
5 Lisa is Mia _____.
6 Clare and Liz are Jessica _____.
7 Poppy, Harry and Mia are Rosie _____.

➡ **Grammar Builder 1A** page 124

3 🎧 **1.12** Listen and check your answers to exercise 2.

4 Work in pairs. Write four more sentences like the ones in exercise 2.

> **LOOK OUT!**
>
> **a** We add **-in-law** for relationships from a marriage.
>
> *father-in-law = your husband's father / your wife's father*
>
> *brother-in-law = your sister's husband / your wife's brother*
>
> **b** We add **step** for relationships from a remarriage.
>
> *stepmother = your father's wife*
>
> *stepsister = your stepfather's daughter /*
> *your stepmother's daughter*
>
> **c** We add **great** to refer to the generation before.
>
> *great-grandfather = your mother's grandfather /*
> *your father's grandfather*
>
> *great-uncle = your mother's uncle / your father's uncle*

5 🎧 **1.13** Read the Look out! box. Then listen to a dialogue about Ella's family photo. Complete the sentence with the correct family member: a, b or c.

This family photo includes Ella's ...

a stepmother **b** great-grandmother **c** brother-in-law

> **RECYCLE!** *have got*
>
> We use *have got* to talk about possessions and family members.
>
> <u>I've got</u> three stepsisters. <u>Have you got</u> a brother?
>
> The third person singular form is *has got / hasn't got*.
>
> <u>She's got</u> two cousins. <u>He hasn't got</u> a sister.
>
> <u>Has he got</u> a stepsister? Yes, <u>he has</u>. / No, <u>he hasn't</u>.

6 Read the Recycle! box. Then complete the questions about Ella's family. Use the correct form of *have got*.

1 _____ Ella's grandfather _____ a sister?
2 _____ Ella's great-aunt _____ children?
3 _____ Ella's sister _____ a husband?
4 _____ Bruno and Maria _____ children?
5 _____ Ella _____ four nieces?
6 _____ Ella's parents _____ a son?

7 🎧 **1.13** Listen again. Answer the questions in exercise 6.

8 Complete the quiz with words from exercise 1. Then do the quiz in pairs.

Famous families

1

Who is this man? Is he Beyoncé's ...

a c _ _ _ _ _ ?
b h _ _ _ _ _ _ ?
c b _ _ _ _ _ _ ?

2

These girls have got a famous f _ _ _ _ _. Who is he?

a Will Smith
b Jay Z
c Barack Obama

3

What is the relationship between these two Hollywood stars – Jon Voight and Angelina Jolie?

a uncle and _ _ _ _ _
b father and _ _ _ _ _ _ _ _
c _ _ _ _ _ _ _ and wife

4

What relationship is this man to Queen Elizabeth II? Is he ...

a her s _ _ ?
b her n _ _ _ _ ?
c her g _ _ _ _ _ _ ?

9 **SPEAKING** Work in pairs. Find out if your partner has got ...

1 a stepbrother
2 cousins
3 a brother-in-law
4 a great-uncle
5 a great-grandmother
6 a step-grandfather

10 **SPEAKING** If the answer is 'yes', find out more information (for example, name and age).

> Have you got a stepbrother?

> Yes, I have.

> What's his name?

> How old is he?

1B Grammar

Present simple (affirmative)

I can use the present simple affirmative correctly.

1 Look at the photo below. Do you know this TV show? Can you name any of the characters?

2 Read the text. Then answer the questions.

1 Which characters in the show work together?
2 Which characters live together?
3 Can you name any other TV shows about friends?

The BiG BANG THEORY

is a TV comedy about a group of friends in Pasadena, California. Leonard and Sheldon are scientists. They work together and they share a flat too. Two other friends from work, Howard and Raj, often visit them. Penny lives opposite. She works in a restaurant. She likes Leonard and Sheldon, but they are very different from her. A lot of the humour comes from this contrast. It's a simple idea for a show, but millions of people watch and enjoy it every week. Clearly, people love shows about friends!

LEARN THIS! Present simple (affirmative)

We use the present simple to talk about:

a something that happens regularly, always or never.
b a fact that is always true.

3 Read the *Learn this!* box. Then complete the table below. The missing words are in the text in exercise 2.

Present simple	
affirmative	
I work.	We work.
You work.	You work.
He / She / It ¹_____.	They ²_____.

4 Find all the other examples of the present simple in the text in exercise 2. Which ones end in *-s*? Why?

5 Complete the sentences about *The Big Bang Theory*. Use the present simple affirmative form of the verbs below.

like live visit watch work

1 Millions of people _____ the show regularly.
2 Sheldon _____ in a flat with Leonard.
3 Raj and Howard _____ with Sheldon and Leonard.
4 Raj and Howard _____ Sheldon and Leonard regularly.
5 In general, people _____ shows about groups of friends.

LOOK OUT!

a Some verbs change spelling when you add *-s* for the third person singular form.

I go	*she go**es***
you watch	*he watch**es***
they study	*she stud**ies***

b The verb *have* is irregular.

we have	*it **has***

6 Read the *Look out!* box. Then complete the text with the present simple affirmative form of the verbs in brackets.

My stepsister Rose is a scientist and she ¹_____ (love) h job. She ²_____ (work) at a university in California – sh ³_____ (study) stars and black holes. Rose isn't Americ but she really ⁴_____ (like) her life in California. Every weekend, she ⁵_____ (go) to the beach. She ⁶_____ (meet) friends there and they ⁷_____ (go) surfing together. Rose ⁸_____ (share) an apartmer with one of her friends, Madison. Madison ⁹_____ (wc in a restaurant and she's often at work in the evening. On those evenings, Rose ¹⁰_____ (watch) DVDs in the apartment she ¹¹_____ (have) dinner with friends in town.

➡ **Grammar Builder 1B** page 124

7 🎧 **1.14** PRONUNCIATION Listen and repeat these third person singular verb forms. Pay attention to the sound of the endings.

A: /z/ or /s/ knows loves visits works
B: /ɪz/ finishes washes uses

8 🎧 **1.15** PRONUNCIATION Listen and repeat these third person singular verb forms. Do they have ending A or B?

comes dances goes likes lives shares
teaches watches

9 SPEAKING Work in pairs. Think of a TV show about a gro of friends or a family. Tell your partner three facts about the show. Use verbs from this lesson. Can your partner identify it?

The main characters are X and Y … They live in …

X loves school and she studies a lot. But Y …

1C
Listening
Spelling and pronunciation
I can distinguish between words with very similar sounds in them.

1 SPEAKING Look at the photo of the Radford family. What is the relationship between the people, do you think?

2 Read the text and answer the questions.

1 What is Noel's job?
2 How many people live in the Radford family home?

A DAY IN THE LIFE OF THE RADFORD FAMILY!

ue and Noel Radford live in a very big house in Morecambe the north of England. The house is big because they've got ineteen children! Their oldest child is 28, and the youngest just a baby.

The day starts at 4 a.m. when Noel, a baker, goes to ork. Two hours later, he comes home and he wakes up the hildren. Sue prepares breakfast and makes twelve packed nches! After breakfast, Noel takes the children to school in a minibus! Noel goes back to the bakery with his eldest aughter, Sophie. She works there too. Then Sue starts on the ousework. She loads the dishwasher, cleans the house and es the washing (nine times a day!). After lunch she goes to e supermarket and she does the ironing. When Noel gets me at 5 p.m., he cooks dinner and the children set the ble. After dinner, Sue helps the children with their homework. e day ends at 10 p.m. when all the children go to bed.

SPEAKING Would you like to have a very large family? Why? / Why not?

VOCABULARY Find seven of the housework activities below in the text in exercise 2.

Housework clean the house cook dinner
do the ironing do the washing go to the supermarket
load / unload the dishwasher set the table
tidy my bedroom wash the dishes

> **Listening Strategy 1**
> In English, you cannot always predict how a word sounds by looking at the spelling. Learning how words are pronounced will allow you to understand them when you hear them.

5 🎧 **1.16** Read Listening Strategy 1. Which red vowel sound in each group of words is different? Listen and check.

1 a school b too c look d cool
2 a grandson b class c father d grandma
3 a wife b China c Italy d like
4 a go b son c photo d hello
5 a eat b meat c seat d great
6 a university b uncle c mum d Hungary

> **Listening Strategy 2**
> Some words sound similar but have very different meanings. Being able to detect the small difference in pronunciation will help you to understand them when you hear them. Use the context to help you too.

6 🎧 **1.17** Read Listening Strategy 2. Then listen and repeat the words. Which word in each pair do you hear first? Pay attention to the different vowel sounds.

1 men man 3 far for 5 live leave
2 cap cup 4 wet wait 6 match March

7 🎧 **1.18** Listen. Which word from exercise 6 does each sentence include? Which other words help you decide?

8 🎧 **1.19** Listen to Ryan and Joanna talking about housework. Are the sentences true or false? Write T or F. Then correct the false ones.

1 Ryan thinks that his bedroom is tidy. ___
2 Joanna tidies her bedroom. ___
3 Ryan hasn't got time to tidy his bedroom every day. ___
4 Joanna's family shares the housework. ___
5 Joanna and Ryan like housework more than homework. ___
6 Joanna has got exams at the moment. ___

9 🎧 **1.20** Read these sentences from the conversation in exercise 8. How are the red sounds pronounced? Listen and check.

1 I tidy my bedroom.
2 My mum does the washing.
3 He's got exams at the moment.
4 He goes to the supermarket too.

10 SPEAKING Work in pairs. Tell your partner about housework in your home. Use phrases from exercise 4. Note down what your partner says.

> I tidy my bedroom and set the table.

> My dad cleans the house.

11 SPEAKING Tell the class about your partner.

> Zak tidies his bedroom and sets the table.

Present simple (negative and interrogative)

I can ask questions about facts and everyday events.

1 SPEAKING Look at the photo. Who are the people, do you think? What are they fighting over?

2 🎧 **1.21** Read and listen to the dialogue. Check your ideas from exercise 1.

Sarah What's this on TV?
Jake I don't know. It's a sitcom, I think. It's really funny.
Tom But Sarah and I want to watch the football! It's Barcelona against Chelsea.
Jake I don't like football.
Sarah But I hate sitcoms! And Tom doesn't like sitcoms either.
Jake Do you want to record the football, then?
Sarah No, I don't! We want to watch it live! Give me the remote!
Jake No! Get off!

3 Read the dialogue again. Study the highlighted forms. Complete the examples in the Learn this! box.

> **LEARN THIS!** Present simple (negative and interrogative)
> **a** We form the present simple negative with *don't* or *doesn't* and the infinitive of the verb without *to*.
> I ¹_____ play football.
> She ²_____ play football.
> **b** We form the present simple interrogative with *do* or *does* and the infinitive of the verb without *to*. We form short answers with *do / does / don't / doesn't*.
> ³_____ you play football?
> Yes, I do. / No, I ⁴_____ .
> Does he play football? Yes, he does. / No, he doesn't.

➡ Grammar Builder 1D page 124

4 Make these sentences negative.
1 My aunt works in London.
  My aunt doesn't work in London.
2 I like rap music.
3 My cousins Emma and Zoe speak Spanish.
4 My stepbrother Nick plays in a volleyball team.
5 Joe and I walk to school.
6 You study Chinese.

5 Write the words in the correct order to make questions. You need to add *Do* or *Does*.
1 live / you / the school / near ?
2 football / your best friend / like ?
3 both work / your parents ?
4 on Friday evenings / you / go out / and your friends ?
5 wear / jeans / you / to school ?

6 SPEAKING Work in pairs. Ask and answer the questions in exercise 5.

> Do you live near the school?

> Yes, I do. / No, I don't.

7 Write true sentences about yourself. Use the present simple affirmative or negative and the phrases below.
1 get up early on Saturdays
  I don't get up early on Saturdays.
2 play ice hockey
  I play …
3 walk to school every day
4 use computers at school
5 watch TV every evening
6 argue a lot with my friends
7 speak French
8 like dancing
9 do a lot of homework at weekends

8 SPEAKING Work in pairs. Ask and answer questions using the phrases in exercise 7. Make a note of the answers.

> Do you get up early on Saturdays?

> No, I don't. Do you get up early on Saturdays?

> Yes, I do.

9 SPEAKING Tell the class about your partner. Use the notes you made in exercise 8.

> Claudia doesn't get up early on Saturdays.

Singular and plural nouns

I can form the plural of a range of regular and irregular nouns.

1 SPEAKING Work in pairs. Who are the people in the photo on the right? What do you know about them?

Posh and Becks

THE BECKHAMS are a famous family from Britain. Becks is the nickname of David Beckham, ex-footballer of Manchester United, Real Madrid and England. Posh is the nickname of his wife, Victoria, a member of the girl-band the Spice Girls.

Victoria is called 'Posh' because she loves posh, expensive clothes. She says she really likes sunglasses too, because it's easy to look cool in them! Now she is a fashion designer. Her company makes very expensive dresses, accessories and jewellery, but also ordinary clothes like jeans and jackets.

David doesn't play football now, but he owns a football team in Miami, Florida. David has got 32 tattoos! He says they are all about the people in his life, his wife and children. David Beckham is a hero to many English football fans.

The Beckhams do a lot of work for charities and they appear a lot on television. They have got four children. Their sons are Brooklyn, Romeo and Cruz, and their daughter is called Harper. The boys are footballers too, and hope to play for England one day.

Read the text. Which family member is missing from the photo?

Read the Learn this! box. Match the nouns highlighted in orange in the text with one of the rules (a–g). Give the singular and plural forms of each noun.

LEARN THIS! Singular and plural forms

a To make the plural of most nouns we add -*s*.
brother → brothers

b If the noun ends in -*s*, -*sh*, -*ch*, -*z*, or -*x*, we add -*es*.
bus → buses   class → classes   dish → dishes
church → churches   watch → watches   box → boxes

c If the noun ends in -*o*, we add -*s* or sometimes -*es*.
photo → photos   potato → potatoes

d If the noun ends in a consonant + -*y*, we change -*y* to -*ies*.
party → parties

e If the noun ends in a vowel + -*y*, we add -*s*.
holiday → holidays

f If the noun ends in -*f* or -*fe*, we change -*f* or -*fe* to -*ves*.
shelf → shelves

g Some nouns have irregular plural forms.
foot → feet   man → men   woman → women

4 DICTIONARY WORK Look at the dictionary entry. How does it show the plural form of the noun?

baby /ˈbeibi/ *noun* (*plural* babies) a very young child:
She's going to **have a baby**. ◇ *a baby boy* ◇ *a baby girl*

5 What is the plural form of these nouns? Use a dictionary to help you.

1 uncle _____
2 address _____
3 day _____
4 video _____
5 match _____
6 life _____
7 lady _____
8 tooth _____
9 mother _____
10 knife _____

LOOK OUT!

a Some nouns are always plural (e.g. *scissors, trousers*).

b Some nouns have no plural form. We call these uncountable nouns (e.g. *homework, information, luggage, help, advice*).

6 Read the Look out! box. Match the nouns highlighted in blue in the text with point a or point b.

7 There are mistakes in some of these sentences. Find them and correct them.

1 My jeans is very old.
2 Put the knifes and forks on the table.
3 I love babies.
4 I'd like some informations about trains.
5 Can I see some photoes of your family?
6 I've got two watches.
7 She's got very big feets.
8 I've got lots of homeworks this evening.

8 Work in pairs. Write three questions about the Beckhams. Do not show your partner.

Is David Beckham American?

9 SPEAKING Work in pairs. Cover the text. Then ask and answer the questions.

Is David Beckham American?   No, he isn't. He's British.

1F Reading
Sibling rivalry
I can understand a text about brothers and sisters.

1 SPEAKING Work in pairs. Read the quotations at the start of the text. Which are true for you or your partner?

> The first one is true for me. I argue a lot with my brother!

> The second / third / fourth one is / isn't true for me. I ...

> **Reading Strategy**
>
> When you want to know if a sentence fits a gap, read the sentences before and after the gap as well as the sentence itself, and ask yourself these questions:
> - Does it make sense?
> - Does it fit grammatically? (Think about tense, pronouns, singular and plural, *this / that*, etc.)
> - Does it match the topic of the paragraph?

2 Read the Reading Strategy. Then match gaps (1–4) in the text with sentences (A–E). Use the questions in the Strategy to check that the sentences fit. There is one extra sentence which does not fit any of the gaps.

A According to the website, the answer is: around the age of 25.

B But other brothers and sisters get on well from an early age.

C We get on well – and we don't argue.

D Give your brother or sister some time alone when they need it.

E Most teenagers have a difficult relationship with their brothers and sisters.

3 Read and listen to the complete text. Check your answers to exercise 2.

4 Work in pairs. Choose the best summary of the text: a, b or c. What is wrong with the other summaries?

a A lot of teenagers do not get on well with their brothers and sisters. However, the relationship is usually good when they are adults.

b Some teenagers get on well with their brothers and sisters. These people usually get on well when they are adults too.

c A lot of teenagers do not get on well with their brothers and sisters. The relationship is usually bad when they are adults too, because people don't change.

> **LEARN THIS!** Adjectives and prepositions
>
> Some adjectives are followed by certain prepositions. Sometimes, more than one preposition is possible.
>
> *excited about   famous for   frightened of*
> *good at   pleased about / with   similar to*

5 VOCABULARY Read the Learn this! box. Then look at the highlighted adjectives in the text. What prepositions follow them? Complete the table.

Adjectives and prepositions

1 angry _____	**4** keen _____
2 different _____	**5** proud _____
3 interested _____	**6** worried _____

6 SPEAKING Interview a classmate who has a brother or sister. Complete these questions with the correct prepositions. Then ask and answer the questions. Give examples.

1 Are you similar *to* your brother or sister?
2 Are you interested _____ the same things?
3 Are you good _____ the same school subjects?
4 Are you keen _____ the same TV programmes?
5 Are your brother or sister's hobbies different _____ yours

> Are you similar to your brother or sister?

> Yes, I am. / No, I'm not.

🎧 1.22 # BROTHERLY LOVE?

'I don't get on well with my brother. He's very different from me and we argue a lot.'

'Sometimes I want to be alone. But my sister is always there!'

'I can't have secrets when my brother is around. He reads my text messages!'

'My sister uses my things – and she doesn't ask me first! I hate that!'

According to the website GettingPersonal.co.uk, these problems are not unusual. ¹___ They argue a lot. In general, teenagers are not worried about their brothers and sisters when things go badly for them. And they are not proud of them when things go well!

But most adults are very keen on their brothers and sisters and have a good relationship. So when does the situation change? ²___ For example, Madison is 28 years old. Her brother, Tyler, is 26. 'I remember big fights, horrible fights with Tyler,' says Madison. 'But now, our relationship is completely different. ³___ We go out together two or three times a month and we have a great time. We're interested in the same things.'

But for teenage brothers and sisters with difficult relationships, what can they do? How can they get on well? Here are a few ideas.

▶ When your brother or sister uses your things, don't get angry about it – learn to share.

▶ Imagine your brother or sister is a friend – and be nice!

▶ Don't tell people your brother or sister's secrets.

▶ ⁴___

Of course, the other answer is: just wait ten years!

Describing people

I can describe my friends.

1 **VOCABULARY** Look at the photos. What do the people look like? Complete the descriptions below.

Describing people blue glasses ~~long~~ moustache short straight wavy

1 She's good-looking with long dark _____ hair.
2 He's got medium-length _____ fair hair and _____ eyes.
3 He's got _____ dark hair, _____, a beard and a _____.

➡ **Vocabulary Builder** Describing people: page 117

2 🎧 **1.23** Read and listen to the dialogue. Identify Tom and Brendan in the photo above.

Amy Do you know Tom?
Toby No, I don't. Is he here?
Amy Yes, he's over there.
Toby Where? What does he look like?
Amy He's tall and he's got short dark hair.
Toby Is he next to Milly?
Amy No, that's Brendan. Tom's got a white T-shirt.
Toby Oh, yes. I see him. Is he your friend?
Amy Yes, he's really nice. Let's go and talk to him.
Toby OK.

3 **SPEAKING** Work in pairs. Choose someone in your class. Describe him or her, but do not say the name. Can your partner guess who it is?

> She's tall. She's got long, straight brown hair.

> Is it Joanna?

4 🎧 **1.24** Listen to three more dialogues at the party. Circle the correct answers.

Dialogue 1
1 Marcus wants to find **Dan** / **Sally**.
2 Sally **is** / **isn't** with Dan.
Dialogue 2
3 Ryan knows **one person** / **lots of people** at the party.
4 George **is** / **isn't** Lisa's brother.
Dialogue 3
5 Lucy thinks it's a **good** / **bad** party.
6 Lucy **likes** / **doesn't like** Kate.

5 🎧 **1.24** Listen again. Correct the mistakes in the descriptions.

1 Dan is quite short, with long red hair. His T-shirt is blue and he wears glasses.
2 George has got a black jacket and blue trousers. He's got curly fair hair and green eyes.
3 Kate is tall, with curly fair hair. Her dress is blue.

6 Imagine you are at a barbecue with your friends. Prepare a dialogue like the one in exercise 2. Then complete the table below.

	first person	second person
Description		
Clothes		

Speaking Strategy
- Speak in a loud, clear voice.
- Look at the other person when he or she is speaking to you and when you are speaking to him or her.
- Listen very carefully to everything the other person says so that you can reply appropriately.

7 **SPEAKING** Read the Speaking Strategy. Then act out your dialogue, using the notes you made in exercise 6.

A personal profile
I can write a personal profile.

1 Read the personal profiles from a student website. What information does each person include? Tick the correct boxes in the table.

	Lauren	James
Family		
Home		
School subjects		
Hobbies		
Ambition		

Introducing your new Head Girl and Head Boy

Hi! I'm Lauren, your friendly new Head Girl. I'm seventeen years old, and I'm in Year twelve.

I live in an apartment. It's very near the school, so I walk to school in five minutes every morning!

I really enjoy school: my favourite subjects are science and art. I'm keen on languages too.

I love films and I watch DVDs with my friends every weekend. My other hobbies are dancing and reading. I like shopping too. Is that a hobby?!

I've got a dog and two cats. I love animals! My ambition is to be a vet. I want to travel too, perhaps before university.

Hello! My name's James. I'm sixteen years old and I'm in Year twelve.

I've got a brother in Year nine. I've got a stepsister too. She's at university.

Music is important to me. I play the guitar and I write songs. I also listen to a lot of music, of course. My favourite singers are Ed Sheeran and Ellie Goulding. I'm also interested in sport. I play football and tennis at the weekend. I'm keen on surfing too, but I'm not very good at it!

I'm creative and hard-working. My ambition is to become a songwriter and write songs for my favourite pop stars.

SPEAKING Work in pairs. Ask and answer the questions.
Student A: Ask about Lauren. Student B: Ask about James.

1 What year is Lauren / James in?
2 What are Lauren's / James's hobbies?
3 What is Lauren's / James's ambition?

3 **VOCABULARY** Which of the personality adjectives below do Lauren and James use to describe themselves? Choose two from the list to describe yourself.

Personality adjectives creative friendly hard-working honest patient polite sensible

➡ **Vocabulary Builder** Personality adjectives: page 117

4 **KEY PHRASES** Complete these phrases from the profiles using the prepositions below. You need to use some prepositions more than once.

at in to with

Giving personal information
I'm ¹_____ Year twelve.   I walk ⁴_____ school.
I watch DVDS ²_____ my friends. She's ⁵_____ university.
I listen ³_____ music.   ⁶_____ the weekend.

Writing Strategy 1
You can use contractions (e.g. *I'm* and *she's*) in letters to friends and family, emails and other informal texts.

5 Read Writing Strategy 1. What contractions can you find in the personal profiles in exercise 1? Say them in full.

I am Lauren ... and I am in Year twelve.

Writing Strategy 2
Always write in paragraphs. A paragraph usually contains two or more sentences about the same topic. When you prepare a piece of writing, make a paragraph plan.

6 Read Writing Strategy 2. How many paragraphs does each profile in exercise 1 contain? Is each paragraph about one topic or more than one topic?

7 Plan a personal profile about yourself. Look at the table in exercise 1 and choose three or four topics you want to include. Make a paragraph plan. Begin like this:

Paragraph 1   Topic: ...
              Information: ...

8 Write your personal profile following your plan from exercise 7. Remember to use contractions.

CHECK YOUR WORK
Have you ...
• followed your paragraph plan?
• used contractions?
• checked your spelling and grammar?

2
School days

2A Vocabulary
Daily routine
I can describe my daily routine at school and at home.

1 VOCABULARY Work in pairs. Match the daily routine phrases with photos (A–H).

Daily routine arrive at school   get dressed   go to bed   have breakfast
have dinner   have lunch   leave school   wake up

2 Write the phrases in the order you do them on a normal school day.

1 wake up,   2 …

> **LEARN THIS! Times**
> 10.00 = ten o'clock   12.00 = midday   2.55 = five to three
> 8.15 = quarter past eight 6.30 = half past six   00.00 = midnight
> 11.20 = twenty past eleven 4.45 = quarter to five

3 Read the Learn this! box. Then say these times.

a 8.45   b 5.15   c 11.00   d 4.25   e 10.55   f 00.15

> quarter to nine

4 🎧 **1.25** Listen to Sofia talking about her daily routine. At what time does she do these things?

1 get up 7.20
2 have breakfast _____
3 arrive at school _____
4 have lunch _____
5 leave school _____
6 have dinner _____
7 go to bed _____

RECYCLE! *do* or *does*

Remember, we use *do* or *does* to form questions in the present simple. We put it before the subject (*she, he, you,* etc.). We use the infinitive without *to*.

Do you have lunch at school?

When does she wake up?

5 **SPEAKING** Work in pairs. Read the Recycle! box. Then check your answers to exercise 4 by asking about Sofia's routine.

What time does she get up?

She gets up at ...

6 **SPEAKING** In pairs, ask and answer questions about your own daily routines. Choose three days of the week from the list (including at least one weekend day).

Days of the week Monday Tuesday Wednesday Thursday Friday Saturday Sunday

What time do you get up on Saturday?

I get up at ...

🎧 **1.26** **VOCABULARY** Match ten of the school subjects with the icons below. Then listen and repeat all the words.

School subjects art and design biology chemistry economics English French geography German history I.C.T. (information and communication technology) maths music P.E. (physical education) physics R.E. (religious education)

8 **SPEAKING** In pairs, compare the subjects in exercise 7 with your own school subjects. Answer the questions.

1 Which subjects from exercise 7 do you do?
2 Do you do any other subjects?

We do English. We don't do economics.

At our school, we also do ...

9 **SPEAKING** In pairs, compare your opinions of the school subjects in exercise 7.

What do you think of maths?

I really like it. / It's OK. / I don't like it. What about you?

10 🎧 **1.27** Listen and complete Tim's timetable for Wednesday, Thursday and Friday. Write the correct school subjects.

	Wednesday	Thursday	Friday
8.20	English	³ _____	Chemistry
9.05	¹ _____	Maths	⁵ _____
9.50–10.30 BREAK			
10.30	Maths	⁴ _____	Maths
11.15	² _____	English	History
12.05–1.00 LUNCH			
1.00	Art	P.E.	English
1.50	R.E.	P.E.	⁶ _____

11 **SPEAKING** Work in pairs. Student A: Look at the timetable below. Student B: Look at the timetable on page 142. Imagine this is your timetable for Monday and Tuesday. Ask and answer questions about the missing lessons.

	Monday	Tuesday
8.20	History	
9.05		Music
9.50–10.30 BREAK		
10.30	Chemistry	
11.15		P.E.
12.05–1.00 LUNCH		
1.00	Maths	
1.50		Economics

What do we have at five past nine on Monday?

French.

have to

I can talk about things that are necessary or compulsory.

BRIT SCHOOL Q&A

The BRIT School near London is for students with one ambition: to get a job connected with performing arts (music, theatre, film, etc.).

Q: How old do you have to be to go to the BRIT School?

A: You have to be between fourteen and nineteen years old to study at the BRIT School. You also have to live in or near London.

Q: Do you have to pay to study there?

A: No, you don't. The BRIT School is a state school so the students don't have to pay.

Q: Do the students have to study all the normal subjects?

A: Yes. As a state school, the BRIT School has to follow the National Curriculum. Classes in performing arts are extra.

1 Read the questions and answers about the BRIT school. Would you like to be a student there? Why? / Why not?

> **LEARN THIS!** *have to*
>
> **a** We use *have to / has to* to talk about things which are necessary or compulsory:
> *We have to do P.E. at school.*
>
> **b** We use *don't / doesn't have to* to talk about things which are not necessary or compulsory. We don't use it to say something is against the rules.
> *You can go home now. You don't have to stay until 4.15.*
> NOT ~~You don't have to use your mobile phone in class.~~ ✗

2 Read the Learn this! box and then look at the table. How many examples of *have to* can you find in exercise 1? Are they affirmative, negative or interrogative?

have to
Affirmative
I / You / We / They have to study music.
He / She / It has to arrive at 9 o'clock.
Negative
I / You / We / They don't have to take exams.
He / She / It doesn't have to be on time.
Interrogative
Do I / you / we / they have to do homework?
Yes, we do. / No, they don't.
Does he / she / it have to help?
No, he doesn't. / Yes, she does.

3 🎧 **1.28** Listen to the text in exercise 1. How are *have to* and *has to* pronounced? Practise saying them.

4 Complete these sentences about your school. Use the affirmative or negative form of *have to*.

1 We _____ do P.E. every week.
2 The head teacher _____ be at school on Saturdays.
3 We _____ wear school uniform.
4 The school _____ stay open at the weekend.
5 We _____ do all our homework on computer.

➡ **Grammar Builder 2B** page 126

5 Look at the pictures of Millie's school day. Then write sentences using the affirmative or negative of *have to* and the prompts below.

1 get up before 7 o'clock
2 make her own breakfast
3 walk to school
4 do P.E. at school
5 take exams
6 stay at school after 3:15

1 *She has to get up before 7 o'clock.*

6 **SPEAKING** In pairs, ask and answer questions about what your partner has to do at weekends. Use *Do you have to ...* and the phrases below.

cook lunch / dinner   do the ironing   do the washing
do your homework   get dressed before lunch   get up ear~~
set the table   take exams   tidy your room

Do you have to cook lunch?   Yes, I do. / No, I don't.

Unusual schools

I can understand numbers, dates and times.

1 SPEAKING Work in pairs. Describe the photo of the classroom. Use the phrases and words below to help you. What is unusual about it?

I can see …   I can't see …

book desk student teacher
whiteboard young / old

2 Complete the fact file with the verbs below. Would you like to go to a 'democratic school'? Why? / Why not?

choose don't go have mark meet take

DEMOCRATIC SCHOOLS

FACT FILE

In democratic schools …

- students ¹_____ the subjects they want to study.
- students don't have to ²_____ to lessons.
- students don't usually have to ³_____ exams.
- teachers don't usually ⁴_____ students' work.
- classes are mixed-ability and often ⁵_____ students of different ages.
- all the students and teachers ⁶_____ to discuss the timetable, school rules, school trips, etc.
- the teachers ⁷_____ make many rules or give many punishments.

LEARN THIS! Saying numbers, dates and times

We often say numbers, dates and times differently from how they are written.

110 = *a hundred and ten* or *one hundred and ten*

1,110 = *one thousand, one hundred and ten*

07.15 = *quarter past seven* or *seven fifteen*

20 May = *the twentieth of May*

April 15 = *April the fifteenth*

1997 = *nineteen ninety-seven*

2005 = *two thousand and five*

2012 = *twenty twelve* or *two thousand and twelve*

07.07.2025 = *the seventh of July, twenty twenty-five*

🎧 1.29 Read the Learn this! box. Then say these numbers, dates and times. Sometimes there is more than one way to say them. Then listen, check and repeat.

1	10.55	6	1 June 1998
2	August 15 2016	7	6.45
3	4.30	8	557
4	1,390	9	20.07.1990
5	150	10	3,260

🎧 1.30 Listen to the sentences A–G. Write the number, date or time that you hear in each sentence.

5 🎧 1.31 Listen to a radio interview with a student at the Brooklyn Free School. Which sentence is not true?

1 Classes at the school are very small.
2 They study the usual school subjects.
3 Nathan doesn't enjoy school.

Listening Strategy

Make sure you know how dates, times and numbers are spoken so that you can identify them when you hear them.

6 🎧 1.31 Read the Listening Strategy. Then listen again. Choose the correct answers (a, b or c).

1 Nathan is ___ years old.
   a 15   b 16   c 17
2 In Nathan's part of the school the students are aged ___.
   a 4–11   b 4–18   c 12–18
3 Nathan's part of the school has about ___ students.
   a 16   b 60   c 66
4 Nathan ___ sits next to students of his own age.
   a sometimes b never   c always
5 The boy who helps Nathan with maths is ___.
   a 11   b 13   c 18
6 Lessons are from ___.
   a 8 a.m. to 3 p.m.   b 9 a.m. to 3 p.m.   c 9 a.m. to 4 p.m.
7 It costs ___ a year to study at the school.
   a $2,000   b $12,000   c $20,000

7 SPEAKING Work in pairs. Compare your school with the Brooklyn Free School. Write five sentences and tell the class.

Our school has … students, but there are only about 120 students in the Brooklyn Free School.

At our school we have to … , but at the Brooklyn Free School they …

2D Grammar
Adverbs of frequency; question words
I can use adverbs of frequency and question words.

1 🎧 **1.32** Read and listen to the dialogue. Which clubs does Maisie go to? Which club does Ben plan to join?

Maisie	Are you a member of a school club?
Ben	No, I'm not. But I'd like to join one. Which clubs do you go to?
Maisie	I often go to photography club. It's always good fun. And I sometimes go to music club.
Ben	Who takes photography club?
Maisie	Mr Carleton, the art teacher.
Ben	I like him. How often does the club meet?
Maisie	Once a week. We usually meet on Fridays, after school. But it's sometimes on Thursday, in the lunch break. Why don't you come along?
Ben	Good idea. Hey, when does the next lesson start?
Maisie	In two minutes. Come on. Mr Baker is always cross when students arrive late!

2 Find four adverbs of frequency in the dialogue in exercise 1. Add them to the table below.

0%	▶	▶	▶	▶	100%
never	hardly ever	¹_____	²_____	³_____	⁴_____

3 Complete the Learn this! box. Use *before* and *after*.

> **LEARN THIS!** **Adverbs of frequency**
>
> **a** We use adverbs of frequency to say how often something happens. We usually put adverbs of frequency ¹_____ the verb.
>
> *I never have breakfast.*
>
> **b** We put adverbs of frequency ²_____ the verb *be*.
>
> *You're always late!*

➡ **Grammar Builder 2D** page 126

4 Put the adverbs of frequency in brackets in the correct place in the sentences.

1 Kate watches TV in her bedroom. (sometimes)
2 Joe is late for school. (often)
3 Harry goes dancing. (never)
4 Hannah does sport at the weekend. (hardly ever)
5 William listens to music in bed. (usually)
6 Ryan is thirsty after football training. (always)

5 Write the words in the correct order to make sentences.

1 **never** / Sally / the dishwasher / loads
2 to my friends / I / text messages / **often** / send
3 is / Jake / at school / hungry / **hardly ever**
4 Harry and Alex / after midnight / go / **sometimes** / to bed
5 tidies / Frank / **usually** / at the weekend / his bedroom
6 late / the school bus / **often** / in the morning / is
7 computer games / Lisa / after school / plays / **always**

6 Rewrite the sentences in exercise 4 so that they are true for you.

I never watch TV in my bedroom.

7 Find five question words in the dialogue in exercise 1 and add them to the Learn this! box.

> **LEARN THIS!** **Question words**
>
> We use question words to ask for information. We put them at the beginning of questions.
>
> *How How many What What time Where Whose*
>
> _____ _____ _____
>
> _____ _____
>
> *What time do you get up?*
> *Where do you live?*
> *Whose book is this?*

8 Read the answers and circle the correct question words to complete the sentences.

1 '**How / When** do you get to school?' 'By bus.'
2 '**Who / Where** are you?' 'In the kitchen.'
3 '**How often / When** do you do your homework?' 'After dinner.'
4 '**Which / How many** subjects do you do at school?' 'Ten.'
5 '**When / Where** do you usually meet your friends?' 'On Friday evenings.'
6 '**Who's / Whose** pencil case is this?' 'My brother's.'

9 Think of possible answers to questions 1–5 in exercise 8 using the *other* question words.

1 'When do you get to school?' 'At 8.30a.m.'

10 Complete the questions with the correct question words.

1 _____ brothers and sisters have you got?
2 _____ do you sit next to in maths lessons?
3 _____ do you travel to and from school?
4 _____ do you live?
5 _____ do you usually go to bed?
6 _____ do you usually eat for breakfast?
7 _____ do you prefer, pizza or pasta?

➡ **Grammar Builder 2D** page 126

11 SPEAKING Work in pairs. Ask and answer the questions in exercise 10.

> How many brothers and sisters have you got?

> I've got one brother and one sister.

Word Skills
Prepositions of time
I can use a variety of prepositions of time.

1 SPEAKING What do you know about British secondary schools? Think about these things.

age of students   mixed / single-sex   name of exams
school day   terms and holidays

LEARN THIS! Prepositions of time 1

a in
*in June   in 2020   in the morning / the afternoon
in (the) spring*

b on
on Friday   on 1 May   on New Year's Day

c at
at 6 p.m.   at night   at New Year   at the weekend

2 Read the Learn this! box. Find the preposition we use with:

1 months
2 times
3 days of the week
4 years
5 festivals
6 seasons
7 parts of the day (*two* answers)
8 a specific day of the year

3 Read what Rachel says about her school and find examples of 1–8 from exercise 2.

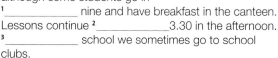

Rachel's Blog
📄 Wednesday 14th 10.40 a.m.

'Students start secondary school when they are eleven, and leave when they are eighteen. Most secondary schools in the UK are mixed.

The school year starts in September and finishes in July. In my school, lessons start at nine o'clock in the morning, although some students go in
¹_____ nine and have breakfast in the canteen. Lessons continue ²_____ 3.30 in the afternoon.
³_____ school we sometimes go to school clubs.

We go to school ⁴_____ Monday ⁵_____ Friday, but not at the weekend. In some private schools, students have school on Saturday morning, but no one goes to school on Sunday.

The school year has three terms. Each term lasts about thirteen or fourteen weeks. We have a two-week holiday at Christmas and the same at Easter. We sometimes have to do homework ⁶_____ the holidays – I hate that.

The end-of-year exams are in the summer, usually in June. I'm in my final year, so next year, in 2019, I have very important exams called 'A levels'. The A level exam results come out on 25 August. That's a very important day, of course, and all the students meet in school to get their results.'

LEARN THIS! Prepositions of time 2

a before
*I have a shower before breakfast.
Ring me before the weekend.*

b after
*I watch TV after dinner.
We have maths after the break.*

c during
My dad works at night, not during the day.

d until
*My mum is in London until tomorrow.
We stay at school until 3.30.*

e from ... to
My dad works from nine to five every day.

4 Read the Learn this! box and translate the examples. Then complete the text in exercise 3 with the correct prepositions. Use each preposition once.

5 SPEAKING How is your school year and school day different from Rachel's?

> Rachel's school year starts in September. Our school year starts in September too.

> In Rachel's school, lessons start at ... , but in our school, they start at ...

6 Circle the correct preposition to complete the sentences.

1 I usually arrive at school **before / on / until** 8.30.
2 I always have a party **at / on / in** my birthday.
3 Do you have dinner **at / to / until** seven o'clock **in / on / during** the evening?
4 I go to computer club **during / before / after** school **on / after / in** Friday afternoon.
5 We have exams **in / during / on** the summer term.
6 Joe always goes to bed **at / from / on** midnight.

7 SPEAKING Work in pairs. Design your ideal school year and school day. Make notes about these things.

1 What time does school start and finish?
2 When and how long are the breaks and lunch hour?
3 Which days do you go to school?
4 When are the holidays and how long are they?

8 SPEAKING Tell the class about your ideal school year and school day. Use the notes you made in exercise 7.

> Our ideal school day starts at 10.30 and finishes ...

Dangerous journeys

I can understand a text about dangerous journeys to school.

1 SPEAKING Look at the photos. Why do these children have to go on dangerous journeys, do you think?

2 Read the introduction to the text. Check your ideas for exercise 1.

3 Read the text. Match texts (1–4) with photos (A–D).

> **Reading Strategy**
>
> When you match sentences to texts, make sure the whole sentence matches the information in the text. Do not just look for one or two words that are in the text and the sentence.

4 Read the Reading Strategy. Then match sentences (A–G) with texts (1–4).

Which group of children …
A sometimes put a family member inside a bag?
B cannot use the bridge across the river?
C travel very fast?
D have to swim across a river?
E have to walk along a dangerous path?
F have a long walk as part of their journey to school?
G travel to school with their head teacher?

The School run 🎧 1.33

B

How dangerous is your journey to school? Perhaps you have to walk across a busy road or ride your bike in traffic. But in general, your journey is probably safe. For some children, it's very different …

1 Banpo Elementary School in China is on a mountain. The path to school is very narrow and dangerous. The children have to walk in a line. When they meet somebody, they have to stand against the mountain while the person passes. For the parents, it is very worrying. Fortunately, the head teacher of the school walks with the children every morning.

2 A group of children in Sumatra, Indonesia, have to cross a wide river every morning on their way to school. The bridge across the river is broken, so about 20 children have to walk across a rope. The rope is ten metres above the water. After that, they have to walk ten kilometres through the jungle! And of course, at the end of the school day, they have to do the same journey again on their way home.

3 Students in Minh Hoa in Vietnam have to cross a river on their way to and from school every day. There are no bridges or boats, so the children swim. They put their books and clothes in large plastic bags so they do not get wet. The bags also help the children to stay safe in the water (the water is 20 metres deep). When they reach the other side, they take their dry clothes out of the bag and put them on.

4 Near Bogotá, the capital of Colombia, some children have to cross a large valley to get to school. At the bottom of the valley is the Rio Negro, a huge river. There is only one way to cross the valley: on a zip wire. That's a metal rope, 800 metres long and 400 metres above the river. The journey is very fast. In fact, it only takes about one minute! Small children cannot travel across the valley alone, so their brother or sister puts them in a bag!

A

5 VOCABULARY Put the highlighted adjectives in the text into four pairs of opposites.

6 VOCABULARY Find these words in the text. Then match them with the pictures below.

In the wilderness boat bridge jungle mountain
path river rope valley

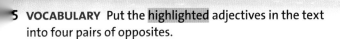

7 Complete the questions about the text using the question words below.

how how many what where which who why

1 In _____ country is Banpo Elementary School?
2 _____ walks with the children on the mountain path?
3 _____ high is the rope across the river in Sumatra?
4 _____ children have to walk across the rope?
5 _____ is Minh Hoa?
6 _____ do the children in Minh Hoa have to swim across the river?
7 _____ is the name of the river near Bogotá?

8 SPEAKING Work in pairs. Ask and answer the questions in exercise 7.

> In which country is Banpo Elementary School?

> It's in …

9 SPEAKING Work in pairs. Imagine you have to do one of the journeys to school in the text. Which one do you choose? Why? Explain your choice to the class.

> I choose journey four because it's …

> I choose journey one because you have to / don't have to …

Giving advice

I can ask for and give advice.

1 🎧 **1.34** **Read and listen to the dialogue between a girl and her friend. Do you agree with the friend's advice? Can you think of any other advice?**

Jade   Hi, Lewis. Can I ask your advice about something?
Lewis   Yes, sure. What's the problem?
Jade   Well, you know that big science project we have to do …
Lewis   Yes …
Jade   Well, Sophie is really worried about it. She wants to copy my work. I feel really bad – and a bit angry. It's my work!
Lewis   Oh, I see …
Jade   What do you think I should do? Should I tell Mrs Jones?
Lewis   No, you shouldn't do that. But you should talk to Sophie. You should explain that copying work is a bad idea and tell her how you feel.
Jade   Yes, you're right. Thanks, Lewis.

2 SPEAKING **Practise reading the dialogue in pairs.**

3 **Read the Learn this! box. Find five more examples of *should* in the dialogue in exercise 1. Are they affirmative, negative or interrogative?**

> **LEARN THIS!** *should*
>
> We use *should / shouldn't* + infinitive without *to* to give advice.
>
> **Affirmative**
> She should take her exam again.
>
> **Negative**
> You shouldn't go outside in this weather.
>
> **Interrogative**
> Should we invite your cousin to the party?

➡ **Grammar Builder 2G** page 126

4 **Read the problems. Complete the two pieces of advice with *should* and *shouldn't*.**

1 You can't do your homework late at night because your brother plays loud music.
  a You _____ talk to your brother.
  b You _____ do your homework very late at night.
2 You feel ill, but want to go to your friend's party.
  a You _____ go to a party with a bad headache.
  b You _____ rest before the party.
3 You hate your birthday present from your aunt.
  a You _____ say thank you for it.
  b You _____ tell her the truth about your feelings.

5 🎧 **1.35** **Check the meaning of the adjectives below. Then listen to four dialogues and complete the sentences with the correct adjective.**

Feelings (adjectives) angry   embarrassed   excited   happy   sad   tired   worried

In dialogue 1, the boy feels _____.
In dialogue 2, the girl feels _____.
In dialogue 3, the boy feels _____.
In dialogue 4, the girl feels _____.

➡ **Vocabulary Builder** Feelings: page 118

6 🎧 **1.35** **Listen again. What advice does the friend give in each dialogue? Match the advice (a–f) with the dialogues. There are two extra pieces of advice.**

Dialogue 1: ___
Dialogue 2: ___
Dialogue 3: ___
Dialogue 4: ___

a 'You should tell your parents how you feel.'
b 'You should send a text message to your friend.'
c 'You shouldn't copy work from the internet.'
d 'You shouldn't stay late at the party.'
e 'You should invite your friend.'
f 'You shouldn't bring your phone to school.'

> **Speaking Strategy**
> Go to the Functions Bank in the Workbook for useful set phrases that you can use in conversations.

7 **Work in pairs. Prepare a dialogue using the prompts below. Use problems from exercise 4 or your own ideas.**

A Greet B. Say that you need advice.

B Ask A what the problem is.

A Explain the problem.

B Give one or two pieces of advice.

A Thank B for the advice.

8 SPEAKING **Act out your dialogue to the class.**

Writing

An announcement

I can write an announcement for a school event.

1 VOCABULARY Match the photo with one of the events below. Is it a good way to raise money, do you think? Why? / Why not?

School events concert   musical   play   school camp
school club   school trip   sports day

➡ **Vocabulary Builder** School events: page 118

2 Read the announcements. Match each with an event from exercise 1. Then check the meaning of all the events.

Cats!

Come to our musical!

Saturday 12 July from 7 p.m. to 11 p.m. in the school hall

Please help us to raise £1,000 for new musical instruments for the school.

We need your help!

Come and see us dance! Come and hear us sing! Fun for all the family! Please bring a friend!

Tickets: £5. Buy your ticket before 30 June and get a 50p discount!

JUDOCLUB

DO YOU ENJOY A CHALLENGE?

Then come to judo club.

We meet every Wednesday after school in the school gymnasium, from 3.30 to 5 p.m.

It's a great way to make new friends and to keep fit!

Are you new to martial arts? Don't worry! We've got a great judo teacher. Everyone is welcome, especially beginners!

Call Sarah on 0990 237789 for more details.

3 Read the Learn this! box. Find nine examples of imperatives in the announcements in exercise 2.

> **LEARN THIS!** Imperatives
>
> We use imperatives to give orders and instructions, and to make requests.
>
> We form affirmative imperatives with the infinitive form of the verb without *to*.
> *Be quiet!   Write the answer in your notebook.*
> *Please sit down.*
>
> We form negative imperatives with *don't* and the infinitive form of the verb without *to*.
> *Don't be silly!   Please don't interrupt.*

4 Complete the sentences with the verbs below. Use affirmative or negative imperatives.

bring   call   forget   miss   put   visit

1 _____ to tell your friends and family!
2 _____ it in your diary so that you don't forget!
3 _____ Dean Richards on 509331 for more information.
4 _____ our website!
5 _____ this event!
6 _____ a friend!

➡ **Grammar Builder 2H** page 126

> **Writing Strategy**
> Make sure that you include all the information required in the task. As you make notes in preparation, tick off the key points in the task as you deal with them.

5 Read the Writing Strategy. Then read the task and make notes using the questions below to help you.

You are organising an event at your school. Write an announcement to publicise the event and encourage people to attend. Remember to include information about the time and place of the event and how people can attend.

1 what is the event?
2 where?
3 date, day and time?
4 what is the purpose of the event?
5 what happens?
6 other information (tickets? phone number? website?)

6 Write an announcement for the event. Use your notes from exercise 5.

> **CHECK YOUR WORK**
> Have you ...
> • used some imperatives?
> • included all the information in exercise 5?
> • checked your spelling and grammar?

Exam Skills Trainer

Reading

> **Strategy**
>
> In multiple-choice questions, the correct option will contain different words from the text, but the words will have the same meaning. It's a good idea to learn different ways of saying the same thing.

1 Read the Strategy. Match A–E with 1–5.

1 I study. _____	**A** I can.
2 I work. _____	**B** I have a job.
3 It's popular. _____	**C** People like it.
4 It's unpopular. _____	**D** I have lessons.
5 It's possible. _____	**E** People don't like it.

2 Read the text. Choose the correct answer, (A–D).

Homeschooling – how does that work?

Oliver Kent is a thirteen-year-old student, but he doesn't go to school. He's homeschooled. His dad is his teacher and teaches Oliver at home.

'People always ask me the same questions,' says Oliver, who lives in London. 'Things like "What time do you have to get up? When do you start? When do you finish? Do you like it?" They don't understand homeschooling, but for me it's normal. I love it! I can get up when I want to, and I have lessons at different times every day.

'Dad doesn't work. I study at home with him, and we sometimes go to museums and talk about what we see. I go swimming three times a week. I have a teacher because Dad can't swim. I'm in a football club too. I have internet lessons on English, maths and politics. Dad teaches me the other subjects.'

Homeschooling is popular in Australia, Canada, New Zealand, the United Kingdom, the United States and many other countries. Can parents homeschool their children in every country in the world? No. Brazil, Greece, Cuba, Turkey and 24 other countries say 'no' to homeschooling.

What about friends? 'People often ask me that question,' says Oliver. 'I have lots of friends. Most of them go to school and that's the right thing for them. My friend Ella is homeschooled by her mum. We can discuss things about homeschooling that other people don't understand.'

Does Oliver think he is different to other thirteen-year-olds?

'Of course not. I watch the same things on TV as other kids my age. I play the same games, I worry about the same things and I eat the same food! I learn the same things. It's just that I learn them in a different way.'

1 Oliver
 A gets up early every day.
 B studies at home every day.
 C doesn't do sport during the week.
 D always finishes school at 4:45 p.m.

2 Oliver's dad
 A has a job in London.
 B doesn't go to museums with Oliver.
 C is good at swimming.
 D doesn't teach Oliver maths.

3 According to the text, what is true about Brazil?
 A Homeschooling is popular.
 B Homeschooling is possible, but it isn't popular.
 C Teachers can homeschool their children.
 D Homeschooling isn't possible.

4 Oliver thinks
 A homeschooling is only for parents who don't have a job.
 B homeschooling teaches children the same things in different ways.
 C he is different from other teenagers.
 D every parent should homeschool their child.

Listening

> **Strategy**
>
> Before you listen, read the task. Think of key vocabulary that is related to the topic and quickly note it down. Some of these words and expressions may appear in the listening.

3 Read the Strategy. For each phrase below, underline three words on the same topic.

1 tidy the classroom
cupboard grandma ice ruler shelf supermarket
2 play a musical instrument
dictionary drums flute geography saxophone ski
3 have a big family
cousin daughter desk eraser niece skateboard
4 describe someone
beard dishwasher economics ironing short straight
5 get up early
copy an answer get dressed have breakfast have dinner play the drums wake up

4 🎧 **1.36** Listen to six people talking about their everyday life. Match speakers 1–6 to A–G. There's one extra letter.

This speaker …
A doesn't have books at school. ___
B can't walk to school. ___
C speaks two languages every day. ___
D has to help his / her parents every day. ___
E can play a musical instrument. ___
F goes to work from 9:00 a.m. until 4:30 p.m. ___
G has extra lessons every day. ___

Use of English

5 Read the Strategy. Read the text below and answer the questions. Do not fill the gaps yet!

1 When is Emily's birthday?
2 When are her sisters' birthdays?
3 Do Emily and her sisters look similar or different?
4 Are Emily and her sisters interested in the same things?
5 Does Emily like her life?

6 Complete the text with the correct answer, (A–C).

Emily and her sisters

Emily Mathias is a normal teenage girl. She lives with her parents and three sisters. She likes animals and she can ¹_____ the cello very well. A cello is like a really big violin. But her family is different from most families. ²_____? Because Emily and her sisters Anna, Mary Claire and Grace are identical quads. They were all born ³_____ 16 February 2000. The four girls ⁴_____ got the same long fair wavy hair and blue eyes, but their personalities are very different. Emily loves horse-riding. Grace ⁵_____ friendly, Mary Claire likes writing and Anna's interested ⁶_____ science.

'Our house is very busy,' says Emily. 'We ⁷_____ to help with jobs at home. Every Monday I do the washing ⁸_____ school. But I'm happy with my life. People often ask me, "⁹_____ are you? Are you Anna?" Sometimes the teacher ¹⁰_____ know. It's funny!'

1	**A** play	**B** plays	**C** to play
2	**A** Where	**B** What	**C** Why
3	**A** in	**B** at	**C** on
4	**A** have	**B** has	**C** are
5	**A** is	**B** does	**C** has
6	**A** in	**B** about	**C** at
7	**A** can	**B** have	**C** got
8	**A** until	**B** during	**C** after
9	**A** Where	**B** How	**C** Who
10	**A** don't	**B** isn't	**C** doesn't

Speaking

7 Read the Strategy. Complete the expressions with the words below.

advice   angry   problem   should (×2)   shouldn't   Thanks

Function	Expressions
Asking if someone is OK	What's the ¹_____?
Saying how you feel	I'm ²_____.
Asking for help	Can I ask your ³_____ about something? What ⁴_____ I do?
Giving advice	✗ You ⁵_____ shout at him. ✓ You ⁶_____ speak to a doctor.
Thanking someone	⁷_____.

8 Work in pairs. Ask and answer questions about one of the problems below.

Your brother isn't at home and he isn't at school.
You can't sleep at night.
You don't want to go to your friend's party.
Your English classes are very difficult.

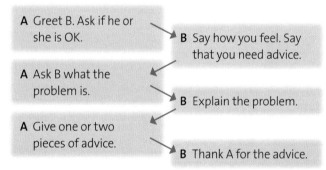

A Greet B. Ask if he or she is OK.

B Say how you feel. Say that you need advice.

A Ask B what the problem is.

B Explain the problem.

A Give one or two pieces of advice.

B Thank A for the advice.

Writing

9 Read the Strategy. Match A–F to 1–6.

1	Do you	**A** a ticket today!
2	Are you	**B** good at football?
3	Do you want	**C** and join us!
4	Come	**D** us to raise money for the school!
5	Buy	**E** play a musical instrument?
6	Please help	**F** to make new friends?

10 Write an announcement for a new school club. Include the information below.

- What is the club (sports? music? film? something else?)
- Where is it?
- What day and time is it?
- What happens at the club?
- Other information (tickets? phone number? website?)

3
Style

Unit map

● Vocabulary
Clothes
Adjectives to describe clothes
Common adjectives

● Word Skills
Adjectives: opposites

● Grammar
Present continuous
Contrast: present simple and
present continuous

● Listening Catwalk fashion

● Reading Teenage pressures

● Speaking Making
arrangements

● Writing An email

● Culture 3 Teens and their
money

3A   Vocabulary
Clothes
I can describe people's clothes.

1 SPEAKING Look at photos A and B. Do you like their clothes? Which are your
favourites? Do you wear similar clothes?

> I like the boy's shirt in photo A.

> I've got a black jacket like the one in photo B.

2 VOCABULARY Match items of clothing 1–13 in the photos with words from the list
below. Check the meaning of the other words.

Clothes boots cap cardigan coat dress hat jacket jeans jumper leggir
pyjamas scarf shirt shoes shorts skirt socks sweatshirt T-shirt tie
tracksuit trainers trousers

3 🎧 **2.02** Listen and repeat all the words in exercise 2.

LOOK OUT!

We often use the word 'top' to mean any kind of shirt, T-shirt, sweater, etc. We sometimes use the word 'bottoms' to refer to the bottom half of a tracksuit, pyjamas, etc.

4 🎧 **2.03** **Read the Look out! box. Then listen and find each person in the photos in exercise 1. Say the name.**

> This person has got black boots and a black top.

> Emma.

5 🎧 **2.04** **Listen to four people talking about their clothes. Which clothes from exercise 2 does each person mention?**

Speaker	Clothes
Archie	tracksuit, trainers
Violet	
Arthur	
Lola	

RECYCLE! Adverbs of frequency

• We use adverbs of frequency to say how often something happens. They usually go before the verb, but they go after the verb *be*.

He usually wears a tracksuit for P.E.

Her socks are often wet.

6 🎧 **2.04** **Read the Recycle! box. Then listen again. Complete sentences 1–5 with the correct adverb of frequency from the list below and the correct present simple form of the verb in brackets.**

always   never   often   sometimes   usually

1 Archie's clothes _____ (be) dirty.
2 Violet _____ (wear) a jacket for school.
3 Violet _____ (get dressed) early on Sunday.
4 Arthur _____ (wear) jeans at the weekend.
5 Lola _____ (change) clothes when she gets home.

7 **Rewrite the sentences in exercise 6 using different adverbs of frequency. Make them true for you.**

I always wear jeans at the weekend.

8 **In pairs, look at the photo at the bottom of the page. Use the colours below to describe items of clothing in the photo.**

(light / dark) beige   black   blue   brown   cream   green   grey   orange   pink   purple   red   violet   white   yellow

> brown boots   a light green shirt

9 **SPEAKING** **Work in pairs. Take turns to be A and B.**

A Imagine you are a person in the photo below. Answer B's questions.
B Ask about A's clothes using '*Have you got … ?*'. Decide which person in the photo he or she is.

> Have you got jeans?   Yes, I have.

> Have you got a red top?   No, I haven't.

> Are you number … ?   Yes, I am. / No, I'm not.

Grammar

Present continuous

I can talk about things that are happening now.

1 SPEAKING Look at the photo. Can you name any music festivals in your own town or region? When do they take place?

2 Read the tweets. Find the name, date and location of the music festival they are describing.

Tweets

@musicnews We're having a fantastic time at #SummerSounds music festival. Finally, it isn't raining!
5:28 p.m. Thursday 4 Aug

@musicnews The sun is shining! We're dancing to @DJSmithy on the main stage. Are you at #SummerSounds in Cardiff? What are you doing? Tweet us!
5:47 p.m. Thursday 4 Aug

3 Read the Learn this! box. What examples of the present continuous can you find in the tweets in exercise 2?

LEARN THIS! Present continuous

a We use the present continuous to talk about events that are happening now.

b We form the present continuous with the present simple of *be* and the *-ing* form of the verb:
I'm singing. They aren't listening.

4 Complete the examples in the table with the correct form of the verb *be*.

Present continuous
Affirmative
I ¹_____ doing my homework.
She ²_____ walking to school.
We ³_____ wearing the same shoes.
Negative
I ⁴_____ watching TV.
She ⁵_____ taking an exam at the moment.
You ⁶_____ helping with the housework.
Interrogative
⁷_____ you going home now? Yes, we ⁸_____. / No, we ⁹_____.
¹⁰_____ she wearing boots? Yes, she ¹¹_____. / No, she ¹²_____.

LEARN THIS! Spelling: *-ing* forms

a We form most *-ing* forms by adding *-ing* to the infinitive without *to*:
eat → *eating*   *go* → *going*

b When the infinitive ends in *-e*, we usually replace *-e* with *-ing*:
dance → *dancing*   *phone* → *phoning*

c When the infinitive ends in a single vowel plus consonant, we often double the consonant before adding *-ing*:
chat → *chatting*   *stop* → *stopping*

5 Read the Learn this! box. Then complete the tweets below with the affirmative form of the present continuous.

Tweets

@musicnews We ¹_____ (sit) in the sun. I ²_____ (take) photos for my Instagram page.

@musicnews I ³_____ (watch) DJSmithy on the big screen, but my friend ⁴_____ (sleep)!

@musicnews We ⁵_____ (have) lunch in our tent. Do you want to join us?

@musicnews I ⁶_____ (look) for my friend. She ⁷_____ (dance) to DJSmithy, but I can't see her. Help!

@musicnews I ⁸_____ (chat) to some friends online.

➡ Grammar Builder 3B page 128

6 🎧 2.05 Complete the phone dialogue. Use the present continuous: affirmative, negative or interrogative. Then listen and check.

Daniel Hi, Elsa. Where are you? What ¹_____ (you / do)?

Elsa I'm in the tent. I ²_____ (look) for my ba

Daniel I've got your bag. Remember? I ³_____ (hold) it now!

Elsa Oh yes. I remember. Where are you?

Daniel I ⁴_____ (sit) on the grass near the mair stage.

Elsa I can't hear any music.

Daniel We ⁵_____ (wait) for the next band. Th ⁶_____ (play) at the moment.

Elsa OK. I ⁷_____ (leave) the tent now.

Daniel ⁸_____ (you / come) to the main stage

Elsa Yes, I am. See you soon.

7 SPEAKING Work in pairs. Mime an activity using the list below or your own idea. Your partner guesses.

dance   play basketball / football / tennis
play the drums / clarinet   ride a bike / a horse
skate   skateboard   ski   sing   swim

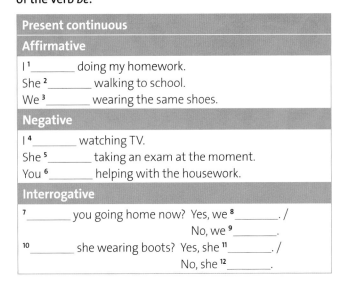

Are you dancing?   Yes, I am. / No, I'm not.

Listening

Catwalk fashion

I can identify stress patterns in two- and three-syllable words.

1 VOCABULARY Put the adjectives into pairs of opposites.

Adjectives to describe clothes baggy casual dark light long long-sleeved patterned plain short short-sleeved smart tight

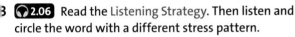

long – short, baggy –

2 SPEAKING Describe the photos. What are the models wearing? Use clothes and colours from lesson 3A and adjectives from exercise 1. Do you like their clothes?

> **Listening Strategy**
> In English, words with more than one syllable have the stress on one of the syllables. This means that the syllable is louder than the others. Being familiar with word stress makes it easier to recognise words when you hear them.

3 🎧 **2.06** Read the Listening Strategy. Then listen and circle the word with a different stress pattern.

1	design	begin	believe	visit
2	Japan	Scotland	Poland	Russia
3	mistake	police	moment	explain
4	model	hotel	hostel	channel
5	always	never	today	often
6	correct	copy	decide	describe

4 DICTIONARY WORK Look at the dictionary extracts below. How are the stressed syllables indicated?

outfit /ˈaʊtfɪt/   **October** /ɒkˈtəʊbə(r)/

July /dʒuˈlaɪ/   **magazine** /ˌmæɡəˈziːn/

audience /ˈɔːdiəns/

5 🎧 **2.07** Underline the stressed syllables in these words. Use a dictionary to help you. Then listen and check.

1	collection	5	dangerous	9	wonderful
2	pyjamas	6	magazine	10	twenty-one
3	understand	7	audience	11	computer
4	disaster	8	amazing	12	seventeen

6 🎧 **2.08** Listen to a radio programme about fashion. Are the sentences true or false? Write T or F.

1 The clothes in the show are for winter and spring. ___
2 Stella and Tonya are wearing summer clothes. ___
3 Tonya is wearing a short jacket, a baggy top and white shorts. ___
4 Stella has got a baggy dress, an orange scarf and boots. ___
5 The third model is a man. ___
6 Martin is wearing yellow and black trainers. ___
7 Martin starts to dance. ___
8 A photographer falls over Martin and the girls. ___

7 🎧 **2.09** Underline the stressed syllables in the highlighted words. Then listen again and check.

1 Good afternoon everyone, and welcome to the show!
2 We are proud to present an exciting new designer: Zizi Malek!
3 Our first models, Tonya and Stella, are coming down the catwalk now.
4 His trousers are difficult to describe. They look a bit like pyjama bottoms!
5 The reporters are taking lots of photographs of him.

8 Work in pairs. Prepare a short 'catwalk commentary'. Make notes for one male model and one female model. Choose the clothes, colours and styles.

9 SPEAKING Present your commentary to the class.

> Our first model, Amy, is coming down the catwalk now. She's wearing a … with …

> She looks great in …

Contrast: present simple and present continuous

I can talk about what usually happens and what is happening now.

1 SPEAKING Ask and answer. How often do you buy clothes? Do you like shopping for clothes?

2 🎧 **2.10** Read and listen to the phone conversation and answer the questions.

1 What does Claire want to buy? _____
2 Where is Joel? Why is he there? _____
3 What does Billy invite Claire to do? _____

Billy Hey, Claire, where are you?
Claire I'm in a clothes shop in town. I'm looking for a new top. But I'm not having much luck. They're all really expensive.
Billy You should go to the department store. They don't cost very much there.
Claire OK. Thanks for the advice.
Billy No problem. Is Joel with you?
Claire No, he's at home. He hates shopping. He never comes with me.
Billy Well, do you and Joel want to go to the cinema on Saturday?
Claire Maybe. Our parents are in the middle of decorating the house and we're helping them. What time's the film?
Billy 7.30 in the evening.
Claire That should be OK. Can I phone you later about it?
Billy Sure. Good luck with the shopping! Try the department store. Bye!

3 Study the examples of the present simple and present continuous in the conversation. Then complete the Learn this! box with the correct tenses.

> **LEARN THIS! Present tense contrast**
> We use the:
> **a** _____ for something that happens regularly, always or never.
> **b** _____ for something happening at this moment.
> **c** _____ for something happening around this time.
> **d** _____ for a fact that is always true.
> **e** _____ with certain verbs that we don't usually use in continuous tenses: *believe, know, hate, like, need, prefer, understand, want,* etc.

4 Complete the sentences with the present simple or the present continuous form of the verbs in brackets. Then match each sentence with rules a–e in the Learn this! box.

1 'Let's go out.' 'No, it _____.' (rain) ___
2 This term we _____ about the Second World War in our history lessons. (learn) ___
3 _____ you _____ what time it is? (know) ___
4 Fish _____ in the sea. (live) ___
5 My parents _____ tennis every Saturday morning. (play) ___
6 I _____ this word. (not understand) ___
7 How often _____ Fred _____ with the housework? (help) ___

➡ **Grammar Builder 3D** page 128

5 Complete the text messages with the present simple or present continuous form of the verbs below.

buy do know look look love get prefer read

> Hi, Chris. What ¹_____ you _____?
>
> I ²_____ for a birthday present for Emma.
>
> Why don't you buy her a CD? She ³_____ music.
>
> I ⁴_____. But she ⁵_____ to download music. She never ⁶_____ CDs.
>
> Well, what about a book? She ⁷_____ a lot.
>
> Good idea. ⁸_____ you _____ ready for her party now?
>
> Yes! I ⁹_____ forward to it!
>
> Me too. See you later, then.

6 SPEAKING Work in pairs. Take turns to say sentences about other students in the class. Use the present simple or the present continuous. Use the verbs below to help you. Can your partner guess who it is?

go hate like live play read sit smile speak study watch wear write

> He's wearing jeans and a red top.

> It's Marcus. She always sits next to Maria.

> It's Clara.

Adjectives: opposites

I can use a variety of adjectives.

1 **SPEAKING** Work in pairs. Describe the photo. What can you see? Where are the people? What are they doing? Use the words below to help you.

verbs make sew sit work
nouns clothes desk factory sewing machine
trousers woman worker

2 🎧 **2.11** Read and listen to teenagers talking about buying clothes. Which person ...

a hasn't got enough money to buy designer labels?
b is wearing something that doesn't cost very much?
c always wants to know where clothes come from before she buys them?
d makes clothes?

It's good that we can buy cheap clothes. I never spend more than £10 on a shirt or trousers, but my clothes are comfortable and I love them. This T-shirt is made in Bangladesh. The workers in the factories there don't get much money. People say that's unfair, but I don't agree. The fashion companies are giving them jobs!' **Ryan**

The large fashion companies don't care about the workers in their factories. The pay is very low and the jobs are often dangerous. It's terrible! We should pay more for clothes. I always look at the label, and I never buy cheap clothes that are made in poor countries.' **Molly**

I haven't got much money and I don't buy designer labels. But I want similar styles. So, I look for cheap copies. It's true that the workers who make the clothes don't get much money, but the cost of living is low in poor countries, so I think it's probably OK.' **Megan**

I think clothes are too cheap. People just wear them a few times and then throw them away! That's wrong. I'm studying Textile Design at school and I hardly ever buy clothes. I usually make them. It isn't very difficult and my clothes always fit and look great! I never throw my old clothes away. I give them to charity.' **Jed**

3 **VOCABULARY** Match the highlighted adjectives in the text with adjectives below that have the opposite meaning.

Common adjectives awful bad different easy expensive false fantastic high new right safe small

4 Work in pairs. Take turns to close your book. Say an adjective from the text or from the list in exercise 3. Your partner says the adjective with the opposite meaning.

high low

> **LEARN THIS!** Negative prefix *un-*
> We can make many adjectives negative by adding the prefix *un-*.
> *friendly – unfriendly kind – unkind happy – unhappy*
> *tidy – untidy usual – unusual necessary – unnecessary*

5 Read the Learn this! box. In Ryan's paragraph find:

a an adjective with the prefix *un-*.
b an adjective that can be made negative with the prefix *un-*.

6 Rewrite the sentences so that they have the opposite meaning. Use the opposite of the underlined adjective.

1 These jeans were very <u>expensive</u>.
2 That yellow shirt looks <u>terrible</u>!
3 My bedroom is always very <u>tidy</u>.
4 It is <u>dangerous</u> to swim in that river.
5 Jason is feeling <u>happy</u> today.
6 My mum works in a <u>small</u> clothes shop.

7 Complete the sentences with adjectives from exercises 2 and 3 and the Learn this! box.

1 That girl is called Saffron. You don't hear that name very often. It's quite _____.
2 The temperature is very _____ – only one degree Celsius.
3 This question is very _____. I can't answer it!
4 You need to get some nice, _____ clothes. All of your T-shirts and jeans have holes in them.
5 That answer is _____. Try again!
6 Leah and Emma's clothes are _____. They're both wearing white tops and brown trousers.

8 **SPEAKING** Work in pairs. Say if you agree or disagree with these statements.

1 Clothes should be more expensive.
2 Fashion companies should pay factory workers more money.
3 People throw away too many clothes.
4 We should make our own clothes.
5 Fashion companies don't care about the workers in their factories.

Do you agree that clothes should be more expensive?

No, I don't. What about you?

9 Do a class survey. How many people agree with each statement in exercise 8?

Teenage pressures

I can understand a text about the pressures on teenagers to look good.

1

2

1 **SPEAKING** Look at photos 1–4. What are the people doing? Use the phrases below. How often do you do these things?

go weight training   put on make-up   straighten your hair   take a selfie

2 Read the text quickly. How many of the writers believe that there is a problem with teenagers and image?

> **Reading Strategy**
>
> When you do a matching task, check your answers by trying to match the extra headings with each paragraph. They should not match any of them.

3 Read the Reading Strategy. Then match paragraphs (1–5) with headings (A–G) below. There are two extra headings.

A Copying a lie?
B Body-building boys
C Enjoying their own style
D Smiling celebrities, worried girls
E From catwalk to clothes shop
F No escape from the camera
G Copying hairstyles from the past

4 Explain why the extra headings in exercise 3 do not match any of the paragraphs.

5 Listen and read. Check your answers to exercise 3.

6 **VOCABULARY** Find the eight highlighted adjectives in the text. Write them as four pairs of opposites.

7 **VOCABULARY** Find four adjectives in paragraphs 1–3 of the text which begin with the negative prefix *un-*.

8 **KEY PHRASES** Complete these phrases for expressing opinions using the words below. The phrases are all in the reading text.

honest   my   really   think   view

Expressing opinions
I ¹_____ believe that …
In my ²_____, …
To be ³_____, …
Personally, I ⁴_____ …
In ⁵_____ opinion, …

9 Match the statements and opinions (a–i) with the people in the texts (1–5).

a Bad photos on social networking sites often get unkind comments. ___
b Most images in magazines and on the internet are not real because the companies change the photos. ___
c Some girls worry a lot about their appearance and this makes them unhappy. ___
d Some boys take drugs to make their bodies look more muscular. ___
e Girls wear make-up to express their personalities. It isn't a problem. ___
f Girls think it's important to look good all the time. ___
g Some boys put their health in danger to try to look good. ___
h A lot of teenage girls are not happy to look natural or a bit untidy. ___
i Teenagers know that the photos in magazines are not rea so it isn't a problem. ___

10 **SPEAKING** Work in pairs. Do you agree or disagree with the opinions and statements in exercise 9?

> I agree with Anna. I think girls worry a lot about their appearance.

> I disagree with … I don't think that .

🎧 2.12

IMPOSSIBLE IMAGES?

1 ___ 'Female celebrities post selfies on social media; millions of teenage girls see them and try to copy them. They want to have the same artificial hairstyles and make-up. I really believe that this is becoming a big problem. Why? Because girls are worrying about their appearance all the time and they're becoming unhappy. And the problem is growing. For example, teenage girls today spend 90% more on make-up than ten years ago.'
Maria Baker, Professor of Sociology

2 ___ 'In my view, social networking websites like Facebook and Instagram are part of the problem. Teenagers take photos of their close friends all the time and then they put these photos on the internet. A bad photo gets unkind comments. So girls now think it's important to look good all the time. Today's teenage girls are embarrassed about looking natural or having untidy hair. They can't relax. I see this problem every day at school.'
Sophie Ellis, Head Teacher

3 ___ 'To be honest, this isn't just a problem for girls. Boys have pressures too. They are surrounded by images of male celebrities with muscular bodies. Suddenly, an ordinary male body is not good enough, they think, so they take dangerous drugs to make their bodies muscular. Others go on unnecessary diets – for example, they buy special drinks because they want to be muscular. They talk about it a lot at the gym.'
Bob French, Gym owner

4 ___ 'A lot of teenagers try to copy images in magazines and on websites. But it's very easy to change photos on a computer. So today's teenagers are trying to copy an image that is not real. However, these tricks are not a secret these days. In fact, some companies are refusing to change their photos. They use hashtags to advertise their "real photos" on Twitter. Some people say social media is part of the problem. Personally, I think it can be part of the solution.'
Luke Woods, Photographer

5 ___ 'In my opinion, people are worrying about this too much. A lot of girls come into my shop and buy make-up. But they aren't copying celebrities. They have their own ideas and their own look. It's a way of expressing your personality. And it can be fun too! Of course some of the images in magazines are fake. Teenagers know that – they aren't stupid!'
Anna Granger, Shop owner

3G Making arrangements

I can make arrangements to meet somebody.

1 Complete the free-time activities with the verbs *play*, *go*, *have* and *meet*. Check the meaning of all the activities.

Free-time activities

1 _____ football / tennis / computer games / cards
2 _____ bowling / ice skating / dancing / rollerblading / swimming
3 _____ to the cinema / to the beach
4 _____ for a walk
5 _____ lunch / dinner in a café
6 _____ friends

➡ **Vocabulary Builder** Free-time activities: page 118

2 🎧 **2.13** Read and listen to the phone call. Find three free-time activities in the dialogue.

Harry	Hi, Imogen. How are things?
Imogen	Hi, Harry. Fine, thanks. What are you doing?
Harry	I'm just doing my homework.
Imogen	Do you fancy going swimming on Saturday afternoon?
Harry	I'm afraid I can't. I'm going shopping with my sister. What about Sunday morning?
Imogen	No, sorry. I'm playing football. How about Sunday afternoon?
Harry	Yeah, I'm free then.
Imogen	OK. What time shall we meet?
Harry	Let's meet at the pool at 2.30.
Imogen	Cool. See you there.

3 Read the Learn this! box. How many examples of the present continuous for future arrangements are there in the dialogue in exercise 2?

> **LEARN THIS!** **Present continuous for future arrangements**
>
> We can use the present continuous to talk about future arrangements.
>
> *What are you doing on Saturday evening?*
>
> *I'm going to the cinema.*

➡ **Grammar Builder 3G** page 128

4 SPEAKING Practise reading the dialogue in exercise 2. Change the highlighted words. Use activities from exercise 1 and your own ideas.

5 🎧 **2.14** Listen to three conversations. Circle the correct answers.

Conversation 1
1 Max is going fishing on **Saturday afternoon** / **Sunday afternoon**.
2 They agree to meet at **Sophie's house** / **the ice rink**.
Conversation 2
3 Amy and Adam arrange to **go shopping** / **have lunch**.
4 They're meeting at **11.30** / **12.30**.
Conversation 3
5 Tommy wants to go to **a musical** / **the cinema** with Caitlin.
6 They're meeting at **7.45** / **8.15**.

6 🎧 **2.15** **KEY PHRASES** Complete the key phrases with the verbs below. Use the correct form (infinitive without *to* or *-ing* form). Listen and check.

come   go   have   meet   see

> Making suggestions
>
> Do you fancy ¹_____ ice skating?
> Shall I ²_____ to your house?
> Why don't you ³_____ lunch with us?
> How about ⁴_____ a film?
> Let's ⁵_____ at the cinema.

7 **KEY PHRASES** Divide the key phrases below into two categories: agreeing to a suggestion and declining a suggestion.

> Agreeing to and declining suggestions
>
> | | |
> |---|---|
> | Cool. | That sounds fun. |
> | Great idea. | Sorry, but I'm busy. |
> | I'm afraid I can't. | Yes, I'd love to. |
> | No, thanks. | |

8 SPEAKING Work in pairs. Prepare a dialogue following the prompts below. Use activities from exercise 1 and key phrases from exercises 6 and 7.

A Greet B. Ask if B wants to do something on a particular day.

B Decline A's suggestion. Give a reason. Suggest another day / part of a day.

A Decline B's suggestion. Give a reason. Suggest another day / part of a day.

B Agree to the suggestion. Ask about the time.

A Suggest a time and place to meet.

B Agree.

> **Speaking Strategy**
>
> In a guided conversation, make sure you look at the other person and listen carefully to what they are saying.

9 SPEAKING Read the Speaking Strategy. Then act out your dialogue to the class.

Writing

An email
I can write an informal email.

1

2

3

4

1 **SPEAKING** In pairs, match photos 1–4 with the words below. Then decide which item is the best present for your partner.

bracelet   headphones   sunglasses   wallet

➡ **Vocabulary Builder** Accessories: page 118

2 Read the task and the email. Answer the questions.

Write an email to your friend in which you:
• describe what you are doing at the moment.
• thank him or her for a present.
• mention a future arrangement.
• suggest an activity to do together.

1 In what order does the email cover the four points?
2 Which paragraph covers two points?

✉ **To:** megan@email.com

Hi Megan,

I hope you're well. Thank you for the bracelet. I'm wearing it now. It's beautiful! My sister loves it too, but she can't borrow it!

I'm in my bedroom at the moment. I'm listening to music and trying to finish my geography project. It isn't going very well! My brothers are playing football in the garden, so I want to go outside too!

Do you fancy going to the cinema on Sunday or meeting for a coffee? I can't go on Saturday because my grandparents are coming to dinner. My dad is cooking his favourite dish – chicken pie.

That's all from me. Please write soon!

Love for now, Poppy

LEARN THIS! Linking words: *and, but, or, so* and *because*

We can use linking words to join words and clauses.

I'm seventeen years old <u>and</u> I live in London. I like P.E. <u>and</u> art.

I like maths, <u>but</u> I don't like history.

Do you want to go to the cinema <u>or</u> do you want to stay at home? Do you want apple juice <u>or</u> milk?

I don't like sport, <u>so</u> I never play football with my brother.

I always wear jeans <u>because</u> I don't like skirts or dresses.

3 Read the Learn this! box. Find examples of all five linking words in the email in exercise 2.

Writing Strategy

There are certain expressions that are used to begin and end an informal email, like *Dear* … and *Best wishes,* … but emails usually include a few other 'social phrases' near the beginning and end. These make the email sound more natural and friendly.

4 **KEY PHRASES** Read the Writing Strategy. Then find four expressions in the email in exercise 2 which you can add to the list below.

Beginning an email
Dear …
Hello … / ¹_____
Near the beginning
² _____
Thanks for your email.
How are you? / How are things?
Near the end
I hope to see you soon.
That's all for now. / ³_____
Please write soon.
Give my love to … / Say hi to …
Ending an email
Lots of love / Love / ⁴_____
Best wishes
Take care

5 Plan an email for the task in exercise 2. Look at the questions below and make notes.

1 What you are doing at the moment? (Imagine you are at home.)
2 What present are you saying thank you for? (Choose an accessory or an item of clothing.)
3 What arrangement(s) have you got? (Use your imagination.)
4 What activity do you want to suggest? (Choose an activity from Lesson G or your own idea.)

6 Write an email following your plan from exercise 5. Remember to include suitable phrases from exercise 4.

CHECK YOUR WORK

 Have you …
• covered all four points in the task?
• used a few 'social phrases'?
• used linking words to join your ideas?
• checked your spelling and grammar?

4

Food

4A Vocabulary

Are you hungry?
I can talk about breakfast, lunch and dinner.

1 SPEAKING Look at the photos. Choose one meal that looks:

a tasty   **b** healthy   **c** quick to make   **d** filling

> The meal in photo 1 looks …

2 🎧 **2.16** **VOCABULARY** Listen and repeat the words in the list. Then match them wi
the photos in exercise 1. Which food items are not in any of the photos?

Food apples beef bread carrots cheese chicken crisps cucumber
fish green / red peppers lamb lemon lettuce melon mushrooms olives
onion pasta peas pineapple potato prawns rice sandwiches sausages
strawberries tomatoes

Photo 1: onions, peas, sausages …

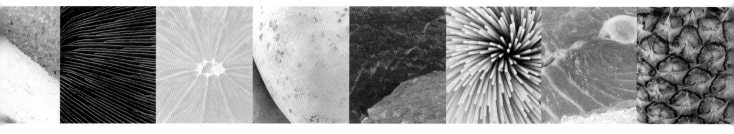

3 Work in pairs. Identify six types of food from exercise 1 in the photos above. Use the phrases below to help you.

It looks like … I think it's … That's definitely …
I agree. / I disagree. / I'm not sure about that.

> **LEARN THIS!** Countable and uncountable nouns
> **a** Countable nouns can be singular or plural:
> strawberry   strawberries
> **b** Uncountable nouns only have a singular form:
> pasta   cheese   bread

4 Read the Learn this! box. Then add the words in exercise 2 to the table below.

Countable nouns	Uncountable nouns
apples,	beef,

➡ **Grammar Builder 4A** page 130

Look at the breakfast menu below. Which five nouns in the menu are countable? How do you know?

breakfast
- cereal
- eggs
- pancakes
- yoghurt
- toast (butter, jam, honey)
- cakes
- bananas
- oranges
- tea
- coffee
- hot chocolate
- milk
- apple juice
- orange juice
- water

café menu

🎧 **2.17** Check your answers to exercise 5. Then, listen and repeat the words in the menu.

SPEAKING Work in pairs. Ask and answer questions about the food in exercises 2 and 5. Find three things you both really like.

> I really like olives. What about you?
> Me too!
> It's / They're OK.
> I don't like it / them.

8 🎧 **2.18** Listen to four people talking about meals. Which question (a–e) is each speaker answering? There is one extra question.

  a What do you have for breakfast and when do you have it?
  b What do you usually have for lunch during the week?
  c What do you have for lunch at weekends?
  d What are your favourite dinners and who cooks them?
  e What do you usually order when you have dinner in a café?

Speaker	1	2	3	4
Question				

> **RECYCLE!** Articles
> Indefinite article: We use *a* or *an* with singular (countable) nouns. We use *some* with plural nouns.
> Definite article: We use *the* with singular and plural nouns.
> We often use the indefinite article when we mention something for the first time and the definite article when we mention it again.
> *We've got some olives and a melon. The melon is on the table, the olives are in the fridge.*

9 Read the Recycle! box. Complete the sentences with *a*, *an*, *the* or *some*.

  Speaker 1 He usually cooks meat, fish or pasta – I think my favourite is [1]_____ fish. My other favourite dinner is my mum's home-made pizza. It's mainly cheese and tomato, but she puts [2]_____ olives on it too.

  Speaker 2 There's [3]_____ café and [4]_____ restaurant in our village, but [5]_____ restaurant is quite expensive, so we usually go to the café. The burgers at [6]_____ café are great: they're really big and they come with lots of chips.

  Speaker 3 I have [7]_____ sandwich and [8]_____ crisps. Sometimes I'm still hungry after [9]_____ sandwich and [10]_____ crisps, so I buy [11]_____ orange or [12]_____ banana.

  Speaker 4 I usually have breakfast, but it's just [13]_____ small cake; I eat it on the bus to school.

10 🎧 **2.18** Listen again and check your answers to exercise 9.

11 **SPEAKING** Work in pairs. Ask and answer the questions in exercise 8.

> What do you have for breakfast and when do you have it?
> I usually have …

there is / there are; *some* and *any*

I can use there is / are *and* some / any *correctly.*

1 Look at the food in the photo. Do you think this person has a healthy diet? Why? / Why not?

2 Work in pairs. Read the text and answer the two questions at the end.

Madison is a student in London. In this photo, you can see the food she buys every week. She tries to choose healthy food. There's some meat and some fish. There are some vegetables too. For snacks, there are some crisps, but there aren't any biscuits or sweets and there isn't any chocolate. There aren't any ready meals because there isn't a microwave in her flat! Now compare this with the food you eat at home every week. Is there a big difference? Are there any things your family and Madison both buy?

3 Complete the table with the correct verb forms. Use the text to help you.

Singular: *there is*	Plural: *there are*
Affirmative	**Affirmative**
There's a melon.	**3** _____ some tomatoes.
Negative	**Negative**
1 _____ a cucumber.	**4** _____ any prawns.
Interrogative	**Interrogative**
2 _____ a melon? Yes, there is. / No, there isn't.	**5** _____ any peas? Yes, there are. / No, there aren't.

4 Look at the photo in exercise 1 again. Complete the sentences below with *there's*, *there are*, *there isn't* or *there aren't*.

1 _____ some apples.
2 _____ a lettuce.
3 _____ a pizza.
4 _____ three peppers.
5 _____ any lemons.
6 _____ a big bottle of water.
7 _____ any bananas.

LEARN THIS! *some* and *any*

a We use *some* and *any* with plural countable nouns and uncountable (singular) nouns.

b We use *some* in affirmative sentences.

We've got <u>some</u> olives and <u>some</u> bread.

c We use *any* in negative and interrogative sentences.

There isn't <u>any</u> cheese. There aren't <u>any</u> eggs.
Is there <u>any</u> beef? Are there <u>any</u> mushrooms?

5 Read the Learn this! box. Then find all the examples of *some* and *any* in the text in exercise 2. Are the nouns countable or uncountable?

6 Complete the sentences with *some* or *any*.

1 I can't see _____ butter on the table.
2 There aren't _____ prawns in the salad.
3 I always have _____ crisps with my lunch.
4 Have we got _____ rice in the cupboard?
5 I'm making _____ pasta. Are you hungry?
6 Are there _____ mushrooms on the pizza?

➥ Grammar Builder 4B page 130

7 Complete the text with the words below.

any (×3)   are   aren't   is   isn't (×2)   some (×2)

There **1**_____ a food market every Thursday morning in my village. I always get there early because after 10 o'clock in the morning, there **2**_____ **3**_____ bread! I always buy **4**_____ vegetables, and I usually get **5**_____ chicken too. There **6**_____ **7**_____ fish, but that's OK because I don't like fish. Th other food depends on the seasons. For example, in winter, there **8**_____ **9**_____ tomatoes. But there **10**_____ always lots of potatoes! I love the market.

8 SPEAKING Work in pairs. Student A: Look at the picture below. Student B: Look at the picture on page 142. Find three differences between the pictures. Ask and answer questions using *Is there ... ?* / *Are there ... ?*

Is there any cereal?   No, there isn't.

Are there ... ?

What a waste!

I can identify and understand unstressed words.

1   SPEAKING   Work in pairs. Describe the photo. Use the words below to help you.

verbs   not need   throw away
nouns   egg   fruit   rubbish bin   vegetables
adjectives   fresh   old

2   Complete the text about freeganism with the words below. Do you find any of the information surprising?

angry   clothes   food   fruit   hungry
meal   rubbish bin   shape

FREEGANISM

In the UK, we throw away seven million tonnes of ¹_____ and drink every year. Supermarkets throw away food that is past its sell-by date, and they also throw away ²_____ and vegetables that are the wrong ³_____ or size! We also waste a lot of food at home because we buy too much, or cook too much for a ⁴_____. And 35% of school lunches go straight into the ⁵_____ too!

Freegans are very ⁶_____ about this. They try not to waste anything. They collect good food that supermarkets throw away, and they eat it or give it to people who are ⁷_____. Freegans recycle and reuse other things too – for example, ⁸_____ and furniture. They want to change the way we live.

LEARN THIS!   Unstressed words

a We usually stress the important 'content words' in sentences (e.g. nouns, names, main verbs, adjectives, question words).
<u>Tom</u> is in the <u>kitchen</u>.
<u>Where</u> is the <u>knife</u>?

b Less important 'functional words' are often unstressed (e.g. prepositions, modal verbs, articles, conjunctions, the verb *be*, pronouns, possessive adjectives).

c The vowel sound in unstressed words sometimes changes to a schwa sound /ə/.
/from/ > /frəm/

🎧 2.19   Read the Learn this! box. Listen and underline the 'content words' in these sentences.

1 Where's the bread?
2 Can you pass me the salt?
3 Dan is in the café.
4 His sister, Sophie, can cook.
5 What's the name of this song?
6 Sushi is from Japan.

Listening Strategy
Unstressed words can be difficult to catch in natural speech. Being able to recognise the unstressed form of words will help you to understand them when you hear them.

4   **🎧 2.20**   Read the Listening Strategy. Then listen. How are the italicised unstressed words pronounced?

1 Pizza's *from* Italy.
2 Here *are* two apples.
3 Where's *your* cup?
4 I *can* help you.
5 I'm going *to* the café.
6 salt *and* pepper
7 Here's *some* cheese.
8 This apple is *for* you.

5   **🎧 2.21**   Listen to an interview with a freegan. Only one of these sentences is correct. Which one?

1 Adam eats food from rubbish bins outside shops.
2 Adam gives food to homeless people.
3 Adam doesn't like spending money on food.

6   **🎧 2.22**   Listen and complete the sentences. How many unstressed words are there in each gap?

1 Adam _____ freegan _____ Luton _____ UK.
2 _____ collects food _____ supermarkets _____ restaurants.
3 _____ collects _____ food three _____ four times _____ week.
4 _____ collect _____ food _____ dark.
5 _____ Adam's friends _____ freegans.
6 _____ never come _____ house _____ meal.

7   **🎧 2.21**   Listen to the interview again. Are the sentences in exercise 6 true or false?

8   SPEAKING   Work in pairs. Say if you agree or disagree with the statements below. Give reasons for your opinions.

1 Freeganism is disgusting.
2 Freeganism isn't safe.
3 Freeganism is a good idea.
4 Freegans should buy food, not take it.
5 Shops and restaurants should throw away less food.

> I agree / don't agree that …

how much / how many, much / many / a lot of, a few / a little
I can talk and ask about quantity.

1 🎧 **2.23** Read and listen to the dialogue. What does Jim want to make? What ingredients does he need?

Sophie What are you doing, Jim?
Jim I'm looking for ingredients. How much flour have we got? How many carrots are there?
Sophie There's a little flour in the cupboard, and there are a few carrots in the fridge.
Jim Good. ... Oh, dear. There isn't much sugar in the bowl. And we haven't got many eggs.
Sophie What do you need them for?
Jim I want to make a carrot cake.
Sophie But you can't cook!
Jim Yes, I can. That isn't very nice!
Sophie Sorry. Look, there's a lot of sugar in the cupboard. And three eggs are enough.
Jim Great ... Oh, hang on. There's only one carrot in the fridge. Can I use a pepper instead?
Sophie I really don't think so!

2 Read the Learn this! box. Underline the examples of *how much*, *how many*, *much*, *many* and *a lot of* in the dialogue.

> **LEARN THIS!** *how much / how many, much / many / a lot of*
>
> **a** We use *how much ... ?* with uncountable nouns.
> *How much rice is there?*
>
> **b** We use *how many ... ?* with countable nouns.
> *How many onions have we got?*
>
> **c** We usually use *a lot of* in affirmative sentences.
> *There's a lot of butter. There are a lot of bananas.*
>
> **d** We use *a lot of*, *much* and *many* in negative sentences.
> *There's isn't much butter. / There's isn't a lot of butter.*
> *There aren't many bananas. / There aren't a lot of bananas.*

3 Complete the questions with *How much* and *How many*.

1 _____ students are there in class today?
2 _____ time do you spend on homework every day?
3 _____ money do you spend every week?
4 _____ DVDs have you got?
5 _____ housework do you do every week?

➡ Grammar Builder 4D   Page 130

4 SPEAKING In pairs, take turns to ask and answer the questions in exercise 3.

> How much time do you spend on homework every day?

> About an hour.

5 Circle the correct answers. Sometimes two answers are possible.

1 We've got **much / many / a lot of** bread.
2 There aren't **much / many / a lot of** books in my bag.
3 I've got **much / many / a lot of** friends.
4 There isn't **much / many / a lot of** milk in the fridge.
5 I haven't got **much / many / a lot of** homework this week.
6 I need **much / many / a lot of** help with this exercise.

6 Read the Learn this! box. Find an example of *a little* and an example of *a few* in the dialogue in exercise 1.

> **LEARN THIS!** *a little* and *a few*
>
> **a** We use *a little* with uncountable nouns.
> *We've got a little butter.*
>
> **b** We use *a few* with countable nouns.
> *There are a few onions.*

7 Complete the sentences with *a little* or *a few*.

1 There's _____ time before the end of the lesson.
2 I've got _____ posters in my bedroom.
3 There are _____ students in the gym.
4 'Would you like some pizza?' 'Just _____, please.'
5 We need _____ prawns for this recipe.

8 Write six sentences about the picture, three true and three false. Use *a lot of*, *a few*, *a little*, *not much* and *not many*.

> There aren't many ...   There's a little ...
> There are a lot of ...   There are a few ...

9 SPEAKING Work in pairs. Take turns to read your sentence to your partner. Correct your partner's sentences.

> There isn't much ...   That's true.

> There are a few ...   That's false. There are a lot of ...

Adjective + preposition

I can use adjective + preposition collocations.

1 SPEAKING Work in pairs. How many foods can you identify in the photo?

JUNK FOOD ADVERTISING

What can we do about junk food adverts for children? The World Health Organisation (WHO) believes that junk food adverts are responsible for a lot of obesity in children. It is very worried about this problem.

American children are used to food and drink adverts on TV. The average teenager watches sixteen every day! But now the food companies are also making computer games with junk food adverts. These games are very popular with children. The adverts are usually for food that is full of fat and sugar, for example burgers, biscuits, sweets and fizzy drinks. Most children are very keen on these foods, but of course they are bad for you. And after they watch the adverts, the children eat on average 45% more junk food.

The food industry says that this is not a problem. The WHO is disappointed with this attitude, because obesity in children is increasing every year. The WHO wants to ban junk food advertising for children in all countries. In Quebec, Sweden and Norway, they are already banned. What do you think?

Read the text. One of these sentences is not true. Which one?

1 After children watch adverts for junk food, they eat more of it.
2 Junk food companies say that there is a problem.
3 In some countries they don't have any TV adverts for junk food.

Do you agree with the WHO that we should ban junk food adverts? Why? / Why not?

LEARN THIS! Adjective + preposition

We use prepositions with some adjectives:
I'm good at maths but I'm bad at art.
I'm interested in history.
France is famous for cheese.

Read the Learn this! box. Then find the adjectives below in the text and write the prepositions that follow them.

1 responsible _____   5 full _____
2 worried _____   6 keen _____
3 used _____   7 bad _____
4 popular _____   8 disappointed _____

5 DICTIONARY WORK Look at the example sentences in these dictionary entries. Identify the prepositions that are used with the adjectives.

---

afraid /əˈfreɪd/ *adjective* If you are **afraid** of something, it makes you feel fear: *Some people are **afraid of** snakes.* ◇ *I was afraid to open the door.*
I'm afraid … a polite way of saying that you are sorry: *I'm afraid I've broken your calculator.* ◇ *I'm afraid that I can't come to your party.*

kind² /kaɪnd/ *adjective* (kinder, kindest) friendly and good to other people. *'Can I carry your bag?' 'Thanks. That's very **kind of** you.'* ◇ *Be **kind to** animals.*
⊃ OPPOSITE **unkind**

---

6 Complete the sentences. Use the prepositions and adjectives below.

at in of to with

1 Are you interested _____ photography?
2 Jason loves football, but he isn't very good _____ it.
3 Kate is disappointed _____ her exam results.
4 Tom is afraid _____ dogs.
5 You should be kind _____ your little sister.

bad kind popular used worried

6 Are you _____ about your exams?
7 RnB music is _____ with a lot of teenagers.
8 Fizzy drinks and sweets are _____ for your teeth.
9 I've got a new phone, but I'm not _____ to it yet.
10 It was _____ of you to help with my homework.

7 Complete the questions with the correct preposition.

1 Which subjects at school are you good _____?
2 Which subjects at school are you bad _____?
3 Outside school, what are you interested _____?
4 What foods do you like that are bad _____ you?
5 What foods do you like that are good _____ you?
6 What food is your country famous _____?

8 SPEAKING Work in pairs. Ask and answer the questions in exercise 7.

> Which subjects at school are you good at?

> I'm good at …

Unusual restaurants

I can understand a text about unusual restaurants.

1 Look at the photos of the restaurants (1–4). In which restaurant ...

a can you see water above the tables?
b can you see fish and water around the tables?
c do the customers sit in hammocks, not chairs?
d is it very dangerous to leave the table?

2 SPEAKING Work in pairs. Would you like to eat in these restaurants? Why? / Why not? Choose a favourite.

3 Read the text. Match the names of the restaurants to the photos. What other restaurants are in the text but not in the photos?

> **Reading Strategy**
> When you have to complete sentences with information from a text, start by deciding which part of the text contains the information you need. Remember that the sentences follow the same order as the text.

4 Read the Reading Strategy. Then read the sentences below, ignoring the gaps. In which paragraph of the text (A–D) can you find the information for each sentence?

1 It is difficult for restaurants in big cities to attract _____. (1 word)
2 A 'gimmick' is something to make your restaurant _____. (1 word)
3 At Ithaa, you can have dinner at a table below the _____ _____. (2 words)
4 You can experience Dinner in the Sky in 45 different _____. (1 word)
5 In Accra, you can have a meal inside an _____. (1 word)
6 At B.E.D. in Miami, there aren't any tables or _____ (1 word) for the customers.
7 At Zauo, the customers don't order their fish, they _____ _____. (2 words)

A Competing for customers

There are hundreds of restaurants in every big city. Often they serve similar food at similar prices – so how do they attract customers? Most restaurants try to offer good food and great service – and they hope customers come back again and again. But some restaurants offer a gimmick – something unusual to make their restaurant different from all the others.

🎧 2.24

B Location, location, location

Sometimes the gimmick is the restaurant's location. El Diablo, on the Spanish island of Lanzarote, is on a volcano. The chef uses heat from the volcano to cook the food. Or how about an underwater restaurant? At Ithaa, a restaurant in the Maldives, you can have dinner five metres below the Indian Ocean and watch sharks and turtles while you eat. Or you can go to the other extreme and choose Dinner in the Sky. Here, customers enjoy their meal at a special table 50 metres in the air. The company has restaurants in 45 different countries. It's an amazing experience – but don't drop your knife or fork!

Out **OF THE ORDINARY**

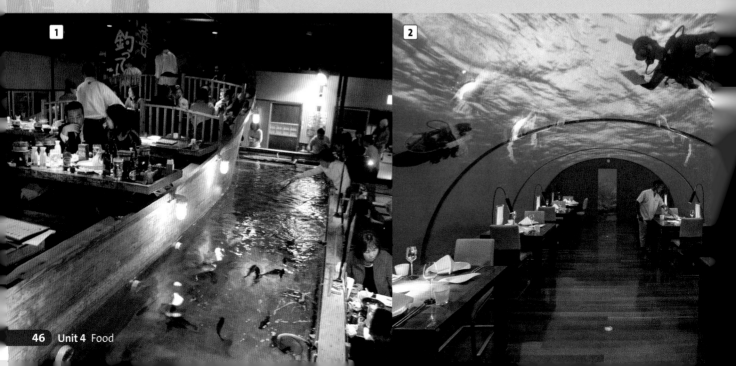

5 Complete the sentences in exercise 4 with information from the text. Write one or two words in each gap.

6 **VOCABULARY** Complete the definitions using the highlighted words in the text.

1 *Service* is the help and attention you get in a restaurant.
2 _____ are people who pay to eat in a restaurant.
3 You use a _____ to cut food on your plate.
4 You use a _____ to hold the food while you cut it.
5 You can use a _____ to carry a lot of drinks at the same time.
6 A _____ cooks the food in a restaurant or café.
7 The _____ is a list of the food and drink you can order.
8 A _____ serves customers in a restaurant.

7 **SPEAKING** Work in pairs. Ask and answer the questions.

1 On what occasions do people generally eat out in your country?
2 What kinds of restaurant are there in your town?
3 Is the service good there, do you think?
4 How often do you eat out?
5 What kind of food do you like to eat when you eat out?

8 **PROJECT** Work in pairs. Invent a restaurant. Then describe your restaurant to the class. The class votes for the best one. Think about:

• how to attract customers.
• the location.
• what kind of food you can order there.
• a gimmick.

C **Are you sitting comfortably?**

People often complain about the seats in aeroplanes: they're uncomfortable and there isn't enough space. So surely a restaurant inside an aeroplane is a bad idea. Well maybe not. In Accra, the capital of Ghana, you can have lunch or dinner inside an old DC-10 aeroplane. The waiter brings your food and drink on a trolley! Other restaurants offer extra comfort. At the Hammock Café in Sri Lanka, there are hammocks instead of chairs. And at B.E.D. in Miami, Florida, there are only beds. On each bed there is a candle and a tray.

D **Work for your food**

People go to restaurants to eat, chat with their friends and relax. But some restaurants ask their customers to work for their food. Zauo is a popular restaurant in Tokyo, Japan. It is a fish restaurant, but the customers do not order their fish from the menu – they have to catch it. Inside the restaurant, all of the tables are on an artificial boat, with water all around. There are different fish in different parts of the water. They choose their fish and then try to catch it!

In a restaurant

I can order food and drink in a restaurant.

1 SPEAKING Describe the photo. What are the people doing? What are they saying, do you think? Use the words below to help you.

look at   menu   order (verb)   restaurant
sit   table   waiter   write

menu

Starters
Red pepper soup • Thai prawn salad • Mushroom pâté

Main courses
Roast beef or lamb • Fish and chips • Vegetable pie

Desserts
Ice cream • Fruit salad • Chocolate cake

2 🎧 2.25 Read and listen to the dialogue. Complete the dialogue with the food that they order from the menu.

Waitress Hi. Are you ready to order?
Woman Yes, we are. I'd like the ¹_____ to start, please.
Waitress And for your main course?
Woman ²_____.
Waitress Fish and chips. Thank you. And for you, sir?
Man I'd like the ³_____ to start, please. Followed by the ⁴_____.
Waitress Thank you. Would you like anything to drink?
Man Can I have an ⁵_____, please?
Waitress Of course.
Woman The same for me, please.
Waitress So that's two orange juices. Thank you.

3 Read the Learn this! box. How many examples of *would like* (affirmative or interrogative) can you find in the dialogue in exercise 2?

LEARN THIS! *would like*

a We use *I'd like …* to ask for something in a polite way.
I'd like some milk, please.

b We use the question form *Would you like … ?* for offers:
Would you like a sandwich?

4 SPEAKING Work in groups of three. Act out the dialogue in exercise 2, but order different food and drinks.

5 🎧 2.26 Listen to dialogues 1–4 between the two customers and the waitress from exercise 2. In which dialogue or dialogues do the customers …

a ask for the menu? _____ and _____
b order / ask for food or drink? _____ and _____
c ask for the bill? _____

6 🎧 2.26 KEY PHRASES Listen again and complete the phrases. Who says them? Write W for the waiter or C for a customer.

Ordering food and drink
Can we have a table ¹_____ _____, please?
Can ²_____ _____ the menu, please?
Is everything ³_____ _____ you?
⁴_____ _____ some water, please.
And ⁵_____ _____, madam?
⁶_____ you _____ a coffee or a tea?
⁷_____ _____ have the bill, please?
⁸_____ _____ include service?
⁹_____ leave a tip.

LOOK OUT!

Drinks are usually uncountable, but they can be countable when we mean 'a cup / glass of …'.

(uncountable) I don't drink coffee.

(countable) Would you like a coffee? *(= a cup of coffee)*

We can't do this with food words. We use partitives like '*a bowl of*', '*a packet of*', etc.

I'd like a bowl of soup.

➡ **Vocabulary Builder** Partitives: page 119

7 Read the Look out! box. Find a countable noun in the dialogue that can also be uncountable. Is it food or drink?

8 SPEAKING Work in groups of three: two customers and a waiter. Look at the menu below. Then prepare a dialogue i which you do three of the following:

- Ask for bread.
- Order drinks.
- Ask for the dessert menu.
- Order a dessert.
- Ask for the bill.

menu

STARTERS
Pea soup ▪ Bread and butter ▪ Cheese and tomato salad

MAIN COURSES
Roast chicken ▪ Sausages and mashed potato ▪ Vegetable pasta

DESSERTS
Pancakes ▪ Fruit salad ▪ Chocolate cake

DRINKS
Apple juice ▪ Hot chocolate ▪ Tea or Coffee

9 SPEAKING Act out your dialogue to the class. Use key phrases from exercise 6 and try not to read from your scri

Writing

An invitation

I can write an invitation.

1

Dear Zak,

It's my birthday next week and I'm having a party to celebrate it. We're going to the beach for a BBQ on Sunday afternoon. That's the 16 August. Would you like to join us? If the weather is fine, bring your swimsuit and a towel. Can you also please bring a few sausages or burgers and some bread rolls for the BBQ?

Put it in your diary!

Love,

Emily x

2

Tom and Alice Bowman

*would like to invite you to
a party to celebrate the New Year
on Saturday 31st January from 8 p.m.*

at 27 Stanton Rd   *RSVP*

3

Hi Denise,

I'm planning a sleepover at my house on Saturday 18 January. Can you come? I'm inviting Laura too, so it should be great fun. Can you please bring some DVDs? I know you've got some good horror and sci-fi movies. My DVDs are all really old!

Come about 6 and you can eat with us too, if you like.

Hope you can come. Let me know!

Take care,

Lisa :)

4

Dear Martha,

Our exams finish at the end of June and I'm having a party to celebrate. It's at the village hall here in Greenwood. I'm inviting everyone in our school year. I'm organising the music, but everyone has to bring something to eat and drink. Can you bring some fruit — maybe some grapes or strawberries?

Hope you can make it.

Love,

Kaylee

1 Read the invitations (1–4) and match one of them with the photo. Which invitation is formal?

2 Find the following information for each invitation:

- the event
- the date and time
- the place

KEY PHRASES Complete the phrases with the words below. They are all in the invitations in exercise 1.

bring can celebrate diary hope
join know make planning

Invitations
I'm having a party to ¹_____ my birthday.
I'm ²_____ a sleepover.
Would you like to ³_____ us?
Can you ⁴_____ some food?
Put it in your ⁵_____!
I ⁶_____ you can come. Let me ⁷_____!
Hope you ⁸_____ ⁹_____ it.
RSVP

Writing Strategy

When you have finished writing, check your work carefully for mistakes. Read once for grammar, once for choice of vocabulary and once for spelling.

4 Read the Writing Strategy. Then check the invitation below and find four mistakes for each category mentioned.

Hi Anna,

I having a party at my hose on 16 Febuary to celebrate my birthday. I'm inviting all my friends so it should be grate fun. You don't have to take any food or drink, but can I please lend your speakers? I've got a lot of music on my MP3 player, but I hasn't got some speakers.

A party starts at 6 p.m. but can you please take the speakers a few hours before that – in the afternoon? Let me now if you can go.

Take care,

Sally

5 Write an informal invitation for one of the occasions below. Include the following information:

- Say why you are holding the party / event.
- Say when and where the party / event is (day, date and time).
- Say what the person you are inviting should do or bring with them.
- Remind them to confirm if they are coming or not.

Christmas   Halloween   New Year's Eve
the end of the exams   the end of the school year
your birthday

➡ **Vocabulary Builder** Parties and celebrations: page 119

CHECK YOUR WORK

Have you ...

- used some key phrases from exercise 3?
- checked the grammar?
- checked your choice of vocabulary?
- checked the spelling?

Reading

1 Read the Strategy. Complete the table with the words below.

~~airport~~ chef ~~curry~~ dish guest peas restaurant restaurant owner sausage scientist ~~sight~~ smell sound sweetshop taste touch ~~TV presenter~~ university

people	places	food	the senses
TV presenter	airport	curry	sight

2 Match gaps (1–7) in the text with sentences (A–H). There is one extra sentence which does not fit any of the gaps.

A For one TV series, he made lots of very large items of food.
B Then there's a fifth one at Heathrow Airport.
C Blumenthal is a British chef and restaurant owner.
D His food always feels interesting when you eat it.
E Or a big sausage with fish, chips and peas inside it?
F I know that the right sound can help food taste better.
G I feel like a child in a sweetshop.
H Yes, he sometimes uses sounds with his dishes.

Blumenthal's Big Ideas about Food

Would you like some chicken curry ice cream for dinner? ¹___ How about a house more than one metre tall made of sweets, biscuits and chocolate for dessert? These are some of the amazing dishes that Heston Blumenthal makes.

²___ He's famous for making very interesting meals. He believes food is fun. 'When I think of a new idea for a meal,' he says, 'I get really excited. ³___ I want guests in my restaurants to feel the same way.'

Blumenthal has lots of restaurants. There's one in London and three more in a town called Bray in the south of England. ⁴___ His restaurants aren't cheap, but his dishes are very special. He takes ideas from many different places and has particular interests in the history of food and the science of food.

Blumenthal's meals don't only taste fantastic, they look, smell, feel and sound amazing too. They sound amazing? Really? ⁵___ The Sound of the Sea, for example, is a seafood soup of fish and prawns served with an i-Pod. Guests can listen to the sound of the sea, seabirds and children's voices as they enjoy their soup. Blumenthal says, 'I did some tests with scientists at Oxford University. ⁶___ '

As well as running five restaurants, Blumenthal is a food writer, chef and TV presenter. ⁷___ He made the world's biggest boiled egg and a teacup he could stand in. What will he think of next?

Listening

3 Read the Strategy. Do these pairs of sentences mean the same (S) or different (D) things? Write S or D.

1 She doesn't have many hats.
She doesn't have a lot of hats. _____
2 There are a few DVDs.
There aren't many DVDs. _____
3 I'm not watching TV.
I never watch TV. _____
4 He's keen on fizzy drinks.
He doesn't like fizzy drinks. _____
5 That isn't kind.
That's unkind. _____
6 I need that pen.
I need a pen. _____

4 🎧 **2.27** Listen to four short recordings. Choose the correct answer (A–D).

1 What are Tina and Emmy both wearing?
   A jeans
   B a long-sleeved top
   C trainers
   D a dress
2 What does the presenter say about the Bath Farmer's Market?
   A There are lots of places to buy clothes.
   B It's a food festival.
   C A festival is happening there at the moment.
   D There aren't many cakes at the market.
3 What does the girl need?
   A some old T-shirts
   B a new T-shirt
   C a patterned T-shirt
   D a plain T-shirt
4 What does James decide to have for lunch?
   A a cheese sandwich
   B cold pasta, cheese and red pepper
   C tomato and red pepper soup
   D pasta and prawns

Use of English

5 Read the Strategy. In sentences 1–6 below, write a word which can complete each gap. Then match the word to the correct part of speech below.

adjective   adverb   article   noun   preposition   verb

1 I never _____ magazines.
2 There's an apple in the _____.
3 He's worried _____ Millie.
4 My sister _____ helps me.
5 It's a _____ fashion company.
6 I need _____ dictionary.

6 Read the text and add ONE missing word in each gap.

Upcycling

Like most people, I know that recycling is good [1]_____ the environment. When I throw plastic, paper, metal or glass [2]_____, I always put it in the recycling box. I [3]_____ put it in the rubbish bin. These days I'm interested [4]_____ upcycling too. That's when you take things that people don't want and make them useful again.

[5]_____'s a shop in my town called 'The Green House'. It sells lots [6]_____ fantastic upcycled furniture. [7]_____ woman who owns the shop upcycles old chairs. She paints them in different colours and they look amazing.

I try [8]_____ upcycle clothes when I can. I make T-shirts from old long-sleeved tops, for example, and I'm good [9]_____ using old jumpers to make scarves. At the moment, my friend and I [10]_____ making a pair of trousers from an old Indian skirt.

Speaking

Read the Strategy. Match answers A–E with questions 1–5.

1 Can we have a table for two, please?
2 I'd like the crab to start, please.
3 Is everything OK for you?
4 And for you, madam?
5 Would you like coffee?

A Yes, thank you. It's very good.
B No, thanks.
C Certainly. And for your main course?
D I'd like the chocolate cake, please.
E Yes, of course. Come with me.

8 Work in pairs or in groups of three.

Students A and B: You are customers. Look at the menu and follow the points below.
Student C: You work at the restaurant. Serve the customers.
- Ask for a table
- Ask for the menu
- Order a main course, and a starter or a dessert
- Ask for the bill

The International Kitchen — *menu*

STARTERS
Thai Crab Soup
Italian Salad

MAIN COURSES
Indian Meat Curry
Japanese pizza

DESSERTS
Turkish Sweets   French Fruit Ice   Russian Honey Cake

Writing

9 Read the Strategy. Add one missing word below to each line.

'm   it   to (×2)   with

1 We're planning a party celebrate New Year.
2 Bring some DVDs you.
3 I organising a film evening.
4 Would you like join us?
5 Hope you can make!

10 You are studying fashion. It's the end of term next week. Write an invitation for your end-of-term fashion party. Include the information below.

- why you are having the party
- when and where it is
- what you want the person you're inviting to wear
- what you want them to bring with them

5

In the city

Unit map

● **Vocabulary**
Places in towns and cities
Prepositions of place
Town and country
Transport

● **Word Skills**
Words that go together

● **Grammar**
Comparatives
Superlatives

● **Listening** Town or country?

● **Reading** Unusual cities

● **Speaking** Asking for and
giving directions

● **Writing** An article

● **Culture 5** New York

● **Vocabulary Builder** page 119
● **Grammar Builder** page 132
● **Grammar Reference** page 133

5A Vocabulary

Places

I can describe places in a city.

1 SPEAKING Work in pairs. Match the photos (1–5) with five of the places in the list below.

Places in towns and cities

airport   bank   bus station   car park   church   cinema   fire station   gym
hospital   hotel   library   mosque   museum   park   police station   post office
shopping centre   square   swimming pool   town hall   train station   zoo

2 🎧 2.28 Listen and repeat all the places in exercise 1.

3 🎧 2.29 Listen. Where are the people? Choose from all the places in exercise 1.

1 _____   3 _____   5 _____   7 _____
2 _____   4 _____   6 _____   8 _____

4 Answer the questions using places from exercise 1.

Where do people go to …
1 report a crime? _____
2 do some exercise? _____
3 catch a train? _____
4 buy some new clothes? _____
5 see some animals? _____
6 play football or have a picnic? _____
7 leave their car? _____
8 see a doctor? _____
9 change pounds into dollars? _____
10 borrow a book? _____

5 Work in pairs. Complete the gaps in the quiz using words from exercise 1.

1 This is a photo of the Blue _____. Where is it?
  a Cairo   **b** Baghdad   **c** Istanbul

2 When you fly to Heathrow _____, which country are you visiting?
  a the USA   **b** England   **c** Australia

3 'Grand Central' in New York is a
  a train _____
  b shopping _____
  c town _____

4 The Marina Bay Sands is an expensive _____ in which city?
  a Singapore   **b** Hong Kong   **c** Dubai

5 Inside Regent's _____ in London there is a famous:
  a hotel   **b** cinema   **c** zoo

6 Work in pairs. Do the quiz in exercise 5.

> **RECYCLE!** *there is / there are*
>
> We use *there's* (*there is*) with singular nouns (including uncountable nouns).
>
> We use *there are* with plural nouns.
>
> The negative forms are *there isn't* and *there aren't*.
>
> There's a bus station, but there isn't an airport.
> There are three banks. There aren't any hotels.

7 🎧 **2.30** Read the Recycle! box. Then listen to a teenager describing his town. Complete the sentences with *there's*, *there are*, *there isn't* or *there aren't*.

1 _____ a gym.
2 _____ a swimming pool.
3 _____ a park.
4 _____ a train station.
5 _____ lots of shops in town.
6 _____ a few banks.
7 _____ a supermarket.
8 _____ a cinema in the town.

8 **VOCABULARY** Check the meaning of the prepositions of place below. Find two pairs of opposites and one pair which mean the same.

Prepositions (place)

behind   between   close to   in / inside   in front of
near   next to   opposite   outside

9 🎧 **2.30** Listen again. Answer the questions.

1 What is the town hall opposite?
2 What is the park next to?
3 Is the shopping centre in town or outside town?
4 What is inside the shopping centre?
5 Where does the speaker live? (Use *between* in your answer.)
6 What is the bus stop close to?

10 **SPEAKING** Work in pairs. Ask and answer questions about your town or a city you know well. Use *Is there a … ?* or *Are there any … ?* and the places below. Then ask another question using the adjectives.

1 hotels? (cheap / expensive?)
2 a swimming pool? (public / private?)
3 a shopping centre? (small / large?)
4 an airport? (inside / outside town?)
5 parks? (busy / quiet?)

> Are there any hotels?

> Yes, there are.

> Are they cheap or expensive?

> There's an expensive hotel and …

5B Grammar

Comparatives

I can make comparisons.

1 SPEAKING Describe the photos. Which is New York and which is Los Angeles? How do you know?

2 Read the internet forum. Which city should Cassie choose, in your opinion?

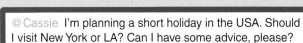

> **@Cassie** I'm planning a short holiday in the USA. Should I visit New York or LA? Can I have some advice, please?
>
> **@Grace** What do you want to do? LA is a more relaxing city. It has wider streets and lower buildings than New York. New York is bigger and noisier. People call it 'the city that never sleeps'.
>
> **@Jack** When are you going? The climate in Los Angeles is better, I reckon – winters are sunnier and summers are more comfortable.
>
> **@Ben** Do you like flying? For Europeans, Los Angeles is further than New York: the flight is four hours longer.

A

B

3 Read the Learn this! box. Then complete the table below with comparative forms from the text in exercise 2.

> **LEARN THIS!** Comparative adjectives
>
> **a** We can compare two things using a comparative adjective and *than*:
> *Today is warmer than yesterday.*
>
> **b** We can also use a comparative form before a noun:
> *We're looking for a bigger house.*

Short adjective	Comparative	Rule
long	1 _____	+ -er
big	2 _____	double consonant + -er
sunny	3 _____	-y → -ier
wide	4 _____	+ -r
Long adjective	**Comparative**	**Rule**
comfortable	5 _____	*more* + adjective
Irregular adjective	**Comparative**	
good	6 _____	
far	7 _____	
bad	worse	

4 Write sentences comparing New York and Los Angeles. Use information from the text in exercise 2 and the comparative form of these adjectives.

1 be / small
   Los Angeles is smaller than New York.
2 be / quiet
3 have / narrow / streets
4 have / tall / buildings
5 have / bad / climate
6 be / near

➡ Grammar Builder 5B page 132

5 Write questions about the cities below using the comparative form of the adjectives.

1 large / Moscow or Paris?
   Which is larger, Moscow or Paris?
2 polluted / Warsaw or Mexico City?
3 expensive / Prague or Tokyo?
4 sunny / Cairo or Istanbul?
5 safe / Cape Town or New York?
6 crowded / Athens or Lisbon?
7 dry / London or Milan?

6 SPEAKING Work in pairs. Ask and answer the questions in exercise 5. Make a note of your answers.

> Which is larger, Moscow or Paris?   Moscow.

7 🎧 **2.31** **PRONUNCIATION** Listen, repeat and check your answers to exercise 6. Pay attention to the pronunciation of: a) the *-er* ending of comparative forms, and b) *than*.

8 Find one mistake in each sentence and correct it.

1 The afternoons are often sunnyer than the mornings.
2 The shops in the town centre are more expensive the shops in the shopping centre.
3 I enjoy maths, but I'm gooder at English.
4 The houses are more expensive and more larger in the west of the city.
5 Big cities are always more exciting that small cities.

9 SPEAKING Work in pairs. Compare places that you know. Use the comparative form of the adjectives below.

attractive busy exciting expensive noisy
rainy safe small sunny warm

> I think Budapest is more attractive than ...

> I agree. / I disagree. I think ...

Town or country?

I can identify the main idea of a listening text.

1 VOCABULARY Divide the words below into 'town' and 'country'. Do some words belong to both groups?

Town and country crowd farm field hill lake office block shopping centre street traffic valley village wood

2 SPEAKING Describe the photos below. Which of the things in exercise 1 can you see?

3 Complete the texts with the comparative adjectives below.

cleaner easier friendlier quieter safer

HE ADVANTAGES OF LIVING IN THE COUNTRY

- It's ¹_____ because there is less crime.
- There isn't much traffic, so it's ²_____ and the air is ³_____.
- People are ⁴_____.
- It's ⁵_____ to be active – to walk, and get out into the fresh air.

better bigger easier more exciting

HE ADVANTAGES OF LIVING IN THE CITY

- It's ⁶_____ to travel round because there are lots of buses and trams. You don't always need a car.
- There's more to do: cinemas, concerts, museums, theatre, etc. It's ⁷_____.
- There are lots of restaurants. The food is ⁸_____ and more interesting.
- There are lots of shops, and they are ⁹_____ so there is more choice.

> **Listening Strategy**
>
> Sometimes it isn't necessary to understand all of the details when you listen, as long as you understand the main ideas. In these cases, focus on what you need to know and do not worry if you do not understand every word.

4 🎧 **2.32** Read the Listening Strategy. Then listen and choose the correct answers. Do not worry if you don't understand everything.

1 What is the speaker talking about?
   a The best place to visit in London.
   b The arrangements for the morning.
   c What they need to take with them.
2 Where are the man and woman going to eat?
   a On the train.
   b At the station.
   c At their house.
3 Why does the tourist decide not to visit the castle?
   a The path isn't safe.
   b It's a long walk.
   c It's already getting late.
4 The speaker's main aim is to
   a compare two different villages.
   b recommend a house that is for sale.
   c recommend a village to live in.

5 🎧 **2.33** Listen and match speakers (1–4) with sentences (A–E). There is one extra sentence. Remember not to worry if you don't understand every word the speakers say.

The speaker
A explains why he / she doesn't like life in the town. ___
B is encouraging people to come and live in the country. ___
C complains that there isn't much to do where he / she lives. ___
D is advertising a radio programme. ___
E would like to have a house in the city and one in the country too. ___

6 SPEAKING Work in pairs. Ask and answer the questions. Use the phrases below to help you.

1 What are the advantages of living in your town or village?
2 What are the disadvantages?
3 Would you like to live somewhere else? Why? / Why not?

An advantage of living in _____ is that there are …
A disadvantage is that …
It's good that you can …
It isn't good that you can't …
I'd like to move to _____ because …
I'd like to stay where I live now because …

5D Grammar

Superlatives

I can use superlative adjectives.

1

2

3

4

1 VOCABULARY Match the photos with four of the forms of transport below. Check the meaning of the other words.

Transport bus car coach motorbike plane ship taxi train tram underground

2 🎧 **2.34** Read and listen to the dialogue. How do they decide to travel from Scotland to London?

Martha We're going to London this weekend. How shall we get there? Train, coach, or plane?

Dan Well, the plane is certainly the quickest and easiest, but it's also the most expensive.

Martha Yes, the train and coach are cheaper. I think the train is the most convenient and the most comfortable.

Dan Overall, I think the coach is the best. It's certainly the cheapest.

Martha But I hate long coach journeys. I always feel sick. I think the coach is the worst option!

Dan OK, let's go by train. Can you ring and book the tickets?

Martha No, let's book online. You get the best deals there.

3 Complete the table with superlative adjectives from the dialogue in exercise 2.

Short adjective	Superlative	Rule
quick	1 _____	+ -est
large	the largest	+ -st
easy	2 _____	-y → -iest
hot	the hottest	double consonant + -est
Long adjective	**Superlative**	**Rule**
convenient	3 _____	*the most* + adjective
Irregular adjective	**Superlative**	
good	4 _____	
far	the furthest	
bad	5 _____	

4 Study the sentences below and complete the rule in the Look out! box with the correct preposition.

1 Who's the most intelligent girl in the school?
2 What's the highest mountain in the world?

> **! LOOK OUT!**
> After a superlative adjective and a noun we often use _____ followed by the name of a place or a group.

5 Complete the quiz. Use the superlative form of the adjective in brackets.

1 What is _____ (sunny) city in the USA?
2 What is _____ (hot) city in Europe?
3 What is _____ (far) capital city from the equator?
4 What is _____ (large) city in Asia?
5 What is _____ (wet) city in Europe?
6 What is _____ (expensive) city in the world?

6 SPEAKING 🎧 **2.35** Work in pairs. Ask and answer the questions in the quiz in exercise 5. Use the cities below. Then listen and check your answers.

Athens Bergen Las Vegas Reykjavik Shanghai Singapore

➧ **Grammar Builder 5D** page 132

7 Compare the different ways of travelling in cities. Give your opinions. Make sentences using comparative and superlative adjectives.

1 quick – buses / walking / bicycles
Bicycles are quicker than walking, but buses are the quickest.
2 convenient – trams / buses / taxis
3 slow – the underground / buses / motorbikes
4 expensive – taxis / buses / trams
5 dirty – motorbikes / bicycles / cars
6 cheap – bicycles / walking / buses

8 Write the questions with superlative adjectives.

1 who / talented / singer in the world?
Who's the most talented singer in the world?
2 who / funny / comedian on TV?
3 what / scary / form of transport?
4 who / good-looking actor in the world?
5 what / good / way to travel to the UK?
6 what / good / way to get round in your town or city?

9 SPEAKING Work in pairs. Ask and answer the questions in exercise 8.

> In your opinion, who's the most talented singer in the world?

> Adele. Do you agree?

> Yes, I do. / No, I think Taylor Swift is more talented.

Word Skills

Words that go together

I can use a range of travel-related collocations.

1 **SPEAKING** Describe the photo. Why is the man running, do you think?

2 Read the text and check your ideas from exercise 1. Would you like to race the tube? Why? / Why not?

3 **KEY PHRASES** Complete the travel collocations. The missing words are all in the text in exercise 2. Check the meaning of all the collocations.

Travel collocations
buy a ¹_____
get to / travel to school / work / London / the shops, etc.
get on / off a ²_____ / a bus / a tram, etc.
get in / out of a car / a taxi / a van, etc.
go up ³_____ / the escalator
go by taxi / bus / tram / train / plane, etc.
take a ⁴_____ / a bus / a train / a tram / a plane, etc.
catch a ⁵_____ / a tram / a train / a plane, etc. (but not a taxi)
miss a train / a bus / a tram / a plane, etc.
go on foot
ride a ⁶_____ / a motorbike / a scooter / a horse
lose your ⁷_____
cross the ⁸_____
drive to work / into town / to London
wait for a bus / a tram / a train, etc.
give somebody a lift

4 Complete the sentences with the verbs below. Use the correct form.

buy   get in   get off   get on   go   ride   take

1 My mum _____ a scooter to work.
2 Open the door, _____ the car and put on your seat belt.
3 'I want to go to the town centre. Where should I _____ the bus?'
  Driver: 'At the next stop.'
4 There aren't any buses. You have to _____ on foot or _____ a taxi.
5 You have to _____ a ticket before you _____ the train.

cross   drive   go up   lose   miss   wait for

6 'What should I do if I _____ the bus?'
  '_____ the next one. They come every five minutes.'
7 Look and listen before you _____ the road.
8 My uncle never _____ to work because he hasn't got a car.
9 'Where's the ticket office?'
  '_____ the stairs. It's on the left.'
0 Joe never _____ his way because he's got a satnav on his phone.

RACING THE TUBE!

The latest craze in big cities with underground trains is 'racing the tube'. The idea is to run faster than an underground train! First you choose two underground stations that are very near to each other. Then you buy a ticket and get on a train that is travelling to the first station. When the train arrives at the station, and the doors open, you get off the train, go up the stairs or escalator – very quickly! – and run to the next station. You can't take a taxi or catch a bus or ride a bicycle. You have to run. But watch out for traffic and don't lose your way! It's easier if someone helps you. For example, when you have to cross the road, they can warn you if cars are coming. When you arrive at the second station, you have to catch the same train. It's more difficult than it sounds!

> **LOOK OUT!** *arrive in* and *arrive at*
> - We use *arrive in* with countries, towns and cities.
>   arrive in Britain / arrive in Oxford
> - We use *arrive at* with buildings or events.
>   arrive at the cinema / arrive at school / arrive at the party
> - We don't use *to* with *arrive*.
>   NOT ~~What time do you arrive to London?~~ ✗
> - We don't use *in* or *at* with *home*.
>   arrive home

5 Read the Look out! box. Find two examples of *arrive at* in the text in exercise 2.

6 Complete the sentences with *in* or *at* or *no preposition (-)*.

1 The train arrives ___ Paddington Station at 10 p.m.
2 Let's have dinner when we arrive ___ the hotel.
3 I usually arrive ___ home at 5 p.m.
4 When do you arrive ___ Budapest?
5 Arrange your visa before you arrive ___ the USA.

7 **SPEAKING** Work in pairs. Ask and answer the questions below. Use collocations from exercise 4 in your answers. Which answers are the same for you and your partner?

1 How do you usually get to school?
2 How do you usually get to: a) the shops, b) your friends' houses?
3 How does your mum or dad get to work?
4 How do you usually go on holiday?
5 How do you usually get to other towns and cities in your country?

Unusual cities

I can understand a text about unusual cities.

1 SPEAKING Look at the photos. Do these cities look like good or bad places to live? Give reasons.

> **Reading Strategy**
>
> When you do a matching task, read all the texts first to get a sense of the overall meaning. Then, go through the questions one by one. Decide which text you think contains the answer and look for it carefully. If you can't find it, look at the other texts.

2 Read the Reading Strategy. Then read the texts (A–C) and match them with the photos (1–4). One of the texts matches two photos.

3 Match each question (1–7) with one of the texts (A–C).

Which text is about a city which …
1 has more than a million inhabitants? _____
2 is easy to travel around? _____
3 is next to a much larger city? _____
4 is less than a hundred years old? _____
5 has a good system of recycling? _____
6 offers high salaries for workers? _____
7 has a lot of green spaces? _____

4 Explain the significance of these numbers and measurements from the texts.

Text A:	1.7 million	400 metres	50 square metres
Text B:	2,000	70	300 km
Text C:	eight million	60,000	90%

> Curitiba has a population of about 1.7 million.

5 VOCABULARY In the texts, find the missing words for the compass points and continents.

Compass points

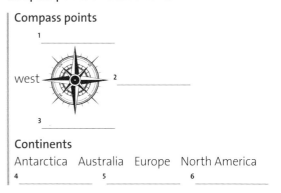

west   2 _____

1 _____

3 _____

Continents

Antarctica   Australia   Europe   North America

4 _____   5 _____   6 _____

6 Work in pairs. Complete the sentences with the correct words from exercise 5.

1 Canada is to the *north* of the USA.
2 Egypt is in the _____ of _____.
3 England is to the _____ of Scotland.
4 Spain is in the _____ of _____.
5 Los Angeles is on the _____ coast of _____
6 Germany is to the _____ of Poland.

7 In pairs, write more sentences like the ones in exercise 6. Include facts about your own country and its neighbours.

8 SPEAKING In pairs, ask and answer questions about the cities in the texts. Use the superlative form of these adjectives.

attractive / ugly   big / small   clean / dirty   near / far

> Which city is the most attractive?

> I think Curitiba is the most attractive.

🎧 2.36

UNUSUAL CITIES
THE GOOD, THE BAD and THE UGLY

A Green city

Curitiba is a medium-sized city in the south of Brazil, the largest country in South America. Why is it unusual? Because many South American cities are very polluted. But Curitiba is the opposite: it is one of the cleanest and 'greenest' cities in the world. In most cities, cars cause a lot of pollution. But in Curitiba, only a quarter of the 1.7 million inhabitants use a car – the others use public transport. That is because the bus system is probably the best in the world. It is called the BRT (Bus Rapid Transport) and it carries two million passengers a day. Tickets are cheap and journeys are fast. And nobody in the city lives further than 400 metres from a bus stop. There are lots of parks in the city: in fact, there are 50 square metres of green space per person!

B Artificial city

Neft Dashlari is a man-made city in the Caspian Sea. It is about 65 kilometres from the east coast of Azerbaijan, in Asia, and it has a population of about 2,000. The most unusual thing about the city is its location – it is in the sea, but not on an island. The ground below the city is completely artificial. Neft Dashlari is about 70 years old and it exists for one reason: oil. The city is in very bad condition. For example, it has 300 kilometres of roads, but only 45 kilometres are safe to use. The bridges are falling into the sea and some of the apartments are under water. But people still live and work there. It is probably one of the worst cities in the world for its inhabitants, but salaries are much higher than in other places.

C Recycling city

Cairo, in the north of Egypt, is one of the biggest cities in Africa. It is the capital and has a population of nearly eight million. Like any city, it creates tonnes of rubbish every day. But amazingly, the city does not employ anybody to collect rubbish. Instead, a group of people called the Zabbaleen collect it. The inhabitants of Cairo pay them a small amount of money for doing this. The Zabbaleen take the rubbish back to their town on the edge of Cairo. It is called Manshiyat Naser and has a population of about 60,000. There, the women and children sort the rubbish by hand. It seems a very slow system, but in fact it works very well. They recycle nearly 90% of the rubbish, which is far better than recycling centres in most western countries. Manshiyat Naser certainly is not one of the most attractive places in Egypt. But thanks to a 2009 film about it, *Garbage Dreams*, it is quite famous – and quite popular with tourists!

Asking for and giving directions

I can ask for and give directions.

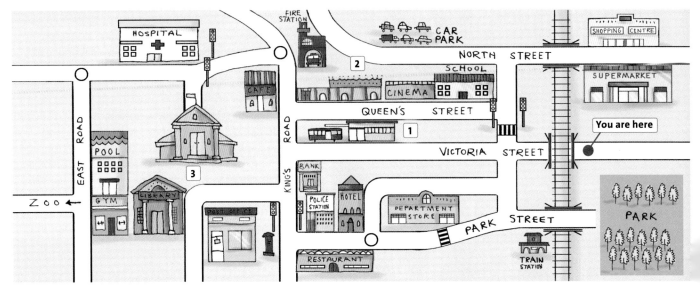

1 Find these things on the map.

bridge   crossroads   roundabout   traffic lights

2 **KEY PHRASES** Match the phrases for giving directions with the diagrams.

Giving directions	Location
Go straight on.	The … is next to the …
Go along King's Road.	It's between the … and the …
Take the first left.	It's opposite the …
Go to the end of the road.	It's on the corner.
Go past the bank.	It's on your right / left.
Turn right at the crossroads.	
Cross the road.	
Go under / over the bridge.	

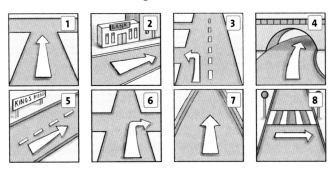

3 🎧 **2.37** Read and listen to the dialogue. Follow the directions and find the museum on the map. Is it 1, 2 or 3?

Girl Excuse me. Can you direct me to the museum, please?

Man Sure. Go along Victoria Street, under the bridge. Take the first right. Then turn left at the traffic lights. Go past the cinema and the museum is on the corner, opposite the café.

Girl Sorry, could you repeat that, please? Go along Victoria Street, under the bridge, …

Man Yes. Take the first right and turn left at the traffic lights. Go past the cinema and it's opposite the café, on the corner.

Girl Thanks very much.

Man You're welcome.

4 **SPEAKING** Look at the map. Ask and answer questions about these places using the phrases for location.

car park   hospital   hotel   post office   swimming pool

> Where's the hotel?

> It's opposite the restaurant. / It's on the corner, next to the police station.

➡ **Vocabulary Builder** In the street: page 119

5 🎧 **2.38** Listen to four dialogues. Follow the directions on the map. Where do the people want to go?

> **Speaking Strategy**
> If you don't understand, ask the person you are talking to to slow down, repeat, or clarify.
> *Could you speak more slowly, please?*
> *Could you repeat that, please?*
> *What does … mean?*

6 🎧 **2.38** Read the Speaking Strategy. Then listen again. Which questions from the Speaking Strategy did each speaker use?

7 **SPEAKING** Work in pairs. Use the map and the prompts below to plan a dialogue.

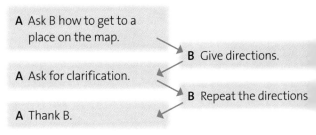

A Ask B how to get to a place on the map.

B Give directions.

A Ask for clarification.

B Repeat the directions

A Thank B.

8 **SPEAKING** Work in pairs. Act out your dialogue for the class.

5H Writing
An article
I can write an article about a town.

1 SPEAKING In pairs, look at the photo of Beverley, a town in the north of England. Compare it to your town or village using the comparative form of these adjectives.

attractive   clean   crowded   exciting

> It looks more / less attractive than my town. It's probably …

➤ **Vocabulary Builder** Describing towns and cities: page 119

2 Read the task and the model text, ignoring the gaps. Think of three similarities between Beverley and your town or village.

Write an article for an international student magazine describing your own town or a town that you know well. Include information which will be appealing to young visitors.

> They both have a shopping centre. They …

A town worth visiting

1 ___ It is a small town, with a population of about 30,000, but it is popular with tourists. They come to explore the narrow streets and to visit the medieval buildings.

2 ___ There are two music festivals every year: a classical music festival in May and a folk music festival in June. There is also a theatre in the town centre. And for nature-lovers, there is a beautiful park called Beverley Westwood. It's the perfect place for a walk or a picnic. There isn't a football stadium in Beverley, but there is a leisure centre and a racecourse.

3 ___ The narrow streets are full of small, interesting shops. There is also a big new shopping centre on the edge of town. And every Saturday, there is a market in the town centre with more than a hundred different stalls.

....
Writing Strategy
Write in paragraphs of two or more sentences. Give each paragraph its own topic and introduce the topic in the first sentence. Plan your paragraphs before you begin writing.
....

3 Read the Writing Strategy. Match the gaps in the model text (1–3) with three of the sentences (a–e) below. There are two extra sentences.

a There are many different forms of entertainment in Beverley.
b It is easy to travel around when you are in Beverley.
c For people who love shopping, Beverley has a lot to offer.
d Beverley, in the north of England, is a very attractive and historic town.
e There is a wide choice of places for eating out, some cheap and some quite expensive.

4 Read the paragraph below. Which of the extra sentences in exercise 3 would be a good opening sentence?

___ For a quick lunch, it's easy to find a tea room or café. There are some good sandwich shops too. In the evening, you can enjoy dinner in one of the town's many restaurants. Some of the pubs offer good food at low prices. And like most towns in Britain, there are also fish and chip shops!

5 Find six different places for eating and drinking in the paragraph in exercise 4.

6 Plan an article about your own town or a town you know well. Choose three of the topics below and write two or three ideas for each topic in the table.

eating out   entertainment   getting around   history   places of interest   places to stay   shopping

Paragraph	Topic	Ideas
1		
2		
3		

7 Write a sentence to introduce each topic that you chose in exercise 6.

8 Write your article using your plan from exercise 6. Begin each paragraph with your sentences from exercise 7.

CHECK YOUR WORK

Have you …
• written in paragraphs?
• started each paragraph with a sentence to introduce the topic?
• checked your spelling and grammar?

6
Going wild

Unit map

● **Vocabulary**
Wild animals
Parts of an animal
Past time expressions
Prepositions of movement
The natural world

● **Word Skills**
Prepositions of movement
and place

● **Grammar**
Past simple affirmative (regular)
Past simple: *be* and *can*

● **Listening** Missing sounds

● **Reading** Stranger than
fiction?

● **Speaking** Photo description

● **Writing** A postcard

● **Culture 6** Yellowstone
National Park

● **Vocabulary Builder** page 120
● **Grammar Builder** page 134
● **Grammar Reference** page 135
● **Extra speaking task** page 142

6A Vocabulary
Wild animals
I can talk about different wild animals.

1 **VOCABULARY** Match the photos A–F with six of the words below. Which of the animals in the list can you find in the wild in your country?

Wild animals bear bee butterfly crocodile dolphin eagle elephant frog giraffe gorilla hippo kangaroo lion monkey shark snake spider tiger whale wolf

2 🎧 **3.02** Listen and repeat all the words in exercise 1.

3 Work in pairs. Decide which animals from exercise 1 you usually see

   a on land *a bear, …*   **b** in water   **c** in the air

4 Match the animals in exercise 1 with the correct category. Then check your answers in pairs.

Insects: _____   Mammals: _____
Birds: _____   Reptiles: _____
Fish: _____   Others: _____

5 Work in pairs. Can you add any more animals to the categories in exercise 4?

5 SPEAKING Work in pairs. Ask and answer questions about the photos above using the words below and the animals from exercise 1.

Parts of an animal ear eye foot (*pl* feet) leg mouth paw tail tooth (*pl* teeth) wing

> What's number 1?

> I think it's a butterfly's wing.

7 🎧 **3.03** Listen and check your answers to exercise 6.

> **RECYCLE! Comparative and superlative forms**
>
> The comparative form of short adjectives ends in -*er*; the superlative form ends in -*est*.
>
> *small – smaller – the smallest*
> *big – bigger – the biggest*
> *rare – rarer – the rarest*
> *pretty – prettier – the prettiest*
>
> With longer adjectives, we add *more* before the adjective to form the comparative and *the most* to form the superlative.
>
> *beautiful – more beautiful – the most beautiful*

8 Read the Recycle! box. Then complete the sentences below with the comparative or superlative form of the adjectives in brackets.

1 Sharks are _____ (dangerous) than crocodiles.
2 Crocodiles are _____ (slow) than most humans on land.
3 Tigers are the _____ (heavy) of the big cats.
4 Giraffes are the _____ (tall) land animals.
5 Dolphins are _____ (intelligent) than gorillas.
6 Baby gorillas are _____ (big) than human babies.

9 🎧 **3.04** Listen to a guide at a wildlife park. Are the sentences in exercise 8 true or false? Write T or F.

10 🎧 **3.04** Listen again. Answer the questions.

1 How many people do sharks kill every year?
2 How fast is a crocodile?
3 How heavy is an adult male tiger?
4 How tall is an adult giraffe?
5 How many words can some gorillas understand?
6 How heavy is a baby gorilla?

11 SPEAKING Work in pairs. Ask and answer questions about the animals below. Use the comparative form of the adjectives. Do you agree with your partner?

1 ugly / a frog or a snake
2 beautiful / a butterfly's wings or a tiger's face
3 frightening / a snake or a spider
4 intelligent / a bee or a bear
5 rare / a tiger or a wolf
6 strong / a crocodile's mouth or a whale's tail

> Which is uglier, a frog or a snake?

> A frog.

> I agree. / I don't agree. I think …

F

E

Past simple (affirmative): regular

I can talk about past events.

SEARCHING FOR THE LOST CITY

The successful Canadian entertainer William Hunt lived and worked in Europe under the name The Great Farini. But he wanted a new challenge and loved the idea of exploration. So in 1885, he sailed to Africa and crossed the huge Kalahari Desert on foot. A photographer travelled with him and photographed the journey. After the journey, they described a lost city in the middle of the desert. Their story caused a lot of excitement and many other explorers studied the photographs and then tried to find the city, but without success. In the end, people stopped looking. Perhaps Farini invented the lost city – nobody knows for sure.

1 🎧 **3.05** Read and listen to the text about exploring the Kalahari Desert. What three different jobs does it mention?

2 Read the Learn this! box. Then look at the highlighted past simple verbs in the text in exercise 1 and match two with each spelling rule (a–d).

> **LEARN THIS!** Past simple (affirmative): regular verbs
>
> The past simple affirmative of regular verbs ends in *-ed*.
>
> **a** With most verbs, we add *-ed* to the infinitive without *to*:
> *work → worked*
>
> **b** If the verb ends in *-e*, we just add *-d*:
> *like → liked*
>
> **c** If the verb ends in *-y*, the *-y* changes to *-ied*:
> *carry → carried*
>
> **d** If the verb ends in a vowel and a consonant, we usually double the consonant before adding *-ed*:
> *chat → chatted*

3 🎧 **3.06** PRONUNCIATION Listen and repeat these past simple forms. In which verbs is the *-ed* ending an extra syllable pronounced /ɪd/? What is the rule?

arrived chatted decided interrupted liked
needed planned visited worked

4 PRONUNCIATION Say the past simple forms of these regular verbs. Pay attention to the endings.

end live start stop travel wait walk want watch

5 Choose the correct verb for each gap. Then complete the text with the past simple affirmative form.

CROSSING THE SAHARA

Michael Asher is a British explorer and the first person to cross the Sahara Desert using only camels. As a young man, Asher **1**_____ (work / arrive) as a police officer and then a teacher. But he **2**_____ (want / wait) to be an explorer. So he **3**_____ (visit / move) to Africa, **4**_____ (live / watch) with an African tribe and **5**_____ (study / start) their language. He **6**_____ (describe / marry) an Italian woman called Mariantonietta Peru. She **7**_____ (plan / love) the idea of exploring too, and together, they **8**_____ (walk / plan) a journey across the Sahara Desert from west to east by camel and on foot. They **9**_____ (train / stop) for three months and then they **10**_____ (start / end) their journey. They **11**_____ (work / travel) about 7,250 kilometres and **12**_____ (arrive / live) at their destination 271 days later. Asher **13**_____ (decide / describe) the crossing in his book *Impossible Journey – Two Against the Sahara*.

➡ **Grammar Builder 6B** page 134

6 Complete the sentences with the past simple affirmative form of the verbs below.

chat live stop travel wait ~~walk~~

1 I walked into town last night.
2 My cousins _____ around Italy last summer.
3 We _____ three hours for a bus.
4 His grandparents _____ in America for years.
5 The rain _____ an hour ago.
6 I _____ to my neighbour yesterday morning.

7 VOCABULARY Add the four underlined time expressions from the sentences in exercise 6 to the list below. Then p[ut] all of the expressions into the correct order (1–10), startin[g] with the most recent.

Past time expressions a few minutes ago last month last week ten years ago three hours ago two months ago

1 *A few minutes ago, 2 …*

8 SPEAKING Work in pairs. Using past simple verb forms from this lesson, tell your partner things you did:

last week ten years ago this morning yesterday

> This morning, I walked to school. I arrived at school. I …

Listening

Missing sounds

I can understand words which are joined together in connected speech.

1 SPEAKING Work in pairs. Describe the photo. Use the nouns below to help you.

bear   chair   grass   paw   sleeping bag   tent

2 Complete the safety advice with the verbs below.

climb   feed   keep   look   rely   run   take   tell   walk

⚠ Safety in the National Park

- ¹_____ someone where you are going.
- Do not ²_____ on mobile phones. You often can't get a signal in the wild.
- ³_____ a map and compass with you.
- Never ⁴_____ bears or other wild animals.
- Don't ⁵_____ food in your tent. Put it in your car or in a box a few metres from your tent.
- If you see a bear, ⁶_____ slowly away from it. Do not ⁷_____. Do not ⁸_____ at the bear's eyes.
- Do not ⁹_____ a tree. Most bears are good climbers.

Listening Strategy

In connected speech, some sounds disappear when we join words together. This is especially true of /d/ and /t/ sounds at the end of a word, when the next word begins with a consonant. The more you listen, the more you will get used to this.

Read the Listening Strategy. Mark one /d/ or /t/ sound in each sentence which might disappear when the sentence is spoken at natural speed.

1 Kate is my best friend.
2 My grandad is an old man.
3 I'm going to the USA next week.
4 It's a cold morning.
5 You must go to the doctor.
6 We camped in Wales last summer.

🎧 **3.07** Listen, check and repeat. Copy the pronunciation.

LOOK OUT! Past simple endings

You may not hear the past simple ending very clearly in connected speech if the following word begins with a consonant.

We played tennis yesterday.   can sound like
We play tennis yesterday.

I cooked dinner last night.   can sound like
I cook dinner last night.

However, we can usually identify past tense forms from the context or from other words in the sentence.

5 🎧 **3.08** Read the Look out! box. Then listen to the two example sentences. How do we know that the verbs are past simple, not present simple?

6 🎧 **3.09** Listen to eight sentences. Say if the verb is present simple, past simple or could be either. How do you know?

7 🎧 **3.10** Listen to four people describing their experiences in the wild. Match the speakers with sentences A–E. There is one extra sentence.

A The speaker describes a problem with a vehicle. ___
B The speaker camped in a beautiful place. ___
C We learn how a mobile helped to solve the problem. ___
D The speaker explains why it's important always to take a phone with you. ___
E The speaker nearly lost some possessions. ___

8 🎧 **3.11** Read these sentences from exercise 7. Mark the /d/ and /t/ sounds that disappear. Then listen, check and repeat.

1 We changed into our swimming trunks behind some trees.
2 We noticed two boys in the wood.
3 Last year my friend Sam and I visited Yellowstone National Park.
4 We closed the car doors.
5 We followed the wrong path.
6 We opened the app.
7 Suddenly, the car slowed down and stopped.
8 My little brother noticed some lions.

9 SPEAKING Work in pairs. Ask and answer the questions.

1 Are there any National Parks in your country?
2 What animals can you see there? Are any of them dangerous?
3 What can you do in the National Parks?

6D Grammar

Past simple: *be* and *can*

I can talk about the past using be *and* can.

1 🎧 **3.12** Read and listen to the dialogue. Where was Molly? Which animals did she see?

Max Were you on holiday last week?
Molly Yes, I was. I was on safari.
Max Lucky you! Was it fun?
Molly Yes, it was amazing. We travelled to Cape Town to visit my uncle and the next day we were in a jeep in the middle of the African plains!
Max Wow!
Molly From the jeep we could see giraffes, elephants and zebras.
Max Could you see any lions?
Molly No, we couldn't. Not there. But later we crossed the plain to a river and there were lions and hippos. It was fantastic. And I wasn't scared!
Max It sounds incredible. Were there any tigers?
Molly No, there weren't. There aren't any tigers in Africa!

2 Complete the Learn this! box. Use the dialogue to help you.

LEARN THIS! Past simple: *be* and *can*

be: Affirmative
I / he / she / it was there.
you / we / they **¹**_____ there.

be: Negative
I / he / she / it **²**_____ there.
you / we / they weren't there.

be: Interrogative and short answers
³_____ I / he / she / it there?
Yes, I / he / she / it **⁴**_____. / No, I / he / she / it wasn't.
Were you / we / they there?
Yes, you / we / they were. / No, you / we / they **⁵**_____.

can: Affirmative
I / he / she / it / you / we / they could swim.

can: Negative
I / he / she / it / you / we / they could not swim.

can: Interrogative and short answers
⁶_____ I / he / she / it / you / we / they swim?
Yes, I / he / we could. / No, she / it / you / they **⁷**_____.

The forms for *could* are the same for all persons.

↪ **Grammar Builder 6D** page 134

3 Complete the sentences with the correct form of *be*.

1 Fran and Harry _____ at school yesterday. Why not?
2 Today is Friday. Yesterday _____ Thursday.
3 '_____ you at the cinema last night?' 'No, I _____.'
4 My keys _____ on the table, but they aren't there now.
5 The science teacher _____ in the lab. She was in the teachers' room.
6 '_____ the weather good when you _____ in France last week?' 'It _____ OK. It was sunny, but it _____ very warm.'

4 Complete the sentences. Use *couldn't* and *because*, and the phrases below.

he was full   I wasn't well   ~~it was raining~~   it was too windy   she wasn't tired   the sea was very rough

1 we / have a barbecue in the garden …
   We couldn't have a barbecue in the garden because it was raining
2 Josh / swim …
3 I / go to school …
4 Liam / finish his burger …
5 we / put up the tent …
6 Harriet / sleep …

5 Complete the dialogue with the correct past simple form of *be* or *can* (affirmative, negative or interrogative).

Zoe Where **¹**_____ you last night? You **²**_____ at Leah's party.
Marcus No, I **³**_____ go to the party. **⁴**_____ it good?
Zoe No, it **⁵**_____.
Marcus Oh, why not?
Zoe The music **⁶**_____ very good, and it **⁷**_____ too loud. I **⁸**_____ hear people talk! And the neighbours **⁹**_____ hear the music. They **¹⁰**_____ very happy! They complained!
Marcus Oh, dear. **¹¹**_____ the food good?
Zoe It **¹²**_____ OK. But at the end of the party I **¹³**_____ find my coat! I think someone else has got it now.
Marcus Oh, no, what a nightmare!

6 Write questions from the prompts. Use the past simple form of *be* and *can*.

1 swim / four
   Could you swim when you were four?
2 count to ten in English / seven
3 write your name / three
4 talk / two
5 walk / one
6 ride a bike / six

7 SPEAKING Work in pairs. Take turns to ask and answer the questions in exercise 6. (If you don't know the exact ages, just guess!)

> Could you swim when you were four?

> Yes, I could. / No, I couldn't.

Prepositions of movement and place

I can use prepositions of movement and place.

SURVIVAL IN THE RAINFOREST

Gileno Vieira da Rocha is a Brazilian engineer. He helps to build roads in the Amazon rainforest. Last year he was in the forest, 300 miles from the nearest big town. When he finished work one day, he decided to walk back to the camp, ten kilometres away. His workmates walked along the usual path. But Gileno decided to take a shortcut. He walked across a field, and into the jungle. But he got lost. He couldn't see any other people and he couldn't return to his workmates. He continued to walk through the trees. He climbed over tree trunks and crawled under bushes. At night he rested in a tree or on the ground. After a few days he was very hungry, but he couldn't find any fruit or animals to eat. So he decided to catch bees and flies for food! Finally, after twelve days, he arrived at a river and started to walk along it. There were people by the river and they helped him. Gileno almost died, but he finally arrived home safely. He was a very lucky man!

1 SPEAKING Work in pairs. Look at the photo and the title of the text. What do you think happened?

2 Read the text and check your ideas.

3 VOCABULARY Match the prepositions of movement with the diagrams. Which six can you find in the text in exercise 2?

Prepositions of movement

across along away from down into off onto out of
over past round through to towards under up

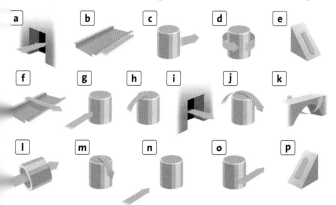

4 Read the Learn this! box. Find three of the examples from the box in the text.

5 Complete the sentences with prepositions from exercise 3 and the Learn this! box. Sometimes more than one answer is possible.

1 We walked _____ some trees to the river and _____ the bridge to the other side.
2 There aren't many wild animals _____ the desert.
3 Go _____ the tunnel and _____ the hill to the top.
4 They sailed _____ the ocean in a large ship.
5 Hastings is _____ the south coast of England.
6 Jake walked _____ the classroom, closed the door and then walked _____ the science lab and sat down.
7 The road doesn't go _____ the mountain. It's too high. It goes _____ it to the other side and back down.
8 We live _____ the sea. I can see it from my bedroom window.

6 SPEAKING Work in pairs. Cover the text and retell the story using the words below. Tell half of the story each.

Student A

1 Gileno Vieira da Rocha / Brazilian engineer / builds roads / Amazon rainforest
2 last year / rainforest / 300 miles / nearest town
3 decide / walk / camp / workmates / walk / usual path
4 Gileno / decide / take shortcut / walk / field / rain forest
5 he / lost / couldn't see / people / couldn't return / workmates

Student B

6 after a few days / hungry / couldn't find / fruit / animals
7 decide / catch bees and flies
8 twelve days / arrive / river / walk / along river
9 there / people / by / river
10 he / almost / die / very lucky man

LEARN THIS! Prepositions of place: *on, in* and *by*

a We use *in* with large areas, e.g. countries and continents, and three-dimensional spaces:
in South America   in Peru   in the jungle / desert
in the air   in a plane

b We use *on* with a surface or a line:
on a lake   on the ground   on the coast
on the edge of the cliff

c We use *by* to mean 'very near to':
by the sea   by a lake   by the river

Stranger than fiction?

I can understand a text about real animals which people thought were myths.

1 **SPEAKING** In pairs, read the paragraph. Then answer the questions below.

Hundreds of years ago, travellers shared stories about strange animals from other parts of the world. But in most people's opinion, these stories were just myths: the animals were not real. However, in a few cases, they were wrong – the animals were real. And hundreds of years later, people proved it!

1 What is a 'myth'?
2 What were people wrong about?

2 Look at the headings (1–4) in the text and match them with the photos (A–D).

> **Reading Strategy**
>
> When you do a multiple-choice task, treat each option as a true or false task. Remember that only one option – the correct answer – is true.

3 Read the Reading Strategy. Then read the first section of the text. Decide if these statements are true or false. Write T or F.

The first people to describe a giant squid were
A the Ancient Greeks. ___
B sailors in the Middle Ages. ___
C two fisherman in 1873. ___

4 Read all of the text. Circle the correct answers (a–c).

1 People finally realised giant squid were real when
  a stories from the Middle Ages matched the stories from Ancient Greece.
  b some fishermen showed the arms of a giant squid to scientists.
  c somebody filmed a video of one.

2 Who first used the word 'gorillae'?
  a Ancient Greeks
  b Africans
  c Germans

3 Scientists realised that the okapi were not a myth when
  a they discovered Ancient Egyptian descriptions.
  b they studied Henry Stanley's description.
  c they received an okapi skin from Henry Johnston.

4 After a pilot discovered Komodo Dragons during the First World War, he
  a shared the story with his friends.
  b informed London Zoo about the animal.
  c tried to catch one.

🎧 3.13

REAL ANIMALS
THAT WERE ONCE A MYTH

A

1 Giant squid

In Ancient Greek times, there were stories about huge sea monsters with very long arms. Similar stories appeared in the Middle Ages. These monsters lived in very deep water, but sometimes they attacked sailors. However, were these creatures real or were they a myth? For hundreds of years, scientists were not sure. But that changed in 1873. A giant squid attacked a small boat near the east coast of North America. The fishermen in the boat used an axe to cut off two of the giant squid's arms. They were six metres long! They showed the arms to the scientists at a local museum. The scientists were amazed! Today, everyone knows that giant squid are real, but people very rarely see them. In fact, only one video exists of a giant squid in its natural habitat.

2 Gorillas

About 2,500 years ago, an Ancient Greek explorer called Hanno travelled to Africa. On one island near the coast, there was a group of strange people with black hair on their faces and bodies. He asked the local people for information about them: they were 'gorillae', they answered. These 'people' were violent, bad-tempered and very strong. And for hundreds of years, there were similar stories about strange creatures – half human and half animal – in the forests of Africa. The first scientific description of gorillas only appeared in the 19th centur And mountain gorillas were a complete mystery until a Germa soldier discovered them in 1902

B

c

3 Okapi

The Ancient Egyptians were familiar with the okapi, a strange creature from the forests of Africa. It looked like a mix between a zebra and a horse. In the 19th century, the famous British journalist and explorer Henry Stanley described the same animal. But was it all a myth? An English politician in central Africa, Henry Johnston, was very interested in Stanley's description. He decided to find the animal. It was not easy, but in 1901 Johnston finally managed to get a complete okapi skin. He sent it to London and the scientists there were amazed. Later, they realised that the okapi is not a type of zebra – in fact, it is a relative of the giraffe.

4 Komodo dragons

During the First World War (1914–18) a pilot crashed into the sea near Indonesia. Luckily, he could swim well. He reached one of the smaller islands. He was safe! Or was he? On the island, he discovered a horrible monster. It looked like a dragon: it was very big with short legs and a long tongue. It attacked and killed large animals for food. The pilot survived and later he described the monster to his friends. They laughed at him! But in fact, the animal was real: it was a Komodo dragon, the largest lizard in the world. In 1927, London Zoo opened its new Reptile House and it included the first pair of Komodo dragons in Europe.

5 VOCABULARY Match the highlighted professions in the text with the definitions below

1 scientists: people who do scientific work.
2 _____: somebody who fights in an army.
3 _____: somebody who writes for newspapers and / or magazines.
4 _____: somebody who goes to new places to discover what they are like.
5 _____: somebody who helps to make a country's laws.
6 _____: people who go out in boats to catch fish.
7 _____: somebody who flies a plane.
8 _____: people who work on a boat.

6 SPEAKING In pairs, choose one of the creatures below and describe it to your partner. What does it look like? Is it big or small? Does it live on land or in water?

The Loch Ness Monster

Bigfoot

Giant Anaconda

7 INTERNET RESEARCH Search online to find out more about one of the creatures from exercise 6. Use the questions below to help you. Then share your answers with the class.

- Are there a lot of stories about it or only a few?
- Where does it live, according to the stories?
- Are there any photos or videos of it?
- Does it really exist, in your opinion?

Photo description

I can describe photos.

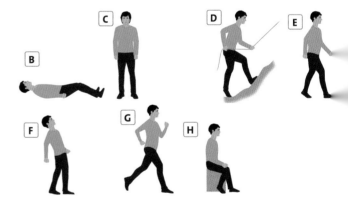

1 SPEAKING Work in pairs. Look at the photos and decide which place looks:

more beautiful   more relaxing   quieter   warmer

2 VOCABULARY In pairs, match some of the words below with one photo or both. Some words do not match either photo.

The natural world beach   cloud   flower   grass ground   moon   mountains   rock   sand   sea   sky snow   stars   sunrise   sunset   tree   water

➤➤ **Vocabulary Builder** The weather: page 120

3 🎧 **3.14** Listen to a student describing the first photo. Which words from exercise 2 does he use?

Speaking Strategy

When you describe a photo, begin by saying what the photo shows in general. Then describe different parts of the photo using phrases like 'in the centre'. Remember to use present tenses in your description.

4 🎧 **3.14** **KEY PHRASES** Read the Speaking Strategy. Then listen again and complete the key phrases using the prepositions below:

in (×2)   at   on

Describing a photo
1 in the centre
2 _____ the background / the foreground
3 _____ the distance
4 _____ the left / the right
5 _____ the bottom / the top

5 Write four sentences describing the second photo in exercise 1. Use words and phrases from exercises 2 and 4.

In the centre, there's …
In the distance, you can see …

6 🎧 **3.15** Listen to another student describing the second photo in exercise 1. Does she say any of your sentences from exercise 5?

7 VOCABULARY Match the phrases in the table with the diagrams.

He's	climbing (up …)
She's	facing (the tree)
They're	looking up / down
	lying (on the ground)
	running
	standing
	sitting (on …)
	walking

8 Look at the photos in exercise 1 again. Which phrases from exercise 7 can you use to describe them? Match two with each photo.

9 Work in pairs. Look at page 142. Choose one photo each. Decide what vocabulary from exercises 2, 4 and 7 you need to describe it.

10 SPEAKING Describe one of the photos on page 142 to your partner. Use words and phrases from this lesson and follow the advice in the Strategy.

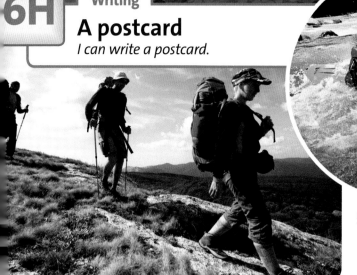

6H

Writing

A postcard

I can write a postcard.

1 VOCABULARY Match the photos with three activities from below. Check the meaning of all the activities. Can you add any others?

Adventure holiday activities abseil cycle
explore kayak surf trek

➥ **Vocabulary Builder** Adventure holiday adjectives: page 120

2 Read the postcards. Match each with three activities from exercise 1.

POST CARD

i Sam,

n having a great time in Vietnam. We arrived three
ays ago and now we're staying in a hostel by a river in
he jungle. The weather is very hot and sunny.

esterday we trekked into the jungle and explored. We
lso looked for monkeys in the trees, but we couldn't
ee any. There were lots of horrible spiders! Yuck!

omorrow morning we're travelling to the beach and in
he afternoon we're surfing. I can't wait!

ay hello to Emma. See you soon.

ove, Milla

---

i Joanna,

his is my second day in Canada. We're staying at a
ampsite near a lake in Ontario. The scenery is really
eautiful. The weather is OK. Yesterday it was really
old and windy, but today it's better.

esterday we kayaked down a river. It was very scary as
ere were lots of rocks. Today I abseiled down a cliff.
at was scary too, but I enjoyed it!

morrow we're cycling to the nearest village to buy
od and drink. I've only got three more days here. ☹

sh you were here!

e for now!

POST CARD

---

3 Answer the questions for each postcard in exercise 2.

1 Which country is the writer in?
2 Where is he / she staying?
3 What's the weather like?
4 What activities did he / she do yesterday?
5 What activities is he / she planning to do?

> **Writing Strategy**
>
> When you write a postcard:
> • Use the present continuous to say where you are staying.
> • Use the past simple to describe activities that you did. Use past time expressions where appropriate.
> • Use the present continuous for future arrangements that you have made.

4 Read the Writing Strategy and find examples of the tenses in the postcards in exercise 2.

5 KEY PHRASES Tick the phrases that the writers use in the postcards in exercise 2.

Postcards
I'm having a great time in ...
This is my third day in ...
The weather is (fabulous / OK / terrible).
We've only got two / three / four more days here.
Wish you were here!
Thinking of you!
Say hello to (David).
Give my love to (your brother).
See you soon.

6 Imagine you are on an adventure holiday. Plan a postcard. Make notes and include the following information.

• which country? Where are you staying?
• describe the weather
• activities you did and when you did them
• activities you are planning to do

7 Write your postcard. Use your notes from exercise 6. Include activities from exercise 1, phrases from exercise 5, and the tenses mentioned in the Writing Strategy.

> **CHECK YOUR WORK**
>
> Have you ...
> • included all the information in the task in exercise 6?
> • used three different tenses and useful phrases?
> • checked your spelling and grammar?

Reading

1 Read the Strategy. Match sentences A–E with intentions 1–5 below.

1 give a reason _____
2 give information about the past _____
3 describe something _____
4 compare things _____
5 give directions _____

A Silver Street is more attractive than East Street.
B It has big wings and a long tail.
C I like living in the house because it's near the gym.
D Come out of the station, cross the square and walk 100 m along Mill Lane.
E 300 years ago, people lived in small houses near the lake.

2 Read the texts and answer the questions (1–3). Choose the correct answer, (A–D).

The heart of Seoul

Seoul is the capital city of Korea. It's 600 years old and it's a large, busy, noisy city. But a small river runs for 5.8 km through the middle of the city. It's called the Cheonggyecheon Stream. The river is older than the city, but for many years the people of Seoul couldn't see it at all because there was a big road over it. Then, in 2003, the government closed the road. They took the road away completely and opened the river again. Now the river is a beautiful place to go for a walk and relax.

1 The text gives readers
  A a list of good places to visit in Seoul.
  B a funny story about a river.
  C reasons why the city needed a big road in 1958.
  D information about the history of a river.

Forest fright

Last year, my family and I visited the Piedras Blancas National Park in the south-west of Costa Rica. We stayed in a small wooden house on a beach near the Pacific Ocean. On the first day, we walked into the rainforest with a guide. It was warm, dark and rainy. Suddenly, a big brown snake appeared on the path in front of us! It was a Hog-Nosed Pit Viper, the most dangerous snake in Costa Rica. We stopped, and luckily the snake moved away. Amazing!

2 What does the boy say about his visit to Costa Rica?
  A He wanted to see a snake.
  B He was interested in the trees in the forest.
  C An exciting thing happened on the first day.
  D He walked over Costa Rica's most dangerous snake.

A Green City Walk

When we were in Paris last month, we walked along the Promenade Plantée. Do you know it? It's a park now, but a hundred years ago it was a train line. The line closed, and then in 1988 two men planned a public garden for the space. They planted trees and flowers and created a beautiful long path through the 12th District. Away from the crowds and the traffic, it was hard to believe we were in the middle of the city.

3 The author of the text
  A invites you to go to a park with her.
  B tells you about the history of a park that she visited.
  C explains why two men wanted to make a park.
  D gives facts about the birds and insects in a park.

Listening

3 Read the Strategy. Add the words below to the correct place in the table.

clean long loud polluted quick quiet safe slow start wait

	similar meaning	opposite meaning
dirty		
noisy		
fast		
short	—	
dangerous	—	
stop		

4 🎧 **3.16** Listen to a conversation between a boy called Stephen and a girl called Myra. Are the sentences true or false? Write T or F.

1 Myra isn't happy with the trams in the city. ___
2 Stephen says it's difficult for trams to move left and right. ___
3 Stephen thinks trams are faster than buses. ___
4 Myra thinks the air in their city is polluted. ___
5 Stephen thinks bikes are bad for the city. ___
6 Stephen thinks trams are noisier than buses. ___

Use of English

5 Read the Strategy. One word in each phrase (1–6) below is wrong. Underline it.

1 **in** ... Spain, New York, a motorbike
2 **get off** ... a bike, a car, a tram
3 **get out of** ... a bus, a taxi, a car
4 **miss** ... your way, the bus, the train
5 **on** ... the ground, Istanbul, a bus
6 **at** ... the museum, the airport, Germany

6 Read the text and choose the correct answer A, B or C to fill the gaps.

City Monkeys

Do you like monkeys? Some people think they're the
¹ _____ animals in the world. In India, however, a lot of people don't want to see monkeys. Their cities have a big monkey problem.

² _____ Delhi, there are tens of thousands of monkeys. They live in the trees and move around the city. They ³ _____ buses and go into people's houses.

Now, people are getting angry with them. In India, people keep water on the roof. The monkeys climb ⁴ _____ people's houses and drink the water. This makes the water dirty, so people can't drink it.

'A few days ⁵ _____, there was a monkey outside my office,' says Gulam Bannerjee. 'At lunchtime, it followed me ⁶ _____ the road to the shop. I ⁷ _____ the fridge and the monkey watched me. I closed the fridge, but then the monkey copied me and got some food. They're very clever! I think they're cleverer ⁸ _____ some people!'

1 **A** funny	**B** funnier	**C** funniest
2 **A** On	**B** In	**C** At
3 **A** miss	**B** get on	**C** cross
4 **A** up	**B** under	**C** past
5 **A** past	**B** last	**C** ago
6 **A** through	**B** along	**C** round
7 **A** opened	**B** opening	**C** open
8 **A** as	**B** than	**C** from

Speaking

7 Read the Strategy. Complete the table with the words below.

afternoon   bridge   city   cloud   cold   evening   ground
park   relax   sit   snow   sunrise   sunset   travel

place	time	weather	activity

8 Choose one of the photos to describe.

Writing

9 Read the Strategy. Circle the correct adjective.

1 It's very **cold / hot**. Yesterday, it was 41°C!
2 I had a **bad / good** day yesterday. I waited 50 minutes for the bus and then I missed my train.
3 It's really **noisy / quiet**! Cars, buses and taxis go past my window all the time and I can't sleep at night.
4 I'm in the **smallest / tallest** building in the city. It's about 650 metres high.
5 We have the **worst / best** room in the hotel. It's clean and comfortable, and we can see the sea from our window.
6 The swimming pool is **fantastic / awful**. It's big and the water is really warm.

10 Imagine you are on a city holiday. Write a postcard to a friend. Include information about:

- the city and the weather.
- where you are staying (e.g. a hotel).
- activities you did and when you did them.
- activities you are planning to do.

7
Digital world

7A Vocabulary
Computing
I can talk about computer equipment.

1 SPEAKING Look at photos 1–6. Does the computer equipment look old or modern? Which things look the oldest / the most modern?

2 VOCABULARY Look at the words in the list. Match them with the items in the photo⟨

Computing (nouns) charger computer headphones keyboard laptop
memory stick monitor mouse printer router speakers tablet webcam

3 🎧 **3.17** Listen and repeat all the words in exercise 2.

4 VOCABULARY Complete the phrases using the verbs in the list. Use each verb only once.

Computing (verbs) connect to delete download enter post print ~~scan~~ surf upload

1 scan a drawing / a photo / a document
2 _____ a comment (on a social networking site)
3 _____ a photo / video (onto the internet)
4 _____ an app / some software / a song / a photo (from the internet)
5 _____ a document / a contact / a photo (from your computer)
6 _____ a Wi-Fi network / the internet
7 _____ your password / your contact details
8 _____ the Web
9 _____ a document / a photo

5 ⏺ 3.18 Listen to four conversations. Which phrases from exercise 4 can you hear?

6 Complete the computer quiz. Use words from exercises 2 and 4.

quiz

1 The computer language for a lot of pages on the internet is:
 a HTTP b HDMI c HTML

2 Which famous American rap star makes Beats _____?
 a Dr Dre b Jay Z c 50 Cent

3 Look at photo A. What is another term for a _____ ?
 a a flash drive
 b a Wi-Fi connector
 c a CD-ROM

A

4 'You can usually _____ a photo from the internet faster than you can upload it.'
 a true b false

5 When you describe a _____ as '300 Mbps' you're talking about its:
 a price b speed c age

6 Look at photo B. This _____ has a 16GB hard drive. What does 'GB' stand for?
 a gigaband b gigabyte
 c gigabar

B

7 When you _____ the Web, what do 'cookies' do?
 a Protect your computer from viruses and hackers.
 b Make the web page the correct size and shape for your phone, tablet, etc.
 c Share information about your visit with the website.

7 Work in pairs. Do the quiz in exercise 6.

> **RECYCLE! Present continuous**
> We form the present continuous with *be* and the *-ing* form of the verb:
> I'm listening. We aren't watching. Is he laughing?
> We use the present continuous to talk about what is happening now, or around now. We also use it to talk about future arrangements.
> I'm learning Chinese. She's leaving tomorrow.

8 ⏺ 3.19 Read the Recycle! box. Then listen to six short conversations and complete the summaries. Use the present continuous (affirmative or negative) form of the verbs from exercise 4.

1 His tablet _____ to Wi-Fi this evening.
2 She _____ a contact from her phone.
3 They _____ a comment on Instagram.
4 He _____ the correct password.
5 She _____ some photos onto her Facebook page this afternoon.
6 They _____ the Web in a café.

9 Decide which sentence from exercise 8 is using the present continuous to talk about the future.

10 ⏺ 3.19 KEY PHRASES Listen again. Match the two halves of these useful phrases.

Computer collocations
1	get	a	your emails
2	click	b	return
3	press	c	online
4	check	d	an error message
5	get	e	a web page
6	visit	f	on a button

11 SPEAKING Work in pairs. Using words and phrases from this lesson, tell your partner:

1 how often you use email and what you use it for.
2 the different ways you use the internet and where you normally are when you get online.
3 other things you use a phone, laptop, tablet or computer for.
4 something that annoys you when you're using a phone, laptop, etc.

> I check my emails a few times a day. I use it for ...

> I use a tablet to ...

> It annoys me when ...

Past simple (affirmative): irregular

I can talk about past events.

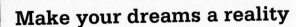

Make your dreams a reality

Imagine that your dream is to fly aeroplanes but you can't afford to go to school or university. What can you do? In today's digital world, the answer is simple: use the internet.

As a boy, George Mel from South Sudan had a dream: to be a pilot. He made flying machines in his garden and tried to fly. Once, he fell off the roof and nearly broke his leg!

When George became a teenager, he went to high school for a few years. However, he had to give up because his family had no money. He found a job and worked hard – but he still dreamed about flying.

He read about aeroplanes on the internet. Secretly, he got some old pieces of wood and metal and began to make an aeroplane in his bedroom. In the end, he built his aeroplane. He drew a Sudanese flag on it and took his work to the South Sudan Air Force. When they saw it, they offered him a job!

1 Read the text. What is unusual about the aeroplane in the photo?

2 Read the Learn this! box. Then find all the past simple forms of the verbs in the text in exercise 1. Which are regular and which are irregular?

LEARN THIS! Past simple (affirmative): irregular

a Many verbs have irregular past simple forms. There are no rules for forming these, you need to learn them.

do – did   speak – spoke   come – came

b The verb *be* is the only verb with two (irregular) past simple forms:

I / he / she it was   you / we / they were

---

3 Match the irregular past simple forms of the verbs in the text with their infinitive without *to*.

1 become _____	6 fall _____	11 make _____
2 begin _____	7 find _____	12 read _____
3 break _____	8 get _____	13 see _____
4 build _____	9 go _____	14 take _____
5 draw _____	10 have _____	

4 Complete the sentences with the past simple forms of verbs from the Learn this! box and exercise 3.

1 I _____ a lot of housework before school yesterday.
2 We _____ a great film at the cinema last night.
3 My sister _____ to Paris for the weekend.
4 I _____ an old memory stick on my bedroom floor.
5 She _____ a lot of photos during the holiday.
6 We _____ to our teacher about the homework.

LOOK OUT!

Several past simple forms end in *-ought* or *-aught*. These endings are pronounced /ɔːt/ (rhyming with *short*).

---

5 Read the Look out! box. Then complete the sentences with the past simple form of the verbs below.

bring   buy   catch   fight   teach   think

1 The British and Americans _____ on the same side in the Second World War.
2 We _____ a new car about a month ago.
3 I _____ about my cousin yesterday because it was her birthday.
4 Aristotle _____ Alexander the Great when he was at school.
5 I _____ my homework to school, but now I can't find it.
6 We _____ the train at six o'clock in the morning.

➡ Grammar Builder 7B   page 136

6 Complete the email with the past simple form of the verbs in brackets. Some are regular and some are irregular.

✉ To: milly@email.com

Hi Milly,
How are you? I hope you ¹ _____ (have) a good weekend.
My weekend ² _____ (be) great. On Friday evening, I
³ _____ (do) all my homework, so I ⁴ _____ (can) relax on
Saturday and Sunday. On Saturday morning, I ⁵ _____ (go)
into town and ⁶ _____ (buy) new speakers for my laptop. In
the afternoon, a friend ⁷ _____ (come) to see me. He
⁸ _____ (bring) a few DVDs, so we ⁹ _____ (stay) at home
and ¹⁰ _____ (watch) them.
On Sunday morning, I ¹¹ _____ (speak) to my cousin on Skype.
Then, in the afternoon, I ¹² _____ (play) football in the park.
Tom and Logan from our class ¹³ _____ (be) there, so it was
fun.
See you soon!
Love, Max

---

7 **SPEAKING** In pairs, tell your partner five things you did last weekend. Make sentences with five different verbs from this lesson.

I broke my dad's printer. I ...

Listening to instructions
I can understand instructions.

1 SPEAKING Work in pairs. Which of these problems have you experienced while using a computer? Can you think of any others? Which problem is the most annoying, in your opinion?

a You've forgotten your password.
b The Wi-Fi connection is very slow.
c You can't access the internet.
d The computer is running very slowly.
e The computer crashes and you lose your work.

2 VOCABULARY Complete the instructions for setting up a printer. Circle the correct verbs.

Setting up your new printer

▶ Take your new printer out of the box and ¹**remove / install** all packaging.
▶ ²**Turn on / Connect** the printer to the power source.
▶ ³**Install / Turn on** the printer. (The green light flashes.)
▶ ⁴**Download / Connect** the printer to your computer with the cable.
▶ ⁵**Upload / Install** the printer software, and ⁶**follow / delete** the on-screen instructions.
▶ ⁷**Remove / Restart** your computer.
▶ ⁸**Enter / Visit** the printer website and ⁹**download / scan** the operating instructions.

> **Listening Strategy**
> When you are listening to a set of instructions, it can help if you can first identify the steps. You can do this by identifying sequencing words (e.g. *first of all, secondly, then*, etc.). This will make it easier to understand the detail when you listen again.

3.20 Read the Listening Strategy. Then listen to the instructions. Number the pictures (A–H) in the correct order.

4 **3.20** VOCABULARY Check the meaning of the sequencing words below. Then listen again. Which sequencing words did you hear that marked the start of each new stage?

Sequencing words after that finally first of all next now secondly then thirdly to start off with

5 **3.21** Listen to three conversations with a computer Help Desk. In each conversation, how many steps are there in the instructions: 3, 4 or 5?

6 **3.21** Listen again and circle the correct words.

Conversation 1
1 The woman asks the man to check the **power source / cable** behind the computer.
2 At first the man forgets his **password / office network**.
Conversation 2
3 The woman finds the missing files **in the recycle bin / on the desktop**.
4 The man tells the woman to drag the **documents / recycle bin** into the folder.
Conversation 3
5 Ben can't use his **memory stick / computer**.
6 Sally works in room **240 / 204**.

7 SPEAKING Work in pairs. What computer problems have you had? How did you solve them?

> I forgot my password. I had to make a new one.

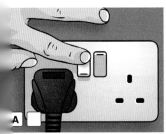

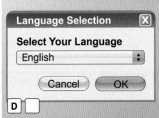

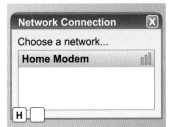

Past simple (negative and interrogative)

I can say what did and didn't happen in the past.

1 SPEAKING Work in pairs. Write down five things you can do with your phone.

> I can send messages.

2 🎧 **3.22** Read and listen to the first part of the dialogue. What was the problem with James's videos?

James Did you go to the music festival in the park last weekend?
Chloe No, I didn't. Did you go?
James Yes, I did. It was fun.
Chloe Did Cool Heart play?
James Yes, they did. They were brilliant.
Chloe Did you take any photos?
James No, I didn't take any photos, but I filmed a few songs. Look …
Chloe I can't hear anything. There's no sound!
James Oh no! It didn't work.
Chloe Did you have your finger over the microphone?
James Yes, maybe. I didn't check. I'm useless with technology!

3 Find all the examples of the past simple negative and interrogative in the dialogue in exercise 2. Then complete the Learn this! box with *did* and *didn't*.

> **LEARN THIS!** Past simple (negative and interrogative)
> **a** We form the past simple negative with _____ + the infinitive without *to*.
> **b** We form the past simple interrogative with _____ + he / they / you, etc. + the infinitive without *to*.
> **c** We form short answers with _____ and _____.

➥ Grammar Builder 7D page 136

4 Make the sentences negative.

1 Tom went to bed before 10 p.m. last night.
2 I caught the bus to school.
3 Sarah had a dream last night.
4 We studied English in primary school.
5 My friend watched TV before school this morning.
6 Sarah and Fred had breakfast this morning.

5 Make questions from the sentences in exercise 4. Use *you* and the past simple.

Did you go to bed before 10 p.m. last night?

6 SPEAKING Work in pairs. Ask and answer the questions in exercise 5.

> Did you go to bed before 10 p.m. last night?

> Yes, I did. / No, I didn't.

> **LOOK OUT!**
> Remember that we don't use *did* / *didn't* to make the past simple negative and interrogative forms of *be* and *can*.

7 🎧 **3.23** Read the Look out! box. Then complete the rest of the dialogue with the past simple negative or interrogative form of verbs in brackets. Listen and check.

Chloe Never mind. Tell me about the festival.
¹_____ (be / you) close to the stage?
James No, I ²_____ (be / not). I ³_____ (not / can) see very well. That's why I wanted to film it.
Chloe What kind of music ⁴_____ (Cool Heart / play)?
James Mostly dance music. They ⁵_____ (not / play) any of their new songs.
Chloe ⁶_____ (be) the other bands good?
James Yes, they were. But I ⁷_____ (not / hear) all of them. I left early because I ⁸_____ (not / want) to miss the last bus.

8 Complete the table with the verbs below. Then tick the things that were true for you yesterday.

be eat go help meet play send surf use

What did you do yesterday?	You	Your partner
1 _____ to the cinema		
2 _____ with the housework		
3 _____ social media		
4 _____ out		
5 _____ your friends		
6 _____ computer games		
7 _____ a lot of texts		
8 _____ the internet		
9 _____ in bed before 11 p.m.		

9 SPEAKING Work in pairs. Take turns to ask and answer questions using the table in exercise 8. Tick the things that your partner did.

> Did you go to the cinema?

> Yes, I did. / No, I didn't. What about you? Did you … ?

10 SPEAKING Tell the class what your partner did yesterday. Use the past simple affirmative and negative.

> Jack went to the cinema. He didn't …

Word Skills
Introduction to phrasal verbs
I can use a range of computer-related phrasal verbs.

First of all, turn on your computers. Type in your passwords and log on. After you complete the test, save your work, and then log off. Finally, shut down your computers.

1 **SPEAKING** Describe the photo. Would you like to learn in a classroom like this? Why? / Why not?

2 Read the Learn this! box. Then find and underline five phrasal verbs in the teacher's speech bubble. Are they transitive or intransitive?

LEARN THIS! Phrasal verbs

a Phrasal verbs consist of a verb and a particle (e.g. *up*, *on*, *in*, *back*, *off*, etc.) They are very common in English.

b Some phrasal verbs are transitive. They take a direct object, e.g.:

subject   verb   direct object

put on: *Alexander puts on his jacket.*

c Some phrasal verbs are intransitive. They do not take a direct object, e.g.:

get up: *I got up at six o'clock.*

3 **VOCABULARY** Match eight of the phrasal verbs below with the pictures. Check the meaning of all the phrasal verbs.

Phrasal verbs: computers

Transitive   back up (your work)   plug in (a printer)
scan in (a document)   shut down (a computer)
turn down (the radio)   turn off (the light)   turn on (the TV)
turn up (the volume)   type in (your username)

Intransitive   break down   log off   log on

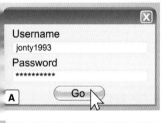

4 **DICTIONARY WORK** Study the dictionary entries. How do you know if the phrasal verb is transitive or intransitive?

turn something off to move the handle or switch that controls something, so that it stops: *Turn the tap off.* ◇ *She turned off the television.*

break down
1 if a machine or car **breaks down**, it stops working: *We were late because our car broke down.*
2 if a person **breaks down**, they start to cry: *He broke down when he heard the news.*

5 Complete the sentences with the phrasal verbs below. Use the correct tense and form.

back up   log on   plug in   shut down
turn down   turn on   type in

1 The music was very loud, so I _____ the volume.
2 I couldn't _____ because I forgot my username and password.
3 Sally _____ her username and password, then pressed enter.
4 Yesterday evening, I _____ all my important documents to a hard drive so that I didn't lose them.
5 Dan closed all the applications and then _____ his computer.
6 I couldn't print the photo because I forgot to _____ the printer and _____ it _____!

6 Work in pairs. Prepare six instructions using transitive phrasal verbs from exercise 3 and a noun. Do not show your partner.

1 *Plug in the computer.*

7 **SPEAKING** Take turns to say your sentences to each other. Your partner acts out the instructions.

Dancing Man

I can understand a text about a social media campaign.

1 SPEAKING Work in pairs. What is 'cyberbullying'? Give one or two examples (real or invented).

2 Read the text, ignoring the gaps. What kind of cyberbullying does the text mention? Is it like the examples you thought of in exercise 1?

> **Reading Strategy**
> When you do a gapped sentence task, think about the order of events within a text. Having a clear idea of the sequence helps you to check that your sentence fits.

3 Read the Reading Strategy. Then put these events into the order in which they happened.

a Cassandra Fairbanks raised money for Sean O'Brien's plane ticket.
b Photos of Sean O'Brien appeared on an internet forum.
c Sean O'Brien threw the ball to start a baseball game.
d Sean O'Brien danced at a gig.
e There was a big party for Sean O'Brien in Hollywood.
f Cassandra Fairbanks started a campaign on Twitter.
g Sean O'Brien appeared on an American TV show.

1 d, 2 …

4 Match gaps (1–4) in the text with sentences (A–E). Use your answers to exercise 3 to help you. There is one extra sentence.

A This quickly raised more than $20,000.
B After one day, they found him.
C Two days later, he returned to England.
D Afterwards, Sean said, 'It was the best night of my life!'
E They wanted to help the man.

5 Read and listen to the complete text. Check your answers.

6 VOCABULARY Match the two halves of these phrases. They are all in the reading text.

1 internet	a media
2 social	b page
3 viral	c account
4 hashtag	d forum
5 fundraising	e campaign
6 Twitter	f story

7 SPEAKING Work in pairs or groups. Think of a campaign you would like to start on social media to make your school, town or environment better in some way. Invent a hashtag for your campaign.

8 SPEAKING Present your campaign to the class. Which is the most popular?

> The aim of our campaign is to …

> We want people to …   Our hashtag is …

🎧 3.24

PEOPLE POWER

In March 2015, a British man went to a gig in London. He liked the music and he began to dance. Because he was a large man, other people noticed his dancing. A few of them laughed and took photos of him. When the man saw their reaction, he stopped dancing and looked sad.

A few days later, the photos appeared on a well-known internet forum. There were comments about the man's dancing and some of the comments were very unkind. The man was a victim of cyberbullying. But that wasn't the end of the story; it was only the beginning.

Cassandra
@CassandraRules   🐦 Follow

Anyone know this man or who posted this? There's a huge group of ladies in LA who would like to do something special pic.twitter.com/DGbu3AXOrB

5:54 PM - 5 Mar 2015

3,444 RETWEETS **3,613** FAVORITES   ↩ 🔁 ★

A group of people on social media, including an American writer called Cassandra Fairbanks, were angry about the cyberbullying. ¹____ They decided to have a huge party for him in California. But they didn't know who he was! However, it quickly became a viral story and Twitter users started a hashtag campaign: #FindDancingMan! ²____ Sean O'Brien was his name. He was originally from Liverpool but lived in London.

Cassandra Fairbanks and her friends on social media began to organise the party for Sean in Los Angeles. They also set up an online fundraising page to pay for Sean's ticket to the USA. ³

They gave the extra money to anti-bullying charities. By this time, the story of 'Dancing Man' was well known. When Sean opened his own Twitter account (@dancingmanfound) he quickly got more than 80,000 followers. Celebrities offered to help with the party and American TV shows wanted to speak to Sean.

The party took place at a nightclub in Hollywood in May 2015. About 1,000 people were there and they danced to music from celebrity DJ Moby. 4 _____ But it was just part of an amazing weekend in the USA. Before the party, he appeared on *Today*, one of the most popular shows on American TV. On the show, he danced with Meghan Trainor. The day after the party, he threw the first ball of an important baseball match. So in the end, a story about cyberbullying became a story about kindness. 'It really shows the power of people,' said Cassandra Fairbanks.

In a shop
I can talk about products and prices.

1 SPEAKING Describe the photo. Where are the people? What are they doing?

2 🎧 3.25 Read and listen to the dialogue. Which phone does the girl buy?

Assistant Hello, can I help you?
Girl Yes, I'm looking for a new smartphone.
Assistant Well, the new SmartTalk 3000 is very popular. Or there's the Micro 4, which is a bit cheaper.
Girl Does the Micro 4 have a good camera?
Assistant Yes, but the camera on the SmartTalk 3000 is better.
Girl And how much are the phones?
Assistant The SmartTalk is £120.50 and the Micro 4 is £89.99.
Girl I'd like the Micro 4, please. Can I pay by debit card?
Assistant Of course. That's £89.99, please ... Can you enter your PIN? ... Would you like a bag?
Girl No, thanks.
Assistant There you are. Thank you very much.
Girl Thanks. Goodbye.

LEARN THIS! Talking about prices

We write	We say
25p	twenty-five p / twenty-five pence
£6.99	six pounds ninety-nine / six ninety-nine
£150	a hundred and fifty pounds

---

3 Read the Learn this! box. Find two prices in the dialogue in exercise 2 and say them correctly.

4 🎧 3.26 VOCABULARY Listen to three conversations in a shop. Answer the questions for each conversation.

1 What product does the customer want to buy?
2 Which features do the customer and the shop assistant mention? Choose from the items below.
3 How much does the customer spend?

Features of gadgets battery life built-in 4G
built-in webcam a case headphones an HDMI port
a memory card slot a motion sensor a SIM card
a touch-screen a USB port Wi-Fi wireless speakers

5 KEY PHRASES Complete the phrases with the words below. Which phrases are said by a shop assistant? Which are said by a customer?

cash change comes credit card help like
looking much next pay PIN receipt would

> **In a shop**
> How can I ¹_____ you?
> I'm just ²_____, thanks.
> ³_____, please!
> How ⁴_____ is it / are they?
> That ⁵_____ to (£10), please.
> How would you like to ⁶_____?
> Can I pay in ⁷_____ / by debit card / by ⁸_____?
> Enter your ⁹_____, please.
> Here's your ¹⁰_____ and receipt.
> Could I have a ¹¹_____, please?
> Would you ¹²_____ a bag?
> ¹³_____ you like anything else?

➡ **Vocabulary Builder** Money and prices: page 120

6 🎧 3.26 Listen again. Which of the phrases in exercise 5 did the speakers use?

7 SPEAKING Work in pairs. Prepare a dialogue following the prompts below. Use the information in the Learn this! box and key phrases from exercise 5.

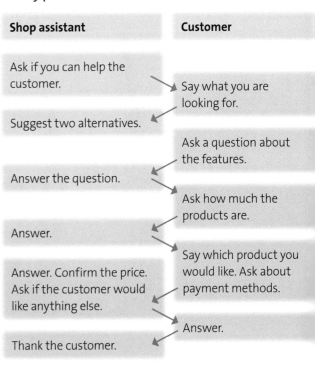

Shop assistant	Customer
Ask if you can help the customer.	Say what you are looking for.
Suggest two alternatives.	Ask a question about the features.
Answer the question.	Ask how much the products are.
Answer.	Say which product you would like. Ask about payment methods.
Answer. Confirm the price. Ask if the customer would like anything else.	Answer.
Thank the customer.	

8 SPEAKING Act out your dialogue to the class.

7H

Writing
A narrative
I can write a narrative.

1 **SPEAKING** Do you have a PIN (personal identification number) for your phone? Think of other situations in which people sometimes need a PIN. Do you find it easy to remember PINs? Do you always use the same PIN?

2 Read the text. Why did the phone become locked when Emily entered her PIN?

Write a story about a time when your phone (or another electronic device) caused problems for you.

LOCKED OUT!

<u>A few months ago</u>, I went out for the evening with my friend Suzie. We planned to have a pizza at a café in town. My dad kindly took us there in his car. 'I can come and get you,' my dad said, 'but don't call too late.'

We had a very nice meal at the café. <u>Afterwards</u>, I tried to call my dad. I entered my PIN, but the phone didn't accept it: I got an error message. I tried again, but the same thing happened.

'This is strange,' I said. I tried a third time; unfortunately, the phone became locked. I couldn't use it.

'Don't worry, Emily, you can use my phone,' said Suzie. Amazingly, the same thing happened to her. She tried three times, but the PIN was wrong and her phone became locked too. I thought very hard and <u>then</u> I remembered something: we had the same type of phone.

'You've got my phone and I've got yours,' I said. 'We swapped by accident. That's why the PIN numbers were wrong!'

Luckily, we saw a boy from our class in the café and told him about our problem. He lent me his phone and I called my dad. So we got home safely <u>in the end</u> – but our phones were locked for three days!

KEY PHRASES Add the underlined time expressions in the model text to the correct group below.

Time expressions for setting the scene
a few weeks ago   ¹_____   last weekend
one day last summer   recently   some time last year
Time expressions for ordering events
a few moments later   ²_____   at that moment
³_____   later   ⁴_____
the next day

4 Read the Learn this! box and answer the questions.

1 Find five adverbs ending in *-ly* in the model text.
2 Find two adverbs that have the same form as the adjective.
3 Are the adverbs use 1) or use 2)?

LEARN THIS! Adverbs

a Most adverbs are formed by adding *-ly* to an adjective:
slow – slowly   *dangerous – dangerously*

b Some adverbs are the same as the adjective. These include: *early   fast   hard   late*

c The adverb related to the adjective *good* is *well*.

We use adverbs in two main ways:

1 to describe a particular verb or action:
verb
She shouted angrily.

2 to describe a situation or event in general:
event
Sadly, he didn't pass his exams.

➡ **Vocabulary Builder** Adverbs: page 120

Writing Strategy
Try to include some direct speech when you write a narrative.
Put quotation marks around the words that the person speaks. Put a comma, question mark or exclamation mark before the closing quotation marks.
'Who are you?' I asked. *'I'm Joe,'* he said.

5 Read the Writing Strategy. Then add the correct punctuation to the direct speech.

1 Have you got my charger she asked.
2 I can't find my memory stick said Tom.
3 Good luck shouted my mum. Thanks I said.
4 It's very late said my friend.
5 Did you see me asked Ben quietly. Yes I replied.

6 Plan your own story using the task in exercise 2. Read these questions and make notes.

- Where were you? Who were you with?
- What kind of device caused the problem? What was the problem?
- What did you do when the problem happened? How did you solve it?
- How did it all end? Did it end well or badly for you?

7 Write your story using your notes from exercise 6. Try to include some direct speech and one or two adverbs. Use time expressions from exercise 3.

CHECK YOUR WORK
Have you ...
- included some direct speech with correct punctuation?
- used at least one adverb?
- checked your spelling and grammar?

8

Be active!

Unit map

● **Vocabulary**
Sports
Future time expressions
Nationalities
Athletics events

● **Word Skills**
Noun suffixes

● **Grammar**
going to
will

● **Listening** Prediction

● **Reading** Against the odds

● **Speaking** Negotiating

● **Writing** An informal letter
● **Culture 8** Football

8A Vocabulary

Sports and hobbies
I can talk about different sports and activities.

1 SPEAKING How often do you do sport? Where do you usually do it?

2 VOCABULARY Match photos (1–6) with six words from the list.

Sports aerobics athletics badminton basketball climbing cycling dancing football golf gymnastics handball ice hockey ice skating judo karate roller skating running skateboarding skiing surfing swimming table tennis tennis volleyball yoga

3 🎧 **3.27** Listen and repeat the words in exercise 2.

> **LEARN THIS!** *play / go / do*
> **a** We normally use *play* with ball games and team sports.
> *play football   play ice hockey*
> **b** We normally use *go* with activities which end in *-ing*.
> *go cycling*
> **c** We normally use *do* for individual activities and combat sports.
> *do athletics   do judo*

4 Read the Learn this! box. Match the sports and hobbies from exercise 2 with the correct verb: *play*, *go* or *do*.

play: badminton, …   go: climbing, …   do: aerobics, …

5 Work in pairs. Can you add any more sports or hobbies to the verbs in exercise 4?

6 SPEAKING Work in pairs. How many of the sports in exercise 2 does your partner d

> Do you do aerobics?   No, I don't. Do you play badminton?

7 Work in pairs. Ask and answer the questions in the Olympics quiz below.

---

1 Which two are connected to the Olympics?

Ⓐ   Ⓑ   Ⓒ   Ⓓ

2 How often do the Olympic Games happen?
a every 2 years   c every 3 years
b every 4 years   d every 5 years

3 When do the Winter Olympics happen?
a the same year as the summer games
b the year after the summer games
c two years after the summer games

4 Which three sports from exercise 2 are part of the Winter Olympics?

5 Complete the names of these Olympic events with words from exercise 2.
a BMX _____
b cross country _____
c synchronised _____
d beach _____

6 Which of these is NOT an Olympic sport?
a handball   b aerobics   c table tennis

7 Match the cities with the Olympic Games for these years.
a 2008 _____   c 2016 _____
b 2012 _____   d 2020 _____
Tokyo   Rio de Janeiro   Beijing   London

---

8 🎧 **3.28** Listen to four speakers. Which sports and hobbies from exercise 2 are they talking about?

Speaker 1 _____   Speaker 3 _____
Speaker 2 _____   Speaker 4 _____

> **RECYCLE! Past simple (affirmative and negative)**
> Regular past simple forms end in -ed.
> *play – played   work – worked*
> Many verbs have irregular past simple forms.
> *do – did   go – went*
> We don't use the past simple form for the negative; we use *didn't* + infinitive without *to*.
> *play – didn't play   go – didn't go*

9 🎧 **3.28** Read the Recycle! box. Then listen again and complete the sentences with the past simple affirmative or negative form of the verbs in brackets. Which verbs are regular and which are irregular?

Speaker 1
a He _____ (fall) over.
b He _____ (injure) himself.
Speaker 2
c She _____ (win) the competition.
d She _____ (enjoy) the experience.
Speaker 3
e He _____ (score) twice.
f His team _____ (lose) the match.
Speaker 4
g She _____ (come) second in one event.
h She _____ (break) a record.

10 SPEAKING Work in pairs. Tell your partner about the last time you took part in a sport or active hobby. Say:
• what sport or hobby it was
• when and where you took part
• who took part with you
• one more thing about the experience (use exercise 9 to give you ideas)

11 SPEAKING Tell the class about your partner.

going to

I can talk about plans.

1 🎧 **3.29** Read and listen to the dialogue. Who is going to take part in the judo competition? Is it …

a Suzie and Dexter?
b Dexter
c Dexter and his cousins?

Suzie What are you going to do this weekend?
Dexter I'm going to take part in a judo competition in Newcastle.
Suzie That's great. Are you going to stay in a hotel?
Dexter No, I'm not. I'm going to stay with my cousins, Luke and Toby. They live very near Newcastle.
Suzie Are they going to be at the competition?
Dexter Yes, they are.
Suzie That's good. You're going to have lots of supporters.
Dexter My cousins aren't going to support me. They're going to take part in the competition!

2 Read the Learn this! box. Find examples of *going to* (affirmative, negative and interrogative) in the dialogue in exercise 1.

> **LEARN THIS!** *going to*
>
> **a** We use *be* + *going to* + infinitive without *to* to talk about plans for the future.
>
> *We're going to have dinner in a restaurant tonight.*
>
> *I'm not going to be at school tomorrow.*
>
> *When are you going to leave?   At five o'clock.*
>
> **b** We often omit 'to go' when we use *going to* with the verb *go*.
>
> *Is he going (to go) cycling?   Yes, he is. / No, he isn't.*

3 Complete the sentences with the correct form of *going to* and the verb in brackets.

1 I _____ (not do) my homework this weekend.
2 We _____ (do) yoga after school.
3 My friend _____ (buy) some new trainers.
4 _____ you _____ (be) at home tomorrow?
5 My parents _____ (not have) a holiday this year.
6 I _____ (meet) friends in town this afternoon.

> ➡ **Grammar Builder 8B** page 138

4 🎧 **3.30** Listen to six dialogues. Write sentences about people's plans for the weekend. Use the affirmative or negative form of *going to* and the verbs in brackets.

1 Charlie (cook) dinner
  Charlie isn't going to cook dinner.
2 Olivia and Sophie (do) schoolwork
3 Bella (send) an email
4 Conrad and Alex (watch) a DVD
5 George (go) cycling
6 Poppy and Alice (play) volleyball

5 **VOCABULARY** Work in pairs. Put the expressions below into the correct order, starting with the soonest. Can you add any other future time expressions to the list?

Future time expressions   in a few days   next month   next week   next weekend   next year   the day after tomorrow   this afternoon   this evening   this weekend   tomorrow   tonight

this afternoon, this evening …

6 🎧 **3.30** Listen to the teenagers again. Then write sentences with *going to* using the names and verbs below and a future time expression from exercise 5.

1 Charlie / go shopping
  Charlie is going to go shopping this evening.
2 Olivia / practise the piano
3 Bella / visit relatives
4 Conrad and Alex / listen to music
5 George / get a new bike
6 Poppy and Alice / have a barbecue

7 Think of plans for these times in the future. Your plans can be real or invented. Make notes.

this evening   this weekend   next week   next year

this evening – visit grandparents

8 **SPEAKING** Work in pairs. Find out your partner's plans and make a note of the answers.

> What are you going to do this evening?

> I'm going to visit my grandparents.

9 **SPEAKING** Tell the class about your partner's plans.

> Leyla is going to visit her grandparents this evening.

Prediction
I can 'listen ahead' and predict what I'm going to hear.

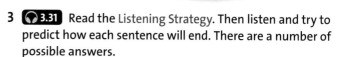

SPEAKING Describe the photos. Where are the men? What are they doing? Use the words below to help you.

at night   climb   dark   high   rock face
rope   sleep   steep   tent

El Capitan

For years, two climbers, Tommy Caldwell and Kevin Jorgeson, dreamed of climbing the Dawn Wall. The Dawn Wall is a one thousand-metre rock face on El Capitan in Yosemite National Park. It is the steepest, most difficult rock face in the world. Tommy and Kevin decided to 'free climb'. That means they use ropes and equipment only to keep them safe and catch them if they fall. They don't use them to climb. They trained hard for six years and then attempted the climb at the end of 2014. People all around the world followed their progress on social media.

Read the text. Answer the questions.

1 What was Tommy and Kevin's ambition?
2 What is the Dawn Wall?
3 What is 'free climbing'?
4 How long did they train before attempting the climb?
5 When did they attempt the climb?

Listening Strategy
When you listen in your own language, you 'listen ahead' and can often predict how a phrase or sentence will finish. Try to do this when you are listening to English too.

3 **🎧 3.31** Read the Listening Strategy. Then listen and try to predict how each sentence will end. There are a number of possible answers.

1 Look at those dark clouds. I think it's *going to rain / going to snow / starting to rain / etc.*

4 **🎧 3.32** Listen to the complete sentences and compare them to your ideas in exercise 3.

5 **🎧 3.33** Listen to the news story about Tommy Caldwell and Kevin Jorgeson. When the recording pauses, write down up to five words that you think will come next. You will hear each part of the story twice.

1 *the sun went down*   5 _____
2 _____   6 _____
3 _____   7 _____
4 _____   8 _____

6 **🎧 3.34** Listen and compare your ideas in exercise 5 with the actual words. Were any of your predictions correct or nearly correct?

7 Work in pairs. Prepare an interview between a journalist and one of the climbers.

Student A You are a journalist. Prepare six questions using the prompts below.
Student B You are Tommy or Kevin. Prepare the answers using the information in the text and the news story.

1 how long / train?
2 when / start to climb?
3 how many hours / climb / each day?
4 get any injuries?
5 where / sleep?
6 biggest danger?

8 **SPEAKING** Work in pairs. Act out your interview for the class.

> How long did you train?

will

I can talk about the future and make predictions.

1 SPEAKING Who competes in the Paralympics? Can you name any Paralympic sports people? What are their sports?

2 Read the text. Are the sentences true or false?

1 Ellie Simmonds is only thirteen years old.
2 She won her first gold medal in 2008.
3 She wants to stop swimming.

ELLIE SIMMONDS

is a British Paralympic swimmer. She's only 1.23m tall, but she says, 'I'm a normal person. I'm just smaller!' She was only thirteen when she won two gold medals in the 2008 Paralympics in Beijing. She won gold again at the London Paralympics in 2012. It was the best moment of her career. 'I will never forget that moment,' she says. Now she is studying at a university in central England. What will she do when she finishes her course? 'I think I'll probably take a short break,' says Ellie. She won't stop swimming – that's certain! She'll be a member of the British Paralympic team for many years to come.

3 Read the Learn this! box. Then find all the examples of the *will* future in the text.

> **LEARN THIS!** *will*
>
> **a** We use *will* to talk about the future and to make predictions.
>
> **b** We form the *will* future with *will / 'll* or *will not / won't* and the infinitive of the verb without *to*. The form is the same for all persons.
>
> **Affirmative**
>
> I'll / she'll / we'll, *etc. see you tomorrow.*
>
> **Negative**
>
> I / he / you / they, *etc.* won't *see us tomorrow.*
>
> **Interrogative and short answers**
>
> When will we see each other again?
>
> Will you be eighteen next July? Yes, I will. / No, I won't.
>
> **c** We don't use the short form *'ll* after names or other nouns, or in short answers.
>
> Ann'll be at the party. ✗ Ann will be at the party. ✓
>
> Will you be at the party? Yes, I'll. ✗ Yes, I will. ✓

➡ **Grammar Builder 8D** page 138

4 Complete the sentences with the correct form of *will / won't* and the verbs below.

be   meet   not arrive   not be   not do   see

1 Dad's train is delayed. He _____ until late this evening.
2 Bye! I _____ you later.
3 I _____ your homework for you!
4 Joe is ill. He _____ at school tomorrow.
5 I _____ you at nine o'clock at the cinema. Don't be late.
6 A: 'It's your birthday tomorrow. _____ you _____ seventeen?'
   B: 'Yes, I _____.'

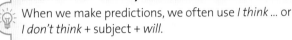

> **LEARN THIS!** *I think / don't think + will*
>
> When we make predictions, we often use *I think …* or *I don't think* + subject + *will.*
>
> I think scientists will discover a cure for cancer.
>
> I don't think scientists will discover a cure for cancer.
>
> NOT I think scientists won't discover … ✗

5 Read the Learn this! box. Find a prediction with *I think* in the text in exercise 2.

6 Make predictions about these possible events. Use *I think* or *I don't think.*

1 England / win the next World Cup
   I think / I don't think England will win the next World Cup.
2 the 2028 Olympics / be in Europe
3 I / go to a live sports event in the next few months
4 Neymar / score more than 30 goals next season
5 Andy Murray / play at Wimbledon next year
6 Spain / win the World Cup in 2026

7 Complete the sentences with *I think I'll* or *I don't think I'll* to make predictions about your future.

1 _____ study science at university.
2 _____ earn a lot of money.
3 _____ get married before I'm 30.
4 _____ have children.
5 _____ buy my own house or flat.
6 _____ have the same friends when I'm 25.
7 _____ stay in this town for the rest of my life.

8 SPEAKING Work in pairs. Take turns to ask and answer questions about the things in exercise 7. Use *Do you think* and make a note of the answers.

> Do you think you'll study science at university?

> Yes, I think I will. / No, I don't think I will.

9 SPEAKING Tell the class about your partner.

> Arda thinks / doesn't think he'll study science at universit

Word Skills

Noun suffixes

I can form nouns with a range of suffixes.

Samar Barakat, a seventeen-year-old teenager from London, is going to cycle through Japan to raise money for Child Chemo House, a charity that helps children who are having treatment for cancer. Her journey will start in Tokyo in July and will end at the headquarters of Child Chemo House in Kobe, 550 kilometres away. Samar's parents gave her permission to do the cycle ride, but they aren't going to cycle with her. Samar is a very independent girl and is not worried about travelling alone. She says she's going to meet friends while she's in Japan, so homesickness shouldn't be a problem. She's doing a lot of preparation and organisation before she starts. She's learning Japanese, and she's researching the route online, looking for accommodation. She doesn't want to cycle in darkness, so at the end of each afternoon, she's going to stop and stay in a cheap hotel or hostel. The journey will take about ten days and she hopes that she will receive lots of donations on her fund-raising web page. It will be an amazing achievement if she's successful.

1 SPEAKING Work in pairs. Look at the photo and the title of the text. What do you think the text is going to be about?

2 Read the text and check your ideas in exercise 1. Do you think this is a good way to raise money? Give reasons.

> **LEARN THIS! Noun suffixes**
>
> **a** We sometimes add *-ment, -ion,* and *-ation* to make nouns from verbs.
>
> *arrange – arrangement   converse – conversation*
> *describe – description*
>
> **b** We sometimes add *-ness* to make nouns from adjectives.
>
> *sad – sadness   happy – happiness*
>
> **c** With some nouns in all these groups, there is a small change in spelling (e.g. *description* and *happiness*).

3 Read the Learn this! box. Then look through the text and find nouns formed from the verbs and adjectives below. Which have a change in spelling?

accommodate achieve dark donate homesick
organise permit prepare treat

4 Make nouns from the verbs and adjectives. Use the correct suffixes: *-ment, -ion, -ation* and *-ness*. Use a dictionary to help you.

1 advertise (verb)   5 fit (adjective)
2 rude (adjective)   6 argue (verb)
3 inform (verb)   7 discuss (verb)
4 suggest (verb)   8 explain (verb)

5 Complete the sentences with the nouns in exercise 4.

1 Can you give me some _____ about trains?
2 I saw a TV _____ for some great football boots. I think I'll buy some.
3 _____ and diet are important if you want to stay healthy.
4 My brother and I had a terrible _____ yesterday. He still isn't speaking to me.
5 In class today, we had a _____ about the dangers of alcohol and drugs.
6 I was surprised at Josh's _____. He upset a lot of people.
7 Can I make a _____? Let's go out for dinner tonight.
8 Our maths teacher told us how to do the calculation, but I didn't understand her _____.

6 SPEAKING Work in pairs or small groups. Imagine you want to raise money for a charity by doing an event similar to the one in the text. Discuss these questions and make notes. Use the phrases below to help you.

help people who …   raise money   start training
support a charity   take part in (an event)

1 Which charity? Why?
2 What event? Why?
3 How will you prepare?
4 How much do you hope to raise?

7 SPEAKING Share your ideas with the class.

> We're going raise money for …
> We're going to take part in …

Against the odds

I can understand a text about inspiring sporting achievements.

1 **SPEAKING** Look at photos (A–D). What do you think the reading text is going to be about? Choose a, b or c.

   a The Paralympic Games and its competitors.
   b Sportspeople with disabilities.
   c The advantages of team sports for disabled people.

2 Read the text and check your answer to exercise 1. Match the photos (A–D) with the paragraphs (1–3). Two of the photos match one paragraph.

> **Reading Strategy**
> Make sure you answer every question in a multiple-choice task. If you are not sure of an answer, try to exclude one option and then guess between the other two. You have a 50:50 chance of being correct!

3 Read the Reading Strategy. Then choose the correct answer a, b, or c.

  1 Christian Haettich became disabled in the year
    a 1976   b 1984   c 1985
  2 Christian Haettich didn't compete in the Paralympic Games in Sydney because
    a he wasn't good enough for the French team.
    b he didn't have the right kind of disability.
    c he preferred to cycle up mountains instead.
  3 Mike Newman's problems with his eyes began
    a when he was eight years old.
    b when he was forty.
    c when he was born.
  4 Mike Newman did not start driving cars until after the age of forty because
    a somebody told him it was not possible.
    b he did not know about the charity for blind people in motor sports.
    c he did not know that blind people could take part in motor sports.
  5 According to the text, which sport did Alana Nichols take part in before her accident?
    a basketball   b skiing   c snowboarding
  6 In which sport has Alana Nichols won her most recent medals?
    a surfing   b basketball   c skiing

4 Answer the questions about the people in the texts. Write *Christian*, *Mike* or *Alana*.

Which person …
  1 became disabled at the youngest age? _____
  2 broke records in 2005 and 2013? _____
  3 took part in a lot of different sports as a child? _____
  4 found it difficult to learn his / her sport? _____
  5 took part in the Paralympic Games? _____
  6 started doing his / her sport after seeing another disabled sports person? _____

UNSTOPPABLE

 3.35

5 VOCABULARY Find four nationality adjectives in the reading texts. Add them to the list below.

Nationalities Australian Brazilian Canadian Chinese Czech German Hungarian Italian Japanese Polish Russian Slovak Spanish Swedish

6 Work in pairs. Look at the endings of the nationality adjectives in exercise 5. Divide them into three groups: *-an*, *-ish* and *-ese*. Which three do not fit?

7 SPEAKING In pairs, ask and answer these questions about the sports people in the text. Give a reason for your answers.

In your opinion, which sportsperson is ...
- the bravest?
- the most talented?
- the fittest?

> I think ... is the bravest because ...

1 THE CYCLIST

In 1976, at the age of fifteen, Christian Haettich had a serious car accident. He lost his left arm and his left leg. For the next few years, he found it very difficult to live with his disability. But in 1984 he saw a man with one leg cycle up a steep hill. 'I can do that,' he thought, and he learned to cycle. It was really difficult – he fell off his bike many times – but he kept trying.

In 1985, he began to compete in races for disabled cyclists. His ambition was to compete in the Paralympic Games in Sydney in 2000 and he trained hard to be in the French team. But then the rules for the competition changed and Christian could not take part because his disability did not match the new rules. So Christian found a new challenge: cycling up mountains. Now he competes in mountain races and cycles around 27,000 kilometres every year!

D

2 THE RACING DRIVER

British driver Mike Newman enjoys breaking speed records. For example, in 2013 he broke two – the land speed and the water speed records. This achievement is more amazing because Mike cannot see. He was born with a serious eye disease and became completely blind at the age of eight.

For many years, Mike did not think it was possible to take part in motor sports. But at the age of forty, he started riding motorbikes and then he tried cars. 'I love the engines, the smells, the noises which come with it,' he says.

He set new land speed records in 2003 and 2005, but in 2010 Metin Senturk, a blind Turkish pop star, went faster. So in 2013, Mike had to set a new record. It is very difficult – and dangerous. Imagine driving a car at 300 kilometres per hour with your eyes closed!

When he isn't breaking records, Mike runs a charity called Speed of Sight. The charity helps other blind people to take part in motor sports.

3 THE SKIER

Alana Nichols was a very sporty child. She loved volleyball and basketball. As a teenager, Alana's ambition was to study sports at university. But then, at the age of seventeen, she broke her back in a serious snowboarding accident. She couldn't walk. For two years, she did not know what to do with her life.

But at the age of nineteen, she discovered a new sport: wheelchair basketball. She became part of the national team for the USA and in 2008 they won a gold medal at the Paralympics in Beijing.

Alana realised that other sports were possible for her too. She tried surfing and kayaking. Then she tried skiing. She trained hard and became part of the American Paralympic team. At the 2010 winter Paralympics, she became the only athlete to win gold medals at the summer and winter Paralympic Games when she won four medals for skiing: two gold, a silver and a bronze. Then, in 2014, she won another silver medal at the winter games.

Negotiating

I can negotiate when discussing plans.

1 **SPEAKING** Match the pictures with three of the sports events from the list. Then tell your partner which events from the list you a) enjoy watching and b) enjoy doing.

Athletics events   100 metres   high jump   long jump
marathon   pole vault   relay   shot put

➡ **Vocabulary Builder** Athletics events: page 121

2 🎧 **3.36** Read and listen to the dialogue. Answer the questions.

1 Which athletics event from exercise 1 do they mention?
2 Which other sports do they mention?
3 Which one do they agree to watch?

Tom Hi, Ryan. It's Tom. Are you going to watch the Olympics on Saturday?

Ryan Yes, I am. But I haven't got any tickets. I'm going to buy them online today.

Tom Shall we go together?

Ryan Good idea. Which events do you want to see?

Tom I think the badminton at the indoor arena will be exciting. Let's go to that.

Ryan I'd rather not. It starts at 8 o'clock in the morning. That's too early! I'd rather see some athletics.

Tom OK. Let's try to get tickets for the stadium. The final of the men's 100 metres is at 12 o'clock.

Ryan I don't think that's a good idea. Those tickets are too expensive. What about swimming at the pool? I think that would be better.

Tom Yes, OK. That sounds good.

Ryan Great! I'll book the tickets.

3 **KEY PHRASES** Add the underlined phrases in the dialogue to category A or B below.

A Rejecting a suggestion
I don't really fancy doing that.
1 _____
2 _____
B Suggesting an alternative
I'd prefer to … .
Do you fancy (+-*ing*) instead?
3 _____
4 _____

4 **SPEAKING** In pairs, take turns to suggest an activity from the list below. Using phrases from exercise 3, your partner rejects the suggestion and suggests an alternative.

go to a café   go to the cinema   go skateboarding
go shopping   go swimming   listen to music   play football
play video games   watch TV

> Do you fancy going swimming?

> I'd rather not. I'd prefer to … .

5 Read the Learn this! box. Find two examples of *too* + adjective in the dialogue in exercise 2.

> **LEARN THIS!** *too* + adjective
>
> We use *too* + adjective to mean 'more than possible'. We often use it to explain why we are rejecting something.
>
> *We can't go to the beach. It's too far.*

➡ **Grammar Builder 8G** page 138

6 🎧 **3.37** Look at the timetable of Olympic events and listen to two teenagers talking about tickets. How many events do they agree to see? Tick the events that they agree to see.

SATURDAY	Pool	Indoor arena	Stadium
08:00	Diving	Badminton	Women's marathon
10:00		Basketball	Men's long jump
12:00	Swimming	Handball	Men's 100 m final
14:00		Gymnastics	Women's pole vault
16:00	Water polo	Volleyball	Men's 400 m relay

> **Speaking Strategy**
> When you are interacting with another speaker, react to what they say in an appropriate way.

7 🎧 **3.37** **KEY PHRASES** Read the Speaking Strategy. Then listen again and complete the phrases the teenagers use for reacting. Use the words below.

mean   right   see   so   that   think

Reacting
You're ¹_____.
I suppose ²_____.
I ³_____ what you ⁴_____.
Do you ⁵_____ so?
Is ⁶_____ right?

8 Work in pairs. Imagine you are planning a day at the Olympics. Look at the timetable in exercise 6, and agree on four events to see. Prepare a dialogue using phrases from exercises 3 and 7.

9 **SPEAKING** Work in pairs. Act out your dialogue to the class.

Writing

An informal letter

I can write an informal letter.

1 **SPEAKING** Look at the photos. What three events does the triathlon combine? Would you like to take part in a triathlon? Why? / Why not?

2 Read the letter. When and where will Emily's triathlon take place?

89 Stover Rd,
Birmingham
B99 7HL

4 July 2016

Dear Henry,

Thanks for your letter. Sorry I didn't reply sooner. My exams finished last week, and tomorrow the summer holidays start.

Guess what! I'm going to take part in a triathlon. It's taking place in Hyde Park in London, and I'm already training for it. I run, swim or cycle every day. You need quite a lot of equipment. My parents bought me a really good bike and helmet for my birthday. I've already got a wetsuit, but I'll need to buy goggles and new running shoes before the race. It's quite a big event and I think there'll be a lot of spectators.

Anyway, that's all for now. Write soon.

Love,

Emily

PS The triathlon is at the end of July. It would be great if you could come and cheer me on!

VOCABULARY Find five of the pieces of sports equipment below in the letter.

Sports equipment bike   boots   goggles   helmet
running shoes   wetsuit

➤ **Vocabulary Builder** Sports equipment and clothes: page 121

Choose the correct words to complete the rules for informal letters.

LEARN THIS! Informal letters

a The writer puts his / her address in the **top-left** / **top-right** corner of the letter.

b We put the date **above** / **below** the address.

c We start the letter with **Hello** / **Dear** and the person's name.

d We add extra information at the end of the letter after the letters **PS** / **SP**.

5 **KEY PHRASES** Add the phrases below to the correct group A, B or C. Which phrases did Emily use in her letter?

Listen, did I tell you that ... / about ...
Oh, and another thing, ...
Sorry, it's ages since I wrote to you.
Maybe you / we could ...
How about (+ -*ing* form)

A Apologising
Sorry I didn't reply sooner.
Apologies for not replying sooner.
B Giving news
Guess what!
You'll never guess what happened ... / I'm going to ...
Good news! ... / Bad news! ...
By the way, did you know that ...
C Making suggestions
Why don't you / we ... ?
It would be great if you could ...
If you like, we / you could ...

Writing Strategy
Spend a few minutes planning and making notes before you start writing your answer.

6 Read the Writing Strategy. Plan a letter to a friend describing and inviting them to a forthcoming sports event that you are going to participate in. Make notes about the following things.

1 What is the event? (e.g. football / volleyball / basketball / ice hockey match)
2 When and where will it take place?
3 How are you preparing for it? What equipment will you need?
4 Who will watch it? (e.g. parents / friends / other spectators)

7 Write your letter. Include your address, date and greetings. Lay out the letter correctly and include phrases from exercise 5.

CHECK YOUR WORK
Have you ...
● included phrases from the Learn this! box?
● followed the model for layout?
● checked the spelling and grammar?

Reading

1 Read the Strategy. Read the statements in exercise 2 and underline the key words.

2 Read the text. Are the sentences true or false? Write T or F.

1 Tricking is a mix of gymnastics and dance. ___
2 There is a long list of rules for tricking. ___
3 Tricking started in sports like judo. ___
4 Trickers post videos of tricks online. ___
5 Trickers only learn tricks from social media. ___
6 The first tricking meeting was in 2010. ___
7 There are trickers all over the world. ___
8 The butterfly twist is easy for beginners. ___

Tricking

A young man jumps, turns his body around in the air and lands on his feet. The movement is beautiful, but the man isn't dancing. Nor is he doing gymnastics, judo or karate. He's tricking.

What exactly is tricking? There's no clear definition. It isn't a sport. It hasn't got any written rules. Trickers are athletes who turn their bodies in new and interesting ways to express themselves.

Tricking started in the USA in the mid-1990s. It developed from the martial arts. Players wanted to challenge themselves to do jumps that were bigger, more powerful and more exciting, so they invented new movements. They called these movements 'tricks'. At that time, the internet was becoming more and more popular. Trickers filmed themselves and shared their new movements on the web, and later on social media.

For a long time, not many people knew about tricking. Trickers used social media to arrange meetings at gyms or outdoor spaces. At these meetings they learned new tricks from each other. Then, people started to do tricking in films and on TV. A character in the 2010 film *Tron* did a few tricks, for example, and there are trickers in some music videos and TV advertisements. Now tricking is a worldwide sport.

Some sports centres now offer tricking courses, but most people still learn tricking from the internet. They usually begin with easier movements such as the 540 kick before learning moves like the flashkick and the butterfly twist which are much more difficult.

Listening

3 Read the Strategy. Match the words below to the gaps in sentences 1–6.

a friend   by the sea   2nd May   two
two o'clock   watch films

1 We usually go cycling in the park or _____.
2 He was born on _____.
3 This tennis match started at _____.
4 I use my computer to check my emails and

_____.

5 You could ask _____ or a teacher for their opinion.
6 I waited for _____ hours for the file to download!

4 🎧 **3.38** Listen to part of a radio report. Add ONE, TWO or THREE words or numbers in each gap.

SuperTech Summer Camps

Most summer camps offer children activities like swimming, fishing, volleyball and [1]_____.

SuperTech Summer Camp offers technology-related events for nine–[2]_____-year-olds.

Courses include web programming, [3]_____ and even how to make a robot.

Some of the course leaders are teachers, others are [4]_____ and scientists.

SuperTech Summer Camps take place at the O'Malley Centre, about [5]_____ km west of Dublin.

Each camp lasts [6]_____, but children can come for more than one camp.

Matthew Day organised the first SuperTech Summer Camp [7]_____.

It costs £[8]_____ per week for a child to go to SuperTech Summer Camp.

Use of English

5 Read the Strategy. Add the correct suffixes to the words below to make people, nationalities and things.

achieve argue China ~~climb~~ discuss farm improve run Sweden swim work

people	nationalities	things
climber		

6 Complete the text with words formed from the words in brackets.

Nick D'Aloisio

Nick D'Aloisio is a successful young computer programmer. In 2011, he created a news story app called Summly. Summly allows users to read the news very quickly. It takes all the important ¹_____ (INFORM) from big news stories and makes them into smaller stories that can fit on one smartphone screen.

People use computer programmes to write the stories, and world-famous ²_____ (ART) and ³_____ (PHOTOGRAPH) Kevin Abosch creates the pictures.

D'Aloisio, who is half ⁴_____ (BRITAIN) and half ⁵_____ (AUSTRALIA), lives in London. He taught himself how to code when he was at school, and developed Summly when he was still a ⁶_____ (TEENAGE).

In 2013, when D'Aloisio was 17, he sold Summly to Yahoo for about \$30 million. So far, Summly is his biggest ⁷_____ (ACHIEVE). What will his next ⁸_____ (INVENT) be?

Speaking

7 Read the Strategy. Are these arguments *for* (F) an option or *against* (A) it? Write F or A.

1 Surfing sounds fun. _____
2 I'm terrible at ice skating. _____
3 It's too cold. _____
4 It would be interesting. _____
5 It would be boring. _____
6 It would be too dark. _____
7 We'd learn something useful. _____
8 I think watching a DVD would be more relaxing. _____

8 You are on an activity holiday abroad. Work with a partner and discuss your preferences. Agree on ONE morning activity, ONE afternoon activity and ONE evening activity.

PROGRAMME OF ACTIVITIES

MORNING
go swimming • do an aerobics class • go shopping play golf • learn to design a website

AFTERNOON
go to the cinema • go cycling • play badminton go climbing • go surfing • learn to design an app

EVENING
watch a DVD • go dancing • play board games play computer games • learn to design a computer game • go ice skating

Writing

9 Read the Strategy. Use the verbs in brackets to complete the sentences below with the present simple, present continuous, past simple or *be going to* + verb.

1 We _____ cycling last weekend. (go)
2 I _____ problems with my computer at the moment. (have)
3 Thank you for your letter. Sorry I _____ sooner. (not / reply)
4 I _____ Adam yesterday. (see)
5 Guess what? I _____ team captain next month. (be)
6 Erica and I _____ about having a party. (think)
7 My dad _____ some old photos of us last week. (find)
8 I _____ a printer. (not / have)

10 Write a letter to a friend about a ticket you won in a competition. Include information about the points below and suggest that your friend comes with you.

- What is the ticket for? (e.g. a holiday, a sporting event, a music festival)
- How did you win it?
- When are you going to go?
- How are you preparing for it?

9

Home sweet home!

Unit map

● **Vocabulary**
Furniture and household items
Parts of a home
Adjectives to describe rooms

● **Word Skills**
do, make, have, take, bring

● **Grammar**
Present perfect (affirmative)
Present perfect (negative and interrogative)

● **Listening** University accommodation

● **Reading** In the middle of nowhere

● **Speaking** Photo comparison

● **Writing** A description
● **Culture 9** The White House

9A Vocabulary

My home

I can describe different kinds of furniture.

1 SPEAKING Look at the photos. Compare the rooms using the adjectives below.

attractive   comfortable   modern   unusual

> I think room A is more attractive than room ...

> In my opinion, room C is the most ...

2 VOCABULARY Match the furniture in the photos with words from below.

Furniture and household items bath bed bin blinds bookcase carpet chair chest of drawers clock cooker cupboard curtains desk dishwasher hi-fi lamp light mirror rug shelves shower sink sofa stool table toilet wardrobe washing machine

3 🎧 **4.02** Check the meaning of all the words in exercise 2. Then listen and repeat.

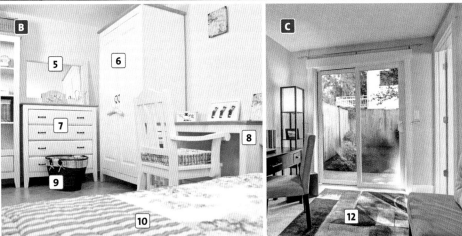

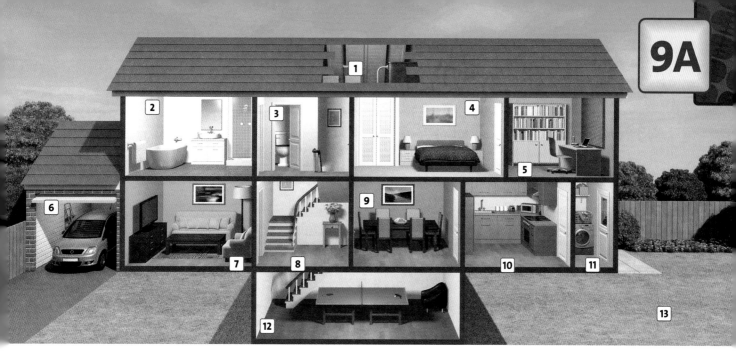

4 SPEAKING Work in pairs. Ask and answer questions about a) your bedroom and b) your living room. Use words from exercise 2. For each room find:

- two things which you both have.
- two things which neither of you has.
- one thing which one of you has but the other doesn't have.

> Is there a chest of drawers in your bedroom?

> Yes, there is. Are there any shelves in your living room?

> No, there aren't.

VOCABULARY Label the parts of the house 1–13 with the words below. What types of room are in the photos in exercise 1?

Parts of a home basement bathroom bedroom dining room garage garden hall kitchen living room loft study toilet utility room

🎧 **4.03** Listen and repeat all the words in exercise 5.

Which items from exercise 2 do you usually find in the parts of the home below? You find some items in more than one part of the home.

bathroom bedroom dining room kitchen living room study utility room

🎧 **4.04** Listen to six short discussions in the same family home. Where is each person, and why does he or she scream? Complete the sentences.

1 The boy is in the bathroom.
   He screams because there's a spider in the bath.
2 The dad is in the _____.
   He screams because _____.
3 The mum is in the _____.
   She screams because _____.
4 The girl is in the _____.
   She screams because _____.
5 The grandad is in the _____.
   He screams because _____.
6 The grandma is in the _____.
   She screams because _____.

RECYCLE! Contrast: present simple and present continuous

- We use the present continuous for events happening now or about now and for future arrangements.
- We use the present simple for habits and routines, and facts that are always true.
- We don't use some verbs with continuous tenses, e.g. *want, believe, understand*, etc.

9 🎧 **4.04** Read the Recycle! box. Then listen again and complete the sentences. Use the present simple or present continuous form of the verbs in brackets.

1 The boy _____ spiders. (not like)
2 The dad _____ the cooker. (clean)
3 Trixie the cat _____ on mum's bed. (lie)
4 The boy _____ to watch the football. (want)
5 The grandad _____ the car. (not fix)
6 The grandma _____ her sun hat. (look for)

10 SPEAKING Work in pairs. Plan your ideal bedroom or your ideal living room. Decide what items of furniture are in it.

> We need a ... so that we can ...

> We should have some ... so that ...

> I agree. / Great idea.

> I'm not sure about that. What about a ... ? Then we can ...

11 SPEAKING Tell the class about the room you planned in exercise 10.

> In our ideal bedroom, there's a ... so that we can ...

Present perfect (affirmative)

I can talk about recent events using the present perfect.

1 Read the email from a student on an exchange programme. Is he enjoying his stay in Germany? How do you know?

To: dad@email.com

To: dad
From: Ben
Subject: I'm in Berlin!
Sent: Mon 14 May 2018 19.55

Hi Dad,

I've arrived safely in Berlin. Kasper and his family met me at the airport. We've just had dinner and now I'm in my bedroom. They've tried to make me feel at home. They've put a photo of London on the wall and they've given me some English books to read! But I really miss my home and my family. Please reply soon! I've sent messages to my friends too, but so far only one person has replied.

Love, Ben

PS I've lost my German dictionary!

2 Read the Learn this! box. Are the highlighted past participles in exercise 1 regular or irregular?

LEARN THIS! Present perfect

a We use the present perfect simple to talk about recent events and give news, especially when the events have an effect on the present.

I can't phone her. She's changed her number.

b We form the present perfect simple with *have* or *has* (*'ve* or *'s*) and the past participle of the verb. The past participle of regular verbs is the same as the past simple form and ends in *-ed*.

We've moved house.

My sister has finished school.

c Irregular verbs have irregular past participles. These are sometimes the same as the past simple form and sometimes different.

I've bought a new bike. (buy – bought – bought)

She's broken her phone. (break – broke – broken)

3 Put the past participles of these verbs into three groups: 1) regular; 2) irregular – same as past simple; 3) irregular – different from past simple. See the list on page 143.

be come do eat feel finish forget give help
learn leave make meet phone play say see sleep
speak spend take tell watch write

Group 1: finished, … Group 2: felt, … Group 3: been, …

➡ **Grammar Builder 9B** page 140

4 Complete the sentences with the present perfect form of the verbs in brackets.

1 What's my password? I _____ _____ (forget).
2 She _____ (try) Greek food but she doesn't like it.
3 It isn't a secret – they _____ (tell) lots of people!
4 I _____ (do) my homework. Can I go out now?
5 Oh no! We _____ (leave) our bags on the train!
6 We can't buy a snack. You _____ (spend) all our money.

LOOK OUT! *just*

We use *just* with the present perfect to emphasise that the event is very recent. We usually put *just* between *have* or *has* and the past participle.

Do you want some pizza? No, thanks. I've just eaten.

5 Read the Look out! box. Find an example of the present perfect with *just* in the email in exercise 1.

6 SPEAKING Work in pairs. Take turns to ask a question from the list below. Your partner invents an answer using *just* and the present perfect.

Why are you …
1 crying?   3 so tired?   5 laughing?
2 so happy?   4 feeling ill?   6 worried?

> Why are you crying?

> Because I've just seen a really sad film.

7 Complete the email with the present perfect form of the verbs below.

eat have help learn meet play send speak

To: dad@email.com

Hi Dad,   Sun 20 May

I hope you are well. I ¹_____ a great first week in Germany! Kasper is really into sport, like me. We ²_____ football and basketball at the park and I ³_____ lots of Kasper's friends. I ⁴_____ German to everyone and I ⁵_____ a lot of new words. The food is really nice. I ⁶_____ just _____ about ten sausages! I ⁷_____ with the cooking a few times too.

love, Ben

PS I ⁸_____ just _____ an email to Mum too.

8 SPEAKING Tell your partner five things you have done this week. Use verbs from this lesson. Can your partner remember all five things and tell the class?

> I've tidied my room. I've …

> Zoltan has tidied his room. He's …

1 SPEAKING Work in pairs. Describe the photo. Then answer the questions.

1 Who are the people?
2 What are they doing?
3 Would you like to live in a place like this? Why? / Why not?

living
TO LEARN

In the UK, most university students live in halls of residence during their first year. A hall is ¹_____ building, owned by the university, with lots ²_____ bedrooms for the students. Students usually share bathrooms and toilets, but some bedrooms ³_____ got their own bathrooms. Some halls have also got kitchens where the students ⁴_____ cook their meals. In others the students only sleep – they go to the university canteen to eat. They are great places ⁵_____ make new friends. In the second and third years of study, most students move out of halls and rent accommodation. They often share a flat or a house ⁶_____ other students. Students can borrow money ⁷_____ the government to pay for their living expenses.

2 Complete the text with appropriate words. Is university accomodation the same for university students in your country? If not, how is it different?

> **Listening Strategy**
> In connected speech, auxiliary and modal verbs (*have, can, want, do*, etc.), prepositions (*to, for*, etc.) and pronouns (*you, he*, etc.) are usually unstressed, and the sounds sometimes change. It isn't necessary to copy this pronunciation when speaking, but it is important to be able to recognise these words in connected speech.

🎧 4.05 Read the Listening Strategy. Then match phrases (1–12) with the way they are pronounced in connected speech (A–L). Listen and check.

1 going to
2 want to
3 have to
4 can you
5 are you
6 do you
7 did you
8 don't know
9 kind of
10 lots of
11 there are
12 can I

A havta
B dunno
C didya
D gunna
E kinda
F dya
G cunya
H lotsa
I wonna
J thera
K cuna
L ah-ya

4 🎧 4.06 Listen and complete the questions.

1 Where _____ live? (*add two words*)
2 What _____ do at the weekend? (*add four words*)
3 What _____ do when you leave school? (*add four words*)
4 _____ speak any languages apart from your own language and English? (*add two words*)
5 _____ pay to study at university in your country? (*add four words*)
6 What _____ job _____ do when you finish your studies? (*add six words*)

5 SPEAKING Work in pairs. Ask and answer the questions in exercise 4. You don't need to copy the pronunciation.

6 🎧 4.07 Listen to the conversation and complete the questions.

1 *Can I* help you?
2 What _____ place _____ looking for?
3 Or _____ looking for your own flat?
4 _____ show me some houses?
5 _____ visit the house?
6 _____ free at the weekend?

7 🎧 4.07 Listen again. Are the sentences true or false? Write T or F.

1 The student has just finished her first year at university. ___
2 She is certain that she wants to live in a flat. ___
3 A house costs between £70 and £130 per person. ___
4 The first house isn't in Bristol. ___
5 The second house isn't in a quiet area. ___
6 The student is free all weekend. ___

8 SPEAKING What are the advantages and disadvantages of sharing accommodation while at university? Use the phrases below to help you.

You can (probably) ...   You don't have to ...
You (probably) can't ...   You (probably) have to ...
be very tidy   cook for others   cook for yourself
make friends   share a living room   share bills
share the housework

9D Grammar
Present perfect (negative and interrogative)
I can talk about recent events.

1 🎧 **4.08 Complete the dialogue with the past participles of the verbs below. Then listen and check.**

do (×2)   finish   hoover
receive   tidy

Mum I've just ¹_____ a text from Uncle Mike. He and your cousins are arriving in an hour. Are you going to tidy your room, Jake?

Jake I've already ²_____ it.

Mum Good. And have you ³_____ the living room yet?

Jake No, I haven't.

Mum I asked you to hoover it this morning. Can you go and do it now, please?

Jake Sarah can do it! What has she ⁴_____ to help? She hasn't done anything!

Mum She's changing the beds. I haven't ⁵_____ decorating Uncle Mike's birthday cake yet. She's going to help me with that too.

Jake Oh, OK. But I haven't ⁶_____ my homework yet. I need to do that first.

Mum No, hoover the living room first, please. Do your homework later.

2 KEY PHRASES Find all the examples of the present perfect negative and interrogative in the dialogue. Then complete the phrases with the correct form of the verb *have*.

Present perfect negative
I / You / We / They ¹_____ arrived.
He / She / It ²_____ arrived.
Present perfect interrogative
³_____ I / you / we / they arrived?
Yes, I / we / they have.
No, I / we / they ⁴_____.
⁵_____ he / she / it arrived?
Yes, he / she / it has.
No, he / she / it hasn't.

3 Write present perfect questions using the prompts below. Then look at the dialogue in exercise 1 and write short answers.

1 Uncle Mike and Jake's cousins / arrive?
   Have Uncle Mike and Jake's cousins arrived? No, they haven't.
2 Mum / receive / a text from Uncle Mike?
3 Jake / tidy / his bedroom?
4 Jake / hoover / the living room?
5 Jake / finish / his homework?
6 Mum / finish / decorating the birthday cake?

➡ Grammar Builder 9D page 140

LEARN THIS! *already* and *yet*

a We use *already* with the present perfect affirmative to say that something has happened (often earlier than expected). We put *already* between *have / has* and the past participle.

'Can you text Tom?' 'I've already texted him.'

b We use *yet* with the present perfect negative to say that something expected hasn't happened, or with the interrogative to ask if something expected has happened. We put *yet* at the end of the sentence.

It's 11 p.m. but Sally hasn't done her homework yet.

Have you tidied your room yet?

4 Read the Learn this! box. Then find examples of sentences with *already* and *yet* in the dialogue in exercise 1.

5 Look at the list of things that need doing before the visitors arrive. Write sentences using the present perfect affirmative with *already* and the present perfect negative with *yet*.

They have already tidied the living room.
They haven't … yet.

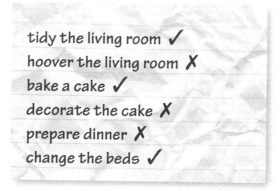

tidy the living room ✓
hoover the living room ✗
bake a cake ✓
decorate the cake ✗
prepare dinner ✗
change the beds ✓

6 SPEAKING Work in pairs. Ask and answer questions about the list in exercise 5. Use the present perfect interrogative with *yet*.

> Have they tidied the living room yet?

> Yes, they have.

7 SPEAKING What have you and your partner done today? Ask and answer questions about the activities below. Make a note of the answers.

buy anything   hand in your homework   have a drink
have a shower   listen to the news   make a phone call
use a computer   watch television

> Have you had a shower?

> Yes, I have. / No, I haven't.

8 SPEAKING Tell another student about your partner.

> Claudia has had a shower. She hasn't …

do, make, have, take, bring
I can use do, make, have, take *and* bring.

1 SPEAKING Describe the photo. How often do you tidy and clean your bedroom?

2 🎧**4.09** Read and listen to three teenagers talking about household chores. Who helps most with the housework: Marvin, Harriet, or James? Who helps least?

↞ ↠ ⟳

@Marvin How do I help round the house? I'm afraid I don't do much housework, actually. I occasionally do the hoovering, but I have to do a lot of homework every evening. It takes ages, so I haven't got time for much housework.

@Harriet My mum is a single parent, so my sister Emma and I try to help her with the housework. We make our beds every morning. Then after we've had breakfast, I usually do the washing up. At the weekend, Emma often does the cleaning while mum and I take the bus into town and do the shopping.

@James I do my best to help with the housework, but it's difficult to find the time. I tidy my bedroom once a week and I sometimes take the rubbish out or help mum to make the dinner. My brother, Max, has a lot of arguments with our parents about housework. He does nothing to help.

VOCABULARY Look at all the red collocations with *do*, *make*, *have* and *take* in the texts. Use them to complete the gaps below.

do ¹housework ²the hoovering ³_____
⁴_____ ⁵_____ ⁶_____
⁷_____ ⁸_____ / something the washing
somebody a favour

make ⁹_____ / breakfast / lunch ¹⁰_____
a mistake friends a phone call an appointment

have ¹¹_____ ¹²_____ a shower a drink
a party a rest a conversation

take ¹³_____ ¹⁴_____ ¹⁵_____
a photo an exam medicine / a pill somebody's advice

4 Circle the correct verbs to complete the sentences.

1 Can you **take** / **make** a photo of us, please?
2 I've **had** / **made** lots of friends at my new school.
3 If you're tired, **have** / **make** a rest.
4 Can you **take** / **do** me a favour?
5 I have to **take** / **make** three exams next week.
6 Don't just stand there! **Do** / **Make** something!
7 Kate **did** / **made** a lot of spelling mistakes in her essay.
8 Would you like to **have** / **do** a game of chess?
9 If you're thirsty, **have** / **take** a drink.
10 I've got a headache. I'm going to **do** / **take** an aspirin.

> ❗ **LOOK OUT!** *bring and take*
>
> The verbs *bring* and *take* both mean 'to move or carry something / somebody with you when you go somewhere'. However, we use:
>
> **a** *bring* when the direction of travel is <u>towards</u> the speaker:
>
> *Please bring me a glass of water.*
>
> **b** *take* when the direction of travel is <u>away</u> from the speaker:
>
> *Don't forget to take your homework to school.*

5 Read the Look out! box. Then complete the sentences with *bring* and *take*.

1 Can you _____ me into town? I've missed the bus.
2 'Don't forget to _____ your P.E. kit to school tomorrow.'
3 I'll _____ you a burger from the takeaway, if you like.
4 _____ a hat and gloves with you when you go out. It's very cold.
5 Please _____ some food and drink to my BBQ.
6 Please _____ this book to Mrs Smith in the teacher's room.

6 SPEAKING Work in pairs. Take turns to ask and answer questions about some of the household chores in the table in exercise 3. Try to give extra information. Make a note of your partner's answers.

> Do you ever do the washing up?

> Yes, I do. I sometimes do the washing up after dinner. / No, I don't. I hate washing up!

7 SPEAKING Tell the class about your partner.

> Matthew sometimes does the washing up after dinner. / He never does the washing up. He hates it.

In the middle of nowhere

I can understand a text about a remote island home.

1 **SPEAKING** Look at photos of Palmerston, an island in the Pacific Ocean. Describe it using the adjectives and nouns below and your own ideas.

Adjectives beautiful clear hot peaceful remote sunny tropical
Nouns beaches ocean palm trees sand

2 Read the text, ignoring the gaps. Would you like to live on Palmerston? Why? / Why not?

> ### Reading Strategy
> To check if a sentence fits a gap, think about any words in the sentence which refer back to people, things, places or situations / events / ideas mentioned in the sentence before the gap. Check that the reference makes sense.

3 Read the Reading Strategy. Then look at the sentences in exercise 4. Does each underlined word refer to people, things, places or situations/events/ideas?

4 Read the text. Match the gaps in the text (1–5) with the sentences (A–G). There are two extra sentences.

  A They then sell <u>them</u> to the ship and buy the things they need.
  B Visitors usually stay <u>here</u> when they are spending some time on the island.
  C <u>They</u> work together, look after each other and share.
  D When you get <u>there</u>, you will get a very warm welcome.
  E It takes four days to reach <u>it</u> by boat.
  F They understand <u>that</u>, but they are not happy about it.
  G <u>This</u> means going abroad to study.

5 Read and listen to the whole text and check your answers to exercise 4. For each gap, decide what the underlined word in the sentence refers to.

In gap 1, 'there' refers to 'the tiny tropical island of Palmerston'.

ISLAND *home*

6 Answer the questions.

1 Why is part of the journey to Palmerston very dangerous?
2 How many buildings are on the main road in Palmerston?
3 How often do the islanders usually receive supplies?
4 What problems do the islanders experience with internet and mobile phone signals?
5 How has the number of people living on the island changed in the past five decades?

7 VOCABULARY Match the two halves of the collocations below. They are all in the text.

1 tropical
2 sandy
3 basic
4 next-door
5 daily
6 free

a beaches
b life
c neighbour
d time
e island
f supplies

8 SPEAKING Work in pairs. Try to include vocabulary from exercise 7 in your role-play.

Student A Imagine you live on Palmerston. Talk to Student B about your daily life there.
Student B You live in a big city. Compare your daily life with Student A. Talk about:

- daily routine
- food and drink
- entertainment (sport, hobbies, etc.)

> In the morning I get up at nine o'clock and walk along the beach to school.

> Really? I catch the bus to school.

... is one of the hardest places in the world to visit. First, you have to ... to Tahiti, an island in the South Pacific Ocean. Then you have to ... avel by boat – for nine days! During that time, you hardly ever see ... other boat or plane. And the final part of the journey is the most ... ngerous, because of the rocks. Over the years, they have caused ... ndreds of boats to sink. You can still see some of the wrecks ... the beaches. But finally, you arrive at the tiny tropical island of ... lmerston, part of the Cook Islands. ¹_____ The islanders love visitors ... d look after them well.

... The island is very beautiful, with white sandy beaches and clear ... e water. There are no cars. The main road in Palmerston is only ... ut a hundred metres long and is made of sand, with only about six ... ldings. There is a small school, but there are no shops. The families ... Palmerston don't use money in their daily lives. ²_____ When you ... out of rice, you ask your next-door neighbour. They only use ... ney to buy things from other countries.

... A ship visits the island twice a year and brings basic supplies, ... rice and fuel. The islanders need money to pay for this, so they ... ch and freeze fish. ³_____ But sometimes the ship doesn't come. ... ently, eighteen months passed without a visit from the ship. But

that wasn't a problem: they could eat coconuts and fish.

These days, the islanders access the internet for one or two hours a day and they can even get a mobile phone signal – sometimes. But everyday experiences, like a visit to the dentist, can be a problem because the island is so remote. The nearest dentist is on Rarotonga, the capital of the Cook Islands. ⁴_____ And when the dentist has finished, you sometimes have to wait six months for a boat home!

Some of the islanders love the remoteness and think their home is paradise, but others have decided to leave. In the past 50 years, the population of Palmerston has dropped from 300 to just 62. About 20 of these are children. Their life is very happy and relaxed, but as they get older, some of them want a university education. ⁵_____ They often plan to come home again after their studies – but in reality, they rarely return.

But, for the people who stay on the island, daily life is easy. Nobody works very hard and there is a lot of free time. In the evenings, children swim in the beautiful blue ocean or play volleyball on the beach. The adults watch TV (there is one TV on the island) or chat. There is a policeman on Palmerston, but there isn't any crime, so he makes musical instruments instead!

Photo comparison

I can compare two photos.

1 SPEAKING Look at the photos above. How many pieces of furniture and household items can you identify?

> I can see a chest of drawers in the second photo.

2 VOCABULARY Find four pairs of opposites in the list of adjectives to describe rooms. Which adjectives would you use to describe the rooms in exercise 1?

Adjectives to describe rooms bright comfortable cosy dark large relaxing small tidy uncomfortable untidy

> ➡ **Vocabulary Builder** Adjectives to describe rooms: page 121

....

Speaking Strategy

In a photo comparison task remember to:

• compare the photos, pointing out any obvious similarities and differences.

• describe the people in the photos and say what they are doing.

• give your opinion and / or speculate about the people and situation.

....

3 🎧 **4.11** Read the Speaking Strategy. Then listen to two students comparing and contrasting photos 1 and 2. Which student followed the advice better? Give reasons for your opinion.

4 🎧 **4.11** **KEY PHRASES** Check the meaning of the phrases. Then listen again. Which phrases did the students use?

Comparing and contrasting
The first photo shows … , whereas the second photo shows …
In the first photo … , but in the second photo …
You can see … in both photos.
Both photos show …

Speculating
It looks as if …
I would say that …
I think … probably …
Perhaps he / she / it / they …
They look (+ adjective) He / She / It looks (+ adjective)

5 SPEAKING Work in pairs. Student A: Look at the two photos below. Student B: Look at the photos on page 142. Compare and contrast the photos. Say which living room you prefer and why.

A description

I can write a description of a home.

1 Read the task and the model texts. Which text matches the photo? How do you know?

Your family has agreed to offer a room to a foreign student for three months. Write a description of your home and the student's room. Include information about the rooms, the location of the home and the activities you do there in your free time.

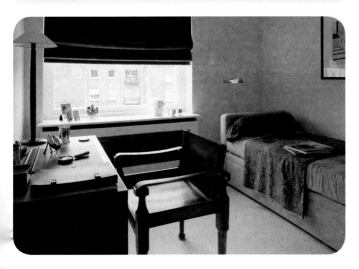

A I live in a fairly modern apartment on the fifth floor. It's a great location because it's right in the middle of the city. You can easily find a café nearby or get the bus to another part of the city.

There are three bedrooms. Your bedroom will be the one at the front of the apartment. The room is a bit small although it's very light. There's a bed, a desk and a chair in the room. The apartment also has two bathrooms, a living room and a kitchen.

In the living room, we have a big 3D TV, so we often lie on the sofas and watch films in the evenings. It's really relaxing! We also have a games console for playing video games.

B I live in a small cottage in a village. It's a bit remote – there are only about 50 houses here and there's only one shop! But there are four buses a day into town and the tickets are not very expensive.

The cottage has a living room, a dining room and a kitchen downstairs. It's extremely cosy in the winter because we always light the fire in the living room. Upstairs, there are three bedrooms. Your bedroom will be the one at the back of the house, so you'll have an amazing view of the countryside.

We often play board games in the evenings. Also, there are lots of books on the shelves. We've got a TV, although we don't watch it much.

Imagine you are choosing a place to stay for three months. Which room in exercise 1 would you choose? Why?

Match the three paragraphs in each text in exercise 1 with the three elements of the task: a) the rooms b) the location c) free-time activities.

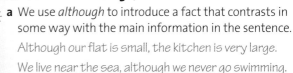

LEARN THIS! *although, because* and *so*

a We use *although* to introduce a fact that contrasts in some way with the main information in the sentence.

Although our flat is small, the kitchen is very large.

We live near the sea, although we never go swimming.

b We use *because* to introduce a reason and *so* to introduce a result.

The flat is on the top floor, so it's very quiet.

The flat is very quiet because it's on the top floor.

4 Read the Learn this! box. Find an example of the three conjunctions (*although*, *because* and *so*) in each text in exercise 1. How do you say these conjunctions in your own language?

5 Circle the correct conjunction to complete these sentences.

1 We can't live in the city centre **although** / **because** it's too expensive.

2 We sometimes go the beach **although** / **so** the sea is too cold for swimming.

3 Our street is in the town centre, **because** / **so** there's a lot of traffic.

4 There's a lot of beautiful countryside, **although** / **so** it's a great place for walks.

5 In the evenings, we usually stay at home **although** / **because** we sometimes visit neighbours.

Writing Strategy

We often use modifiers like *very* or *fairly* before adjectives when we are writing a description. Modifiers make the description sound more natural.

The apartment is very / fairly modern.

6 **VOCABULARY** Read the Writing Strategy. Which modifiers can you find in the texts in exercise 1. What adjectives are they with?

Modifiers a bit extremely fairly pretty quite really (not) very

➡ **Vocabulary Builder** Modifiers: page 121

7 Plan an answer to the task in exercise 1. Make notes for each element (a–c in exercise 3). Include adjectives and modifiers in your notes.

8 Write your description following your plan from exercise 7. Use conjunctions to join ideas together within each paragraph.

CHECK YOUR WORK

 Have you ...
- used conjunctions correctly?
- included modifiers in your description?
- checked your spelling and grammar?

Exam Skills Trainer

Reading

> **Strategy**
>
> Make sure you read the whole of each paragraph before you start to match the headings. The extra heading will contain a word or phrase that matches part of one or two paragraphs, but only the correct heading will match the whole of the paragraph.

1 Read the **Strategy**. Read each paragraph of *Homes in Mexico* and answer the questions.

   1 Which paragraphs in the text contain the word *rich*?
   2 Which paragraphs in the text contain the word *big*?
   3 Which paragraph matches the whole meaning of heading F?

2 Read the text. Match the headings (A–F) to the gaps (1–5). There is one extra heading which does not fit any of the gaps.

   A European-style houses, old and new
   B Old houses in many colours
   C Small houses for Mexico's richest people
   D New houses, old style
   E Colours have made life better
   F Big houses for rich people

Homes in Mexico

Mexico has forests and beaches, high mountains and lowlands. It has very rich people and very poor people. It isn't surprising then that there are so many different kinds of homes in Mexico.

1 _____

There are modern blocks of flats in Mexico's towns and cities, but a lot of Mexican people prefer to live in houses. In the old areas of town you can see traditional houses. Their outside walls are painted bright green, yellow, orange and blue. The houses haven't got gardens, but there's usually a small outside space at the back where you can sit and relax. People can talk to their neighbours easily because the houses are next to each other.

2 _____

Some people in Mexico have built modern *adobe* houses. They look like houses from ancient Mexican cultures. They are small and simple, with red walls and small windows. Inside they are cool and comfortable, even when the weather's hot.

3 _____

Some rich people in Mexico live in Spanish *villas*. These houses may be modern or old, but they all have white walls, red roofs, wooden doors and lots of windows. The walls in the kitchens and bathrooms are usually blue. Some Spanish villas have beautiful gardens.

4 _____

Other very rich people live in very big, beautiful houses called *haciendas*. In the past, rich families owned haciendas and all of the land around them. They used the land for growing coffee and sugar. Lots of people worked there, but only the family who owned the land lived in the big house.

5 _____

Not everyone in Mexico can live in a beautiful house, but in one town where life is difficult for many people, the government has paid a group of street artists to paint more than 200 new houses in bright colours. The houses make a 20,000 m² picture. 'It's fantastic,' says Ana Flores, who lives in the area. 'It's helped young people believe that a better future is possible.'

Listening

> **Strategy**
>
> Read the instruction and the options in multiple-choice questions carefully before you listen. Then guess what the general topic of the listening is about.

3 Read the **Strategy**. Read the questions in exercise 4. What is the best summary of the listening text?

   1 Three teenagers tell us about their new homes.
   2 Three teenagers describe their homes and bedrooms.
   3 Three teenagers talk about their experiences of moving house.

4 🎧 **4.12** Listen to part of a radio report about moving house. Choose the correct options, A, B, or C.

   1 Which feelings does the presenter talk about?
     A excitement, happiness, worry
     B sadness, anger, worry
     C excitement, sadness, worry
   2 Caitlin, Ahmed and Josie
     A moved house three months ago.
     B have moved house recently.
     C moved house a long time ago.
   3 Caitlin
     A has felt unhappy in her new house.
     B doesn't like her bedroom.
     C has been to visit her old school.
   4 Ahmed
     A started his new school last week.
     B has already decorated his bedroom.
     C thinks his bedroom is too dark.
   5 Josie
     A has felt very sad in her new house.
     B hasn't spoken to her old friends.
     C has made some new friends.

Exam Skills Trainer

Use of English

5 Read the Strategy. Match the verbs below to 1–5.

do have make share take

1 _____ your bed / friends / a phone call
2 _____ an argument / a rest / breakfast
3 _____ your best / the cleaning / your homework
4 _____ a pizza / the bills / a room
5 _____ someone's advice / an exam / medicine

6 Read the email and complete each gap with ONE word.

Hi Matt,

Help! Why did I decide to have ¹_____ party? It's four o'clock and I'm still getting the house ready! I ²_____ tidied the living room, but there's still a lot to do! I ³_____ cleaned the floors yet, and I need to finish making the food.

⁴_____ Darren phoned you? ⁵_____ he be here this evening? Does he know the party starts ⁶_____ eight o'clock?

Can you ⁷_____ me a favour? I've done the shopping, but I ⁸_____ a mistake at the supermarket – I forgot to buy some bread! Can you get some?
See you later.

Vicky

PS I've decorated the cake so we don't need to worry ⁹_____ that. ☺

PPS Oh no! I've ¹⁰_____ remembered something else! I need to clean the bathroom!

Speaking

7 Read the Strategy. Write the adjectives in the correct place in the table.

attractive awful cosy light relaxing ugly
uncomfortable untidy

Positive	Negative

8 Compare and contrast the two rooms below. Where do you study at home? Where do you relax?

Writing

9 Read the Strategy. Complete the sentences with the words below.

at in nearby next on upstairs

1 There are two big rooms _____ the second floor.
2 There's a swimming pool _____. It takes about five minutes to walk there.
3 There's a small bathroom downstairs, and there's a bigger bathroom _____.
4 The kitchen is _____ the front of the house.
5 I live _____ a small village.
6 The house is _____ to a park.

10 Think of a home that you know well (but not your own home). Write a description. Include information about the points below.

- who lives there
- the location
- the rooms
- when you last went there and what you did

🎧 4.13

A NORMAL LIFE

Prince William is the grandson ¹_____ Queen Elizabeth II and the eldest son of Prince Charles and Princess Diana. He and his wife, Kate, live in a large apartment in Kensington Palace in London with their two young children, George and Charlotte. They also have a home in Norfolk in the east of England.

William works hard but he ²_____ got a normal job. Instead, he has a lot of royal duties: he meets foreign kings, queens and presidents and he helps a lot of different charities. He is famous all around the world, but he ³_____ want his home life to be special or different.

Kate also has a lot of royal duties. But like her husband, she ⁴_____ a normal life too. She goes shopping in the local supermarket, and she sometimes meets friends and has coffee with them. She always buys her own clothes. Sometimes she buys expensive designer clothes, but she often goes ⁵_____ normal clothes shops.

William and Kate are happy together and they love their apartment in London and their quiet home in the country. Kate's hobbies are cooking, walking their dog Lupo and playing with her children. William and Kate are proud ⁶_____ their young children. They think they have got a wonderful family!

1 SPEAKING Look at the photos. Which members of the British Royal Family can you name?

2 USE OF ENGLISH Read the magazine article and complete the gaps with one of the words below.

1 **a** of	**b** for	**c** with
2 **a** isn't	**b** hasn't	**c** doesn't
3 **a** doesn't	**b** does	**c** isn't
4 **a** want	**b** wants	**c** doesn't want
5 **a** for	**b** in	**c** to
6 **a** of	**b** at	**c** by

3 Read the first paragraph of the article and complete the family tree.

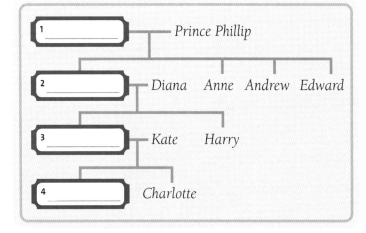

1 _____ — Prince Phillip

2 _____ — Diana Anne Andrew Edward

3 _____ — Kate Harry

4 _____ — Charlotte

4 Read the whole article and answer the questions.

1 Who is William's grandmother?
2 Where do William and Kate live?
3 Where is their other home?
4 What are William's royal duties?
5 Where does Kate buy food?
6 What does Kate like doing?

5 VOCABULARY Match the highlighted words in the text with words below that have the opposite meaning.

busy   cheap   old   sad   small   west

6 🎧 4.14 Listen to three people talking about the British Royal Family. Match each speaker (1–3) with two of the sentences below (A–F).

Which speaker …
A is not sure that all the stories about the Royal Family are true? ___
B thinks the Queen is good for tourism? ___
C is happy that the Queen does not smile a lot? ___
D likes looking at photos of the Royal Family? ___
E doesn't know what the members of the Royal Family do? ___
F thinks Harry sometimes does silly things? ___

7 INTERNET RESEARCH Choose one of the people in the family tree in exercise 3. Find out about him / her. Write a few sentences about him / her.

8 SPEAKING Work in pairs. Draw a family tree for your family. Tell your partner about your family.

> This is my mum. She's a nurse. This is my sister. She's 21.

The University of Oxford

1 SPEAKING Look at the photos. Where are the students? Match photos A–D with the phrases below.

at their degree ceremony   in a college room
in the dining hall   in the library

2 Read the fact file about the University of Oxford and questions A–E below. Match each of the questions with the correct paragraph 1–5 in the fact file.

▶ 4.15 THE UNIVERSITY OF OXFORD
THE FACTS

The University of Oxford is about a thousand years old. It is famous all over the world, but why is it so well known?

1 ___
Yes. There are over 22,000 students at Oxford: about 12,000 of these are undergraduates and 10,000 are postgraduate students. Around 25% of the population of the city of Oxford are students.

2 ___
In lots of ways. Firstly, the university has more than 30 different colleges. Secondly, students wear special gowns for exams and other important university events. Finally, the degree ceremony is in Latin, the language of the ancient Romans.

3 ___
Yes, it does. Two of the most famous buildings are the Bodleian and the Sheldonian. The Bodleian is the university library and has over eleven million books. At the Sheldonian, concerts, lectures, degree ceremonies and other university events take place.

4 ___
Yes! These include David Cameron and 25 other UK prime ministers, 27 Nobel prize winners, famous scientists such as Stephen Hawking and 120 Olympic gold medallists.

5 ___
This is the publishing department of the university. It sells over 110 million books each year and is famous for the Oxford English Dictionary. There are about 300,000 words in this dictionary and it weighs more than 60 kilos!

A Are there many famous students?
B How is Oxford different from other universities?
C Does the university have many famous buildings?
D What is Oxford University Press?
E Are there lots of students at the university?

3 VOCABULARY Match the highlighted words in the fact file with the definitions (1–6) below. (Most of the words are plural in the fact file.)

1 somebody with a first degree doing further studies at university _____
2 somebody studying for their first degree _____
3 the number of people who live in a particular area _____
4 somebody who leads the government of their country _____
5 a lesson for a large group of university students _____
6 a long item of clothing that people wear for some formal occasions _____

4 🎧 4.16 Listen to five University of Oxford students. Which students are not from the UK?

5 🎧 4.16 Listen again. Match speakers (1–5) with sentences (A–F) below. There is one extra sentence.

Which speaker ...
A is worried about starting at Oxford? ___
B is excited about starting at Oxford? ___
C is not keen on studying for a degree? ___
D is a postgraduate student? ___
E is friends with other people from their own country? ___
F is not the first person in his / her family to study at Oxford? ___

6 SPEAKING Discuss this question in pairs or small groups: Do you want to go to university? Why? / Why not?

7 INTERNET RESEARCH Find out about the University of Cambridge on the internet. Write down at least three interesting facts about the university. Compare your answers with the rest of your class.

Teens and their money

1 SPEAKING Work in pairs. How much money do you spend on the things below?

apps and games   clothes   films and music   food and drink
jewellery   make-up and accessories   shoes

> I spend a lot of my money on …

> I spend some money on …

> I don't spend much on …

> I spend nothing on …

2 Look at the pie charts. Are the sentences true or false? Write T or F.

1 In the USA, young people spend more money on apps, games and electronics than on food and drink. ___
2 They spend more money on music and films than on make-up and accessories. ___
3 Amazon is the most popular shopping website. ___

3 USE OF ENGLISH Read and complete the text. Write one word in each gap.

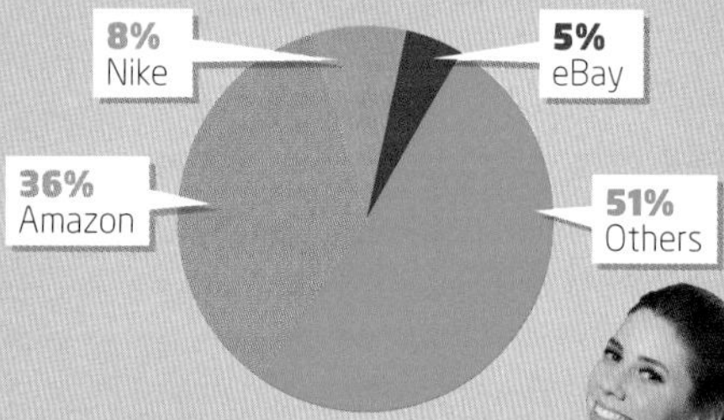

4 Read the text again and choose the best summary, a, b or c.

a American teenagers spend most of their money online, not in high street shops.
b Spending money on clothes is more important for American teenagers than spending money on entertainment.
c American teenagers spend more on clothes than on anything else, but food and entertainment are also important.

5 🎧 **4.18** Listen to four British teenagers talking about how they spend their money. How many of them mention spending money on video games?

6 🎧 **4.18** Listen again. Match the speakers to the activities. There is one sentence that doesn't match any of the speakers.

Which speaker …
a spends a lot of time with friends? _____
b only buys clothes that aren't expensive? _____
c isn't interested in fashion? _____
d likes buying smart clothes? _____
e buys most things online? _____

7 SPEAKING Work in pairs. Discuss the questions.

- How is the way you spend money different from the way American teenagers spend money?
- Do you often shop online? Why? / Why not? If you shop online, what do you buy?

🎧 **4.17**

$PENDING HABITS

How ¹_____ American teenagers spend their money: on clothes, or food, or apps? Let's find out.

How teenagers spend their money

figure 1

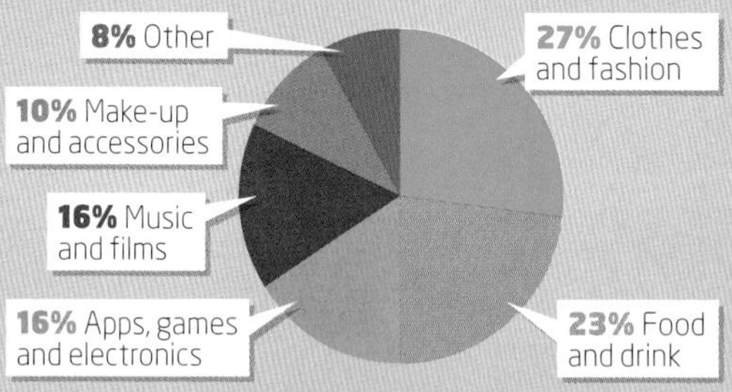

- **8%** Other
- **10%** Make-up and accessories
- **16%** Music and films
- **16%** Apps, games and electronics
- **27%** Clothes and fashion
- **23%** Food and drink

Style is important for American teenagers, so ²_____ isn't surprising that they spend nearly 40% of their money ³_____ clothes and make-up (see figure 1).

However, teenagers don't just buy clothes in shops. Over 80% ⁴_____ teenagers shop online for fashionable clothes. Amazon is their favourite shopping site, but Nike and eBay are also popular (see figure 2). Teens particularly like to buy shoes on the internet. That's because there ⁵_____ many fashionable shoe shops in town centres. There is more choice on shopping websites – and

for many teenagers, it is very important to wea the 'right' brand!

But young people aren't only interested ⁶_____ clothes and fashion. A lot ⁷_____ teenagers me in coffee shops and restaurants, and they spen 23% of their money there on food and drink.

When you add together the percentages for apps, games, electronics, films and music, you ⁸_____ see that American teenagers spend a lo of their money on entertainment too.

Favourite shopping websites

figure 2

- **8%** Nike
- **5%** eBay
- **36%** Amazon
- **51%** Others

British food

1 VOCABULARY Match the names of the dishes below with the photos A–D. Which of the dishes would you like to eat?

fish and chips   roast beef and Yorkshire pudding
sausages and mashed potato   strawberries and cream

2 USE OF ENGLISH Complete the article about food in Britain. Write one appropriate word in each gap.

🎧 **4.19**

BEST OF BRITISH!

UNLIKE FRANCE OR ITALY, Britain is not famous for the quality of its food. And the truth is, British people are very keen ¹_____ food from other countries. There are Indian and Chinese restaurants in nearly every town in ²_____ UK – and other types of international food are popular too. However, according to a recent survey, British people are also keen on traditional British food and usually have one ³_____ two favourite British dishes.

A traditional Sunday lunch with roast beef and Yorkshire pudding is very popular, and so is a full English breakfast. (This is not just bacon and eggs, of course. It also includes sausages, tomatoes, mushrooms and toast.) Another favourite, ⁴_____ survey says, is sausages and mashed potato – or 'bangers and mash', as people often call it.

Sometimes, favourite dishes have a connection with a special time or place, and often the food seems to taste better because ⁵_____ that connection. For example, a hot pie is the perfect food when you're watching a football match. But when you're watching tennis at Wimbledon, you want a bowl ⁶_____ strawberries and cream.

So what is the nation's favourite British food, according to the survey? The answer is: fish and chips – especially take-away fish and chips in paper. And especially when you're eating it by the sea!

Read the text again and answer the questions.

1 Which two types of restaurant are very common in British towns?
2 What is a full English breakfast?
3 What is another name for sausages and mashed potatoes?
4 What do people like to eat at football matches?
5 Where do people like to eat strawberries and cream?
6 Where does fish and chips taste best, according to the survey?

4 🎧 **4.20** Listen to a radio interview about modern British cuisine. Which two adjectives from the list best describe this kind of food?

beautiful   fresh   simple   unhealthy

5 🎧 **4.20** Listen to the interview again. Circle the best answers.

1 Which kind of food from the 1970s do they discuss?
   a nouvelle cuisine
   b cuisines from other countries
   c modern British cuisine
2 How is modern British cuisine different from other styles of cooking?
   a It takes a new look at traditional recipes.
   b The meals are very small.
   c The recipes use traditional herbs and spices.
3 Which of these dishes is a Modern British cuisine recipe?
   a traditional roast lamb
   b duck with orange sauce
   c duck with cherries or pistachio nuts
4 What extra information do some Modern British cuisine menus include?
   a Which herbs and spices the food contains.
   b Where the ideas for the dishes come from.
   c How far away the ingredients come from.

6 SPEAKING Work in pairs or small groups. Discuss these questions.

1 Which do you prefer: traditional food from your country or food from other countries?
2 Are some traditional dishes disappearing in your country? If so, why do you think this is happening?
3 Do you agree that some food tastes better at certain times or in certain places? Give examples.

7 INTERNET RESEARCH Search the internet for British recipes. Find a recipe that you like. Then work in pairs or small groups and describe your recipes.

New York

1 SPEAKING Work in pairs. How much do you know about New York? Decide if these sentences are true or false. Write T or F. Can you correct the false sentences?

1 New York is the capital of the USA. ___
2 The population of New York is about 8.5 million. ___
3 People speak around 800 different languages in New York. ___
4 The Golden Gate Bridge is in New York. ___
5 The Empire State Building is in New York. ___
6 The United Nations Headquarters is in New York. ___
7 The White House is in New York. ___

2 🎧 **4.21** Listen and check your answers.

3 Read the tourist guide to New York City. Match headings A–F below with paragraphs (1–5). There is one extra heading.

A The Statue of Liberty
B The view from the top
C The Brooklyn Bridge
D Central Park
E Visit a museum
F Times Square

🎧 **4.22**

NEW YORK
THE TOP FIVE THINGS TO DO

NEW YORK is one of the world's most interesting and exciting cities. There are parks, rivers, and famous buildings; there are great shops and interesting museums too. It is home to about 8.5 million people – more than any other city in the USA. About 55 million visitors come to New York every year. Why do they come?

4 🎧 **4.23** Listen to the interview with Gloria Estrada. Answer the questions.

1 What event is she looking forward to?
2 How many people are taking part in the event?
3 When is the event?

5 🎧 **4.23** Listen again. Are the sentences true or false? Write T or F. Correct the false sentences.

1 Gloria lives in Bogotá. ___
2 She runs seven times a week. ___
3 This is her first marathon. ___
4 She is nineteen years old. ___
5 She doesn't think that marathons are very tiring. ___
6 She is starting to feel more at home in New York. ___

6 SPEAKING Work in pairs. A British friend is coming to your country. You are meeting him / her in a city that you know well. Agree on the top three places to visit, and give reasons. Use the phrases below to help you.

> I want to take him / her to ... because ...

> ... is interesting. Let's take him / her there.

> I know. Why don't we take him / her to see ... It's really ...

7 INTERNET RESEARCH Choose an American city from the list below, or use your own ideas. Find the 'top three' things to do there. Write a paragraph about each attraction, saying why it is good to visit.

Boston   Miami   New Orleans   San Francisco   Washington, D.C.

 ___

Day or night, the view from the top of One World Trade Centre, the tallest building in the USA, is fantastic. You can see islands, bridges, and some of the most famous buildings in the world.

 ___

This is New York's busiest place. Over 300,000 visitors come here a day. People sell art and jewellery on the street, and you can buy cheap tickets for Broadway musicals and plays. Don't miss this place!

 ___

This is one of the most surprising places in the city. What can you do here? Visit the zoo or the castle. Walk or jog on the grass and along the paths. Look at the beautiful lakes and gardens. In the winter, you can go ice skating, and in the summer, you can watch a Shakespeare play. There's something for everyone.

 ___

Are you interested in art? What about science, history, or space travel? Between East 82nd and East 105th Streets, there are eight amazing museums and art galleries. Don't miss one of the great educational centres of the world.

 ___

A gift from the people of France in 1886, this is perhaps the city's most famous tourist attraction. It is a symbol of hope and freedom for people who arrive in America to start a new life.

Yellowstone National Park

1 SPEAKING What is a national park? Are there any national parks in your country? Can you name them?

2 VOCABULARY Match the words below with the correct definitions.

canyon   expedition   extraordinary   pond   protect   variety

1 a deep valley _____
2 very surprising or unusual _____
3 an organised trip, often to an unknown place _____
4 a number of different kinds of the same thing _____
5 a small area of water _____
6 to make sure something is safe _____

3 Complete the article with the correct forms of the words in exercise 2.

A LAND OF FIRE AND ICE

🎧 **4.24**

[I]n 1809, John Colter, a hunter, travelled to a new part of the United States: the mountains and forests of Wyoming. He [d]iscovered an amazing place. It was an ¹_____ land [o]f ice and fire. When he returned home, he talked about his [a]dventures – but nobody believed him!

[C]olter described amazing scenes. There were ²_____ [o]f water – but they boiled! There were trees that appeared to be [s]tone. There were holes in the ground that suddenly exploded, [li]ke fountains of boiling water. Everywhere there was the strong [s]mell of sulphur.

[C]olter walked deep into the forests. He watched and studied an [a]mazing ³_____ of animals, including bears and wolves. [H]e climbed high mountains and explored beautiful lakes and [ri]vers. There were high waterfalls and deep ⁴_____ with [ye]llow rocks on each side. In fact, the name of this place comes [fr]om those rocks: Yellowstone.

[Fi]fty years later, the US government organised three scientific ⁵_____ to Yellowstone. They wanted to find out what [w]as really there. Finally, people started to believe John Colter's [st]ories. They realised Yellowstone was a beautiful and unusual [pl]ace, and asked the government to ⁶_____ it. So in [18]72, President Ulysses S Grant signed a new law: Yellowstone [w]as now the first national park in the world.

4 Read the article. Are these sentences true (T) or false (F)? Write T or F.

1 John Colter was the first person to go to Yellowstone. _____
2 Colter talked to nobody about his adventures in Yellowstone. _____
3 Colter noticed a strange smell in Yellowstone. _____
4 The name 'Yellowstone' comes from the colour of the lakes and rivers there. _____
5 The government sent expeditions to Yellowstone in 1872. _____

5 SPEAKING Work in pairs or small groups. Discuss this situation.

You are walking in the forest when you meet a bear. What do you think is the best thing to do?

6 🎧 **4.25** Listen to the interview. Compare your ideas from exercise 5 with the woman's actions.

7 🎧 **4.25** Listen to the interview again. Circle the correct answers.

1 The woman
   a wanted to be ready if she met a bear.
   b was not aware that there were bears in Yellowstone.
   c wanted to meet a bear.
2 The woman remembered reading that running away from a bear is
   a never a good idea.
   b the best thing to do.
   c only a good idea if you are quick.
3 When the woman moved backwards, the bear
   a started to move backwards too.
   b was frightened and moved away quickly.
   c moved quickly towards the woman.
4 In the end, the bear
   a pushed the woman to the ground.
   b walked around the woman and then moved away.
   c stayed still and the woman moved away.

8 SPEAKING Discuss this question in pairs or small groups: Is it important to have national parks? Why? / Why not?

9 INTERNET RESEARCH Find out about a national park in your country or a neighbouring country. What is special about this area? Are there any special animals in the park? Are there any special places or sights? Share the information with the rest of your class.

British scientists

1 SPEAKING Work in pairs. Discuss these questions. How many famous scientists from your country can you name? Why are they famous?

> He / she discovered / invented ...

2 Read the text about Isaac Newton. Complete the timeline of Isaac Newton's life.

1642 ▼	Newton was born on 25 December. He lived with his ¹_____ from an early age.
1654 ▼	He started to go to ²_____.
³_____ ▼	He started to study at Cambridge University.
1665 – ⁴_____ ▼	The University of Cambridge closed. Newton returned ⁵_____.
1669 ▼	He became Professor of ⁶_____ at Cambridge.
⁷_____ ▼	He published his book, *Principia Mathematica*.
⁸_____	Newton died

🎧 **4.26** ISAAC NEWTON was born on Christmas Day in 1642. Newton's father died before he was born. His mother got married again, and Newton lived with his grandmother. At the age of twelve, he started school and seven years later, in 1661, he went to Cambridge University. There he began to study light and colour. He invented a new type of telescope and was the first person to discover that white light is a mixture of all the colours. After four years at Cambridge, the plague arrived in Britain. The plague was a terrible illness that killed thousands of people. The university closed and Newton returned home. While he was at home he continued to think and to work. One day, he was sitting under an apple tree in his garden, and an apple fell on his head. Newton said that is how he discovered gravity. It's certainly a good story, but we aren't sure if it is true! He returned to Cambridge in 1667 and two years later he became a Professor of Mathematics. Starting in 1684, Newton wrote his greatest work: *Principia Mathematica*, which he published in 1687. Isaac Newton died in October 1727, at the age of 84. His work is still important, nearly 300 years after his death.

3 Find the past tenses of these verbs in the text.

1 be _____
2 get _____
3 go _____
4 begin _____
5 fall _____
6 say _____
7 become _____
8 write _____

4 🎧 **4.27** Listen to an interview about the astronomer Caroline Herschel. Choose the best summary.

1 She was German but mostly lived in Britain. She built telescopes and discovered planets with her brother, who was her assistant.

2 Born in Germany, she worked as assistant to her more famous brother. However, she was responsible for some important discoveries.

3 She worked as assistant to her brother. They spent most of their lives in Germany and together discovered comets, nebulae and the planet Uranus.

5 🎧 **4.27** Listen again. Answer the questions.

1 How much younger than William was Caroline?
2 What did Caroline do for William before she became his assistant?
3 How many comets and nebulae did she discover?
4 What did she successfully calculate?
5 How old was she when she died?

6 SPEAKING Work in pairs. Decide on your top three discoveries and inventions. Choose from the list below or use your own ideas.

aeroplanes cars computers DNA electricity evolutio
gravity the internet microscopes nuclear power
penicillin printing the telephone telescopes
television the wheel writing X-rays

> I think the invention / discovery of ... is the most important because ...

> ... is more important because ...

7 SPEAKING Work in pairs. Tell the class about your choices from exercise 6.

> Our first / second / third choice is ... We chose it because ...

8 INTERNET RESEARCH Find out about a famous scientist from your country. Write a short article about them, include information about:

- why you chose this person.
- the person's life.
- how important their ideas are today.

8 Culture

Football

SALARIES PER YEAR IN THE UK		AVERAGE FOOTBALLER SALARIES IN EUROPE (PER WEEK)	
Top footballers	£15 million	Premier League (UK)	£43,700
Prime Minister	£150,000	Bundesliga (Germany)	£28,000
Doctor	£78,000	Serie A (Italy)	£25,300
Teacher	£37,000	La Liga (Spain)	£23,300

1 SPEAKING Work in pairs or small groups. Look at the information in the tables above. What do you find most surprising? Why?

2 Read the opinions below. Who thinks footballers are paid too much?

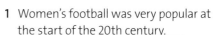

 4.28

Do footballers earn too much?

First of all, footballers' careers are short. They can play for fifteen years, if they're lucky, but the average career lasts for only eight years – and a career can end suddenly at any time with a bad injury. Also, only a few footballers earn really big salaries. Most footballers play in the lower leagues. They earn a good salary while they are playing, but when they stop, they need to find another job – they certainly won't have enough money to last for the rest of their lives. Yes, some footballers earn extraordinary amounts of money. But that is true for other jobs too. The best actors, the best singers and the best lawyers all earn millions. Why shouldn't the best footballers?

PHILIP JAMESON FOOTBALL JOURNALIST

In one month, a top footballer can earn about the same as the Prime Minister earns in one year! Is that right? I don't think so – but I don't blame the players, I blame the clubs. They want success on the pitch, but it is also big business. The best footballers make money for their clubs even when they aren't playing football. Real Madrid paid £80 million for Cristiano Ronaldo. In the next nine months fans paid £100 million for kits with Ronaldo's name on the back. Football is not about sport any more – not at the highest level. It's about money.

KAREN FLORY FOOTBALL FAN

3 VOCABULARY Match the highlighted words in the text with the definitions below. Write the singular forms. (Some words are plural in the text.)

1 _____: a group of teams who play sport against each other
2 _____: an organisation that includes a sports team and all the people who work with them.
3 _____: someone who loves football.
4 _____: the shorts, shirt and socks that members of a sports team wear.
5 _____: the area of grass where football matches take place.
6 _____: money you earn each year for doing your job

4 Read the opinions in exercise 2 again. Who do you agree with most?

5 🎧 **4.29** Listen to an interview with Nick Wheeler, a football journalist. Which sentence is true?

1 Women's football was very popular at the start of the 20th century. ___
2 The England women's football team is probably the best in the world. ___

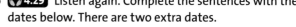

6 🎧 **4.29** Listen again. Complete the sentences with the dates below. There are two extra dates.

1895   1920   1921   1969   1972   1991

1 The first women's football match was in _____
2 The first women's football World Cup was in _____
3 Women footballers stopped using men's pitches in _____
4 The English Women's Football Association started in _____

7 SPEAKING Read the statements below. Give each statement a mark from 1–5, where 1 = *I completely agree* and 5 = *I completely disagree*. Then discuss your answers in pairs or small groups.

1 Female footballers should get the same money as male footballers. ___
2 Football is boring compared to many other sports. ___
3 There is too much football on television. ___

8 INTERNET RESEARCH Find out about one of the women's football teams in your country or abroad.

- What are the players' salaries?
- How many people go to watch the matches?
- How much do the tickets cost?
- How successful are they?

The White House

1 SPEAKING Work in pairs or small groups. Who lives in this building? In which country and city is it?

2 USE OF ENGLISH Read the White House information sheet. Choose the correct words to complete the text.

1 **a** of	**b** at	**c** for
2 **a** a	**b** some	**c** the
3 **a** in	**b** into	**c** onto
4 **a** more	**b** later	**c** then
5 **a** At	**b** On	**c** In
6 **a** a	**b** the	**c** one

3 Read through the information again and answer the questions.

1 Who decided where to build the White House?
2 Who was the first President to live in the White House?
3 When did people start calling it the White House?
4 How long has the Oval Office been the President's office?
5 What sports facilities has the White House got?
6 How many people visit the White House each week?

4 VOCABULARY Match the words below with 1–7 in the picture.

ceiling   clock   fireplace   painting   statue   wall   window

5 🎧 **4.31** Listen to the tour guide. In what order do they visit these rooms?

the Cabinet Room   the Oval Office   the Roosevelt Room   the secretary's office

---

🎧 **4.30**

Welcome to the White House!

In 1789, George Washington became the first President ¹_____ the United States. Two years later, he chose this place to build the President's house. Unfortunately, Washington died before ²_____ house was ready, so the first person to live there was the second President, John Adams. He moved ³_____ the house with his wife, Abigail, in 1800. Since then, every President has lived there.

Over the years, there have been many changes. The British set fire to the house in 1814 during a war between the two countries. Three years ⁴_____, President Monroe organised the repairs. In 1901, President Roosevelt named the house the 'White House' and the next year, he started a programme to modernise it. This included building a new part of the house: the West Wing. ⁵_____ 1909, William Taft created the Oval Office in the West Wing, and this has been the President's office since then.

The White House has 132 rooms, 35 bathrooms, eight staircases, three lifts, a swimming pool, a tennis court, a jogging track and a private cinema. It receives 30,000 visitors ⁶_____ week. While it is the home of the US president and his (or her) family, the White House is also a museum of American history.

6 🎧 **4.31** Listen again. Answer the questions.

1 What is the 'Fish Room' now called?
2 Who changed the name of the room?
3 Where does the President meet with his staff?
4 Which room is next to the Oval Office?
5 Why does the tour guide mention the clock in the Oval Office?
6 Who chooses the paintings for the Oval Office?

7 SPEAKING Work in pairs. Imagine you can build a dream home. Read the questions and discuss your ideas.

- Where is it?
- How many rooms has it got?
- What different rooms has it got?
- What do the rooms contain?

8 INTERNET RESEARCH Find out about a famous state building in your country. How old is it? Who lived or work there in the past? Who lives or works there now? Can the public visit? Write a fact file.

V Vocabulary Builder

Introduction

IA Numbers and ordinals

1 SPEAKING Say the odd numbers 1–49 around the class. Then say the even numbers 2–50.

> one, three, five …

> two, four, six …

2 🎧 **4.32** Listen and read the ordinals in the Learn this! box.

> **LEARN THIS!** Ordinal numbers and dates
> 1st first 2nd second 3rd third 4th fourth 5th fifth
> 6th sixth 7th seventh 8th eighth 9th ninth 10th tenth
> 12th twelfth 20th twentieth 22nd twenty-second
> 31st thirty-first
>
> 1st July = 'the first of July'

3 SPEAKING Say these dates.

1 2nd June	4 12th February	7 3rd January
2 22nd November	5 21st April	8 23rd July
3 5th August	6 19th October	9 6th December

IC Musical instruments

4 Match the pictures with eight of the words below.

bass guitar cello clarinet drums flute
guitar / electric guitar keyboard oboe organ piano
saxophone trombone trumpet violin

A

B

C

D

E

F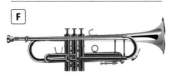

G

H

Which instruments from exercise 4 do you usually find …

1 in a pop or rock group?   2 in an orchestra?

Unit 1

1G Describing people

1 Complete the Learn this! box with the adjectives below. Check the meaning of all the words.

attractive a beard curly eyes long hair
medium height slim

> **LEARN THIS!** Describing people
> She's tall / short / ¹_____.
> He's ²_____ / medium weight / overweight.
> She's good-looking / ³_____.
> He's got ⁴_____ / a moustache / glasses.
> She's got blue / brown / green / dark ⁵_____.
> He's got ⁶_____ / medium-length / short hair.
> She's got fair / brown / red / grey / dark ⁷_____.
> She's got straight / ⁸_____ / wavy hair.

2 Write short descriptions of the people in each photo.

A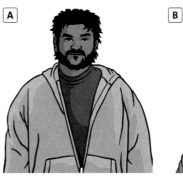

B

3 Write four sentences that describe you, your friends or your family. Describe two or more features (eye, hair, height, build, etc.) of the person in each sentence.

1H Personality adjectives

4 Put the personality adjectives below into the correct group: a) positive or b) negative.

brave creative friendly hard-working honest lazy
mean moody patient polite rude selfish sensible

positive	negative

5 Circle the best adjective to complete the sentences.

1 A **lazy** / **mean** person hates hard work.
2 A **friendly** / **sensible** person usually makes good decisions.
3 An **honest** / A **hard-working** person does not tell lies.
4 A **brave** / **polite** person does not get scared easily.
5 A **moody** / **selfish** person does not think about other people.
6 A **patient** / **creative** person does not get angry about waiting.

V Vocabulary Builder

Unit 2

2G Feelings

1 Label the pictures with six of the adjectives below.

angry bored embarrassed excited guilty happy
sad scared surprised tired worried

A

B

C

_____

D

E

F

_____

2 Match the other five adjectives from exercise 1 with the definitions.

1 People get _____ when something really good is about to happen.
2 People get _____ when they do something wrong or make a mistake.
3 People often feel _____ after they do something bad.
4 People feel _____ when something unusual happens and they don't expect it.
5 People feel _____ when they are waiting in a long queue.

2H School events

3 Complete the sentences with the school events below.

concert jumble sale musical open day
parents' evening play raffle school camp school club
school trip sports day

1 On an _____, students and parents come and visit the school for the first time.
2 Students sing and dance in a _____.
3 Students play music at a _____.
4 At a _____, people can buy old things very cheaply.
5 At a _____, students' mums and dads come to the school and meet the teachers.
6 In a _____, people buy tickets and hope to win prizes.
7 After school, students can go to a _____.
8 At a _____, students play games and have races.
9 On a _____, students visit interesting places with their teachers.
10 At a _____, students spend several days in the countryside and do outdoor activities.
11 In a _____, students act.

Unit 3

3G Free-time activities

1 Complete the table with the words below.

board games books bowling cards chess
computer games dancing dinner in a café DVDs
fishing football for a walk friends ice skating
lunch in a restaurant magazines a musical instrument
music rollerblading skateboarding swimming tennis
to the beach to the cinema TV

play		go	
1 _____	5 _____	8 _____	13 _____
2 _____	6 _____	9 _____	14 _____
3 _____	7 _____	10 _____	15 _____
4 _____		11 _____	16 _____
		12 _____	17 _____
have		**meet**	
18 _____	19 _____	20 _____	
listen to		**watch**	
21 _____		22 _____	23 _____
read			
24 _____	25 _____		

3H Accessories

2 Label the pictures with six of the words below.

belt bracelet earrings gloves headphones necklace
purse ring sunglasses wallet watch

A

B

C

_____

D

E

F

_____

3 Complete these sentences with the other words from exercise 2.

1 You can listen to music with _____.
2 A piece of jewellery you wear _____ on your wrist
3 You use a _____ to tell the time.
4 You need _____ when the weather is sunny.
5 You wear a _____ around the top of your trousers

Vocabulary Builder

Unit 4

4G Partitives

1 Complete the phrases using the words below.

bread   crisps   jam   lemonade   orange juice   soup   tea
~~water~~

1 a glass of *water*
2 a loaf of _____
3 a bowl of _____
4 a packet of _____
5 a cup of _____
6 a carton of _____
7 a jar of _____
8 a can of _____

2 Complete these phrases with a partitive (*glass*, *bowl*, etc.) from exercise 1. Several answers are possible.

1 a _____ of cereal
2 a _____ of sugar
3 a _____ of milk
4 a _____ of coffee
5 a _____ of biscuits
6 a _____ of honey

4H Parties and celebrations

3 Match the pictures with the types of celebration below.

barbecue   birthday party   end-of-exams party
fancy-dress party   New Year's Eve party   street party

A

B

_____

C

D

_____

E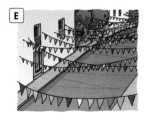

F

_____

Unit 5

5G In the street

1 Match the things in the picture (1–12) with the words below.

bridge   bus shelter   crossroads   cycle lane   lamp post
pavement   pedestrian crossing   phone box   roundabout
square   T-junction   traffic lights

2 Complete the sentences with words from exercise 1.

1 It was raining so we waited for the bus in the _____.
2 The safest place to cross the road is the _____.
3 There are two _____ over the river.
4 The _____ were red so the car stopped.
5 It's much safer to ride your bike in the _____.
6 'I need to call my mum, but I've forgotten my mobile.'
   'Don't worry. There's a _____ over there.'
7 'Walk on the _____, not on the road!'

5H Describing towns and cities

3 Put the adjectives below into five pairs of opposites.

~~attractive~~   boring   clean   crowded   exciting   historic
modern   polluted   quiet   ~~ugly~~

attractive / ugly, …

4 Compare the place you live with these cities. Use the comparative form of adjectives from exercise 3.

The place I live, _____, is:

1 _____ than New York.
2 _____ than London.
3 _____ than Tokyo.
4 _____ than Istanbul.

Unit 6

6G The weather

1 Match the weather adjectives with the icons below.

cloudy   cold   hot   rainy   snowy   stormy   sunny
warm   windy

2 Describe the weather in these pictures. Use two different words from exercise 1 for each picture.

3 Answer the questions.

1 What is the weather like today?
2 What was the weather like yesterday? / last Sunday? / on your birthday?
3 What is the weather usually like in December / August?

6H Adventure holiday activities

4 Match the pictures with eight of the adventure holiday activities below.

abseil   bungee-jump   climb   cycle   explore
go caving   kayak   kite-surf   swim   surf   trek
watch wildlife   windsurf

Unit 7

7G Money and prices

1 Match the currencies with the countries.

1 yen	a China
2 dollar	b UK
3 pound	c Japan
4 euro	d USA
5 yuan	e most European Union countries

2 SPEAKING Say these prices.

1 99p   4 5p
2 £1.37   5 £4.99
3 £250   6 £75.85

3 🎧4.33 Listen and write the prices.

1 75p   4 _____
2 _____   5 _____
3 _____   6 _____

7H Adverbs

4 Write the adverbs for these adjectives.

1 loud _____   4 fast _____
2 bad _____   5 dangerous _____
3 good _____   6 slow _____

5 Complete the sentences with adverbs from exercise 3.

1 He's working _____.
2 She's singing _____.
3 He's playing the guitar _____.
4 They're running _____.
5 She's cycling _____.
6 He's talking _____.

V Vocabulary Builder

Unit 8

8G Athletics events

1 Match the photos with three of the athletics events below.

100 metres   5,000 metres   10,000 metres
cross-country running   discus   hammer   high jump
hurdles   javelin   long jump   marathon   pole vault   relay
shot put   triple jump

 **A**
 **B**
 **C**

_____   _____   _____

2 Write the events from exercise 1 in the correct group. One of the events can go in two groups.

Running	Throwing	Jumping
100 metres	discus	high jump

8H Sports equipment and clothes

3 Label the photos with the sports equipment below.

ball   bat   bike   boots   gloves   goal   goggles   helmet
net   racket   running shoes   shirt   shorts   skates   socks
trainers   wetsuit

 A
 B
 C
 D

_____   _____   _____   _____

 E
 F
 G
 H

_____   _____   _____   _____

Which items of sports equipment in exercise 3 do you
a) wear and b) hold?

Match the sports equipment with different sports.

1 ball *football, volleyball*
2 skates _____
3 racket _____
4 gloves _____
5 helmet _____
6 net _____
7 wetsuit _____
8 bat _____

Unit 9

9G Adjectives to describe rooms

1 Complete the adjectives with *a, e, i, o, u* and *y*.

1 br _ ght
2 cl _ _ n
3 c _ mf _ rt _ bl _
4 c _ s _
5 d _ rk
6 d _ rt _
7 l _ rg _
8 m _ d _ rn
9 _ ld-f _ sh _ _ n _ d
10 r _ l _ x _ ng
11 sm _ ll
12 t _ d _
13 _ nc _ mf _ rt _ bl _
14 _ nt _ d _

2 Describe the following rooms in your home. Use three adjectives for each one.

1 the living room
2 your bedroom
3 the kitchen

9H Modifiers

> **LEARN THIS!** Modifiers
>
> - Modifiers (*fairly*, *very*, etc.) come before an adjective and make the meaning stronger or weaker.
>   It's 5°C today. That's cold.
>   It's 10°C today. That's fairly cold.
>   It's –5°C today. That's very cold.
> - We only use *a bit* or *not very* when the adjective is after a noun.
>   My bedroom is not very large. ✔
>   **NOT** ~~We've got a not very large kitchen.~~ ✗
> - We can use *quite* with adjectives before or after the noun. However, when the adjective is before the noun, we put *quite* before the indefinite article *a / an*.
>   Our flat is quite old.   We live in quite an old flat.

3 Read the Learn this! box. Then add the modifiers below to the table.

a bit   extremely   fairly   not very   pretty   quite   rather
really   very

Make the adjective stronger	Make the adjective weaker
extremely	a bit

4 Complete the sentences with a suitable modifier. Sometimes more than one answer is possible.

1 That Aston Martin sports car is _____ expensive. It costs over €200,000!
2 We live in a _____ small cottage.
3 These shoes are _____ small. They're size 42 and I need a 43.
4 He's _____ late. The lesson started 30 minutes ago!
5 Their house isn't beautiful but it's _____ attractive.
6 This room is _____ warm. I need to put a jumper on.

Grammar Builder

IB *be*

1 Complete the text with the correct affirmative form of *be*.
➻ I.1, I.2

> My name **1**_____ Joe. I **2**_____ from Glasgow in Scotland. I **3**_____ sixteen years old. This **4**_____ a photo of my family. I **5**_____ on the left. My sister **6**_____ on the right. My parents **7**_____ teachers.

2 Make the sentences negative. ➻ I.1, I.2

1 I'm from the USA.
2 My teacher is British.
3 I'm at home.
4 You are sixteen years old.
5 It is cold today.
6 My friends and I are in a maths lesson.

3 Write the words in the correct order to make questions. Then match the questions with the answers (a–f). ➻ I.1, I.2

1 we / in / are / school?
2 today? / very / is / it / hot
3 you / from / China? / are
4 your / teachers? / are / parents
5 eighteen / Stella / is / old? / years
6 Sam / is / in / his bedroom?

a No, he isn't.
b Yes, it is.
c No, they aren't.
d Yes, we are.
e Yes, she is.
f No, I'm not.

IB *have got*

4 Circle the correct words to complete the sentences.
➻ I.3, I.4

1 I **has got / have got** a little brother.
2 My teacher **hasn't got / haven't got** blue eyes.
3 We **hasn't got / haven't got** computers in our classroom.
4 My best friend **has got / have got** three sisters.
5 You **has got / have got** black hair.
6 My parents **hasn't got / haven't got** a car.

5 Write true sentences about yourself with the affirmative or negative form of *have got*. ➻ I.3, I.4

1 a bike
  I've got a bike. / I haven't got a bike.
2 a laptop
3 a pet
4 a smartphone
5 a TV in my bedroom
6 an English dictionary

6 SPEAKING In pairs, ask and answer the questions in exercise 5. ➻ I.3, I.4

Have you got a bike?
Yes, I have. / No, I haven't.

IC *can*

7 Write sentences with *can* or *can't*. ➻ I.5, I.6

1 Jack / ride a bike ✗
  Jack can't ride a bike.
2 They / speak French ✗
3 We / swim ✓
4 Ben and Sam / ski ✓
5 You / play the piano ✗
6 My friend / play tennis ✓

8 In pairs, ask and answer questions about the activities in exercise 6. ➻ I.5, I.6

Can you ride a bike?
Yes, I can. / No, I can't.

ID Articles: *the, a / an, some*

9 Write the correct article, *a, an* or *some*. ➻ I.7, I.8, I.9

1 _____ bike
2 _____ old man
3 _____ books
4 _____ computers
5 _____ orange
6 _____ children
7 _____ easy exercise
8 _____ pen
9 _____ dictionary
10 _____ cats

10 Write the correct article, *a, an, some* or *the*.
➻ I.7, I.8, I.9, I.10

1 I've got _____ flute and _____ saxophone. I can play _____ flute, but I can't play _____ saxophone.
2 I've got _____ rabbits and _____ goldfish. _____ rabbits' names are Floppy, Blackie and Fred. _____ fish's name is Goldie.
3 At home we've got _____ old piano and _____ drums. _____ piano is in the living room and _____ drums are in m[_] brother's bedroom.
4 We've got _____ computers and _____ interactive whiteboard in the classroom. _____ computers are old, but[_] _____ interactive whiteboard is new.

ID *this / that / these / those*

11 Circle the correct words to complete the sentences. ➻ I.11

1 'Are **that / those** your DVDs?'
  'Yes, they are.'
2 '**This / That** is my friend Marcus.'
  'Nice to meet you, Marcus.'
3 'Is **this / these** your phone?'
  'No, it isn't.'
4 **That / Those** is my pencil.
5 **That / Those** are my trainers over there.
6 **This / These** exercises aren't very difficult.

Grammar Reference

be

I.1

Affirmative	Negative
I am	I am not
you are	you are not
he / she / it is	he / she / it is not
we / you / they are	we / you / they are not

Interrogative	Short answers
Am I ... ?	Yes, I am. / No, I'm not.
Are you ... ?	Yes, you are. / No, you aren't.
Is he / she / it ... ?	Yes, she is. / No, it isn't.
Are we ... ?	Yes, we are. / No, we aren't.
Are you ... ?	Yes, you are. / No, you aren't.
Are they ... ?	Yes, they are. / No, they aren't.

I.2 Short forms

I am → I'm   you are → you're
we are → we're   they are → they're
I am not → I'm not   is not → isn't   are not → aren't

- We use short forms after most pronouns: *I, you, he, she, it, we, they, that* and *there*. We also use them after question words: *what, who, where*, etc. But we don't use them after most nouns, or after the pronouns *this, these* or *those*.
  We're at school. That's my classroom. Where's the gym?
  NOT ~~My friends're at home.~~ ✗ → My friends are at home.
- We don't use short forms in affirmative short answers.
  Yes, I am.   NOT ~~Yes, I'm.~~ ✗

have got

I.3

Affirmative	Negative
I have got (short form = *I've got*)	I haven't got
he / she / it has got (short form = *he's got*)	He / She / It hasn't got
you / we / they have got (short form = *you've got*)	you / we / they haven't got

Interrogative	Short answers
Have I got ... ?	Yes, I have. / No, I haven't.
Has he / she / it got ... ?	Yes, he / she / it has. / No, he / she / it hasn't.
Have you / we / they got ... ?	Yes, you / we / they have. / No, you / we / they haven't.

I.4 We use *have got* to talk about possessions and family.
I've got a bike.   She's got a dog.
Have you got a brother? No, but I've got a sister.
We also use *have got* to describe people's appearance.
They've got blue eyes.   He's got long legs.
What colour hair has she got?

can

I.5

Affirmative	Negative
I / You / We / They / He / She / It can walk.	I / You / He / She / It / We / They can't walk. The full form of *can't* is *cannot*.

Interrogative	Short answers
Can I / you / we / they / he / she / it swim?	Yes, I can. / No, I can't.
	Yes, she can. / No, she can't.
	Yes, they can. / No, they can't.

I.6 We use *can* to:
- talk about ability.
  I can ski. My friend can't ride a bike.
  Can you speak French?
- ask for permission.
  Can I borrow your pen, please?   Yes, you can.

Articles: *the / a / an / some*

I.7 We use the indefinite article (*a* or *an*) with singular nouns only.
a book   a computer
We can use the definite article *the* with all singular and plural nouns.
the table   the chairs   the water

I.8 We use *an* instead of *a* when the next word begins with a vowel sound. This means most words beginning with *a, e, i, o* and *u* and a few words that begin with silent *h*.
an egg   an Indian restaurant   an hour
Some words that begin with the letter *u* do not start with a vowel sound, they start with /j/.
a university   a useful book   a US city

I.9 We can use *some* with plural nouns when we don't know, or we don't want to say, exactly how many.
I've got a pen and some pencils.

I.10 We use *a* or *an* when we mention something for the first time.
I've got a phone in my pocket.
We use *the* when we mention it again.
The phone isn't mine.

this / that / these / those

I.11 We use *this* and *that* with singular nouns. We use *these* and *those* with plural nouns.
this book   that book   these books   those books
We use *this* and *these* with objects near to us.
This is a DVD, not a CD.   These are my pencils.
We use *that* and *those* with objects that are further away.
That's our car.   Those are tall trees.
We use *this* to introduce people.
This is Emma.

Grammar Builder

1A Possessive 's

1 Complete the second sentence so that it means the same as the first. Use possessive 's. ➡ 1.1

1 My dad has got a cat. It's white.
My _____ is white.
2 Jack has got a sister. She's at university.
_____ is at university.
3 My teacher has got a bike. Where is it?
Where is my _____ ?
4 Ted's parents have got a boat. It's big.
Ted's _____ is big.
5 My grandparents have got a flat. It's in London.
My _____ is in London.

1B Present simple (affirmative)

2 Write sentences in the present simple affirmative.
➡ 1.2, 1.3, 1.4

1 my cousin / work / in Sweden
My cousin works in Sweden.
2 I / love / comedy shows
3 my best friend / live / with his grandparents
4 my dad / teach / English
5 we / listen / to music / at home
6 my sister / go / to school / by bus
7 I / enjoy / school
8 my dad / study / ancient languages

3 Look at the table. Complete the sentences about the people's regular activities. ➡ 1.2, 1.3, 1.4

Who?	What?	Where? / When?
1 Joanna	sing	in the bedroom
2 Tom & Ann	play tennis	in the garden
3 Connor	meet friends	after school
4 Liam & Evie	visit relatives	every weekend
5 Rachel	have a shower	every evening
6 Daniel	skateboard	in the park

1 *Joanna sings in the bedroom.*

4 Use the table to make five more sentences. Combine the names, activities and time / places in different ways.
➡ 1.2, 1.3. 1.4

Connor plays tennis in the bedroom.

1D Present simple (negative and interrogative)

5 Write all the negative and interrogative forms of the verb *work* (*I, you, he / she / it, we, you, they*) in the present simple. ➡ 1.5, 1.6, 1.7

Negative: I don't work. You …
Interrogative: Do I work? Do you … ?

6 Complete the sentences with *don't* or *doesn't*. ➡ 1.5

1 My dad _____ drive to work.
2 My brother _____ like cats.
3 I _____ do my homework in the living room.
4 We _____ have lunch at school.
5 You _____ listen to me!
6 She _____ go to work by car.

7 Write the words in the correct order to make questions.
➡ 1.6, 1.7

1 school? / does / like / Henry
2 their uncle / do / visit / at weekends? / Liam and Steven
3 your / you / tidy / bedroom? / do
4 a lot / does / it / rain / in Scotland?
5 ride / does / a horse? / Vicky
6 Italian? / and Fred / do / speak / you

8 Match the answers (a–f) with the questions in exercise 7.
➡ 1.6

a ___ No, I don't.
b ___ Yes, she does.
c ___ No, he doesn't.
d ___ No, we don't.
e ___ Yes, they do.
f ___ Yes, it does.

9 Look at the table and write questions and short answers about Ed and Emma. ➡ 1.6, 1.7

	Ed	Emma
speak Italian	yes	no
live in a big house	no	yes
study biology at school	yes	yes
like dancing	no	no

1 Ed / speak Italian?
Does Ed speak Italian? Yes, he does.
2 Emma / live in a big house?
3 Ed and Emma / study biology at school?
4 Emma / speak Italian?
5 Ed / live in a big house?
6 Ed and Emma / like dancing

10 Complete the questions with *Do* or *Does*. ➡ 1.6, 1.7

1 _____ you live near the school?
2 _____ your best friend like football?
3 _____ your parents both work?
4 _____ you and your friends go out on Friday evenings?
5 _____ you wear jeans to school?
6 _____ your teacher speak French?

11 SPEAKING Work in pairs. Ask and answer the questions in exercise 10. ➡ 1.6, 1.7

Do you live near the school?
Yes, I do. / No, I don't.

Grammar Reference

Possessive 's

1.1 We add *'s* to a name or noun to show possession or a family relationship.
Monica's car is blue.
I know Sam's sister.

We just add an apostrophe (') to plural nouns ending in *-s*.
my brothers' friends   (BUT *my children's toys*)

Present simple (affirmative)

1.2

Affirmative
I / You / We / They work
He / She / It works

1.3 Spelling rules for 3rd person singular (*he / she / it*)
Most verbs: add *s*
play+ -s → plays

Verb ends in *-ch / -s / -sh / -o*: add *-es*.
watch + -es → watches
go + -es → goes

Verb ends in consonant + *-y*: *-y → -ies*.
study   -y → -ies → studies

The verb *have* is irregular. The 3rd person singular form is *has*:
He has lunch at home every day.

1.4 We use the present simple:
*   for something that happens regularly, always or never.
    I play football every day.
    School finishes at 3 p.m.
    I never watch sport on TV.
*   for a fact that is always true.
    My sisters share a bedroom.
    Lions live in Africa.

Present simple (negative)

1.5

Negative
I don't play
You don't play
He / She / It doesn't play
We don't play
You don't play
They don't play

Full forms
I don't play = I do not play
He doesn't play = He does not play

We form the negative with *don't* or *doesn't* and the infinitive without *to*.

Present simple (interrogative)

1.6

Questions	Short answers
Do I work?	Yes, I do. / No, I don't.
Do you work?	Yes, you do. / No, you don't.
Does he / she / it work?	Yes, he does. / No, he doesn't.
Do we work?	Yes, we do. / No, we don't.
Do you work?	Yes, you do. / No, you don't.
Do they work?	Yes, they do. / No, they don't.

1.7 We form present simple questions with *do* or *does* and the infinitive without *to*.
Do you like maths?
Does he like maths?

Note: we don't use the third person singular form of the main verb.
NOT *Does he likes maths?* ✗

Grammar Builder

2B *have to*

1 Write sentences using the prompts. Use the affirmative or negative of *have to*. ➦ 2.1

  1 my sister / walk / to school ✗
    My sister doesn't have to walk to school.
  2 we / speak English / in class ✓
  3 I / sing / in my music lessons ✗
  4 my brother / work / at weekends ✗
  5 my brother and I / share / a bedroom ✓
  6 I / do the ironing / at home ✓
  7 my little sister / go to bed / early ✓
  8 my mum / use a computer / at work ✗

2 Complete the questions using the verbs below. ➦ 2.1, 2.2

  be do get up go help practise

  Do you have to …
  1 _____ before nine o'clock on Saturdays?
  2 _____ to school on Saturdays?
  3 _____ a lot of homework at weekends?
  4 _____ with the housework at weekends?
  5 _____ home before midnight on Saturdays?
  6 _____ a musical instrument at weekends?

3 SPEAKING In pairs, ask and answer the questions in exercise 3. ➦ 2.1, 2.2

  Do you have to get up before nine o'clock on Saturdays? Yes, I do. / No, I don't.

2D Adverbs of frequency

4 Complete the adverbs of frequency. Use *a, e, i, o, u* and *y*. ➦ 2.3

  1 n _ v _ r   4 _ l w _ _ s
  2 s _ m _ t _ m _ s   5 h _ r d l _ _ v _ r
  3 _ s _ _ l l _   6 _ f t _ n

5 Complete the table with the adverbs of frequency in exercise 4. ➦ 2.3

  1 _____ [•][•][•][•][•]
  2 _____ [•][•][•][•][ ]
  3 _____ [•][•][•][ ][ ]
  4 _____ [•][•][ ][ ][ ]
  5 _____ [•][ ][ ][ ][ ]
  6 _____ [ ][ ][ ][ ][ ]

6 Write sentences about Millie. Use the correct adverb of frequency. ➦ 2.3, 2.4

  1 do sport after school [•][•][•][•][ ]
    Millie usually does sport after school.
  2 meet her friends in town after school [•][•][•][ ][ ]
  3 do her homework on the bus [•][•][ ][ ][ ]
  4 be hungry at break time [•][•][•][•][•]
  5 take the bus to school [•][ ][ ][ ][ ]
  6 be late for school [ ][ ][ ][ ][ ]

2D Question words

7 Match the questions (1–5) with the answers (A–E). ➦ 2.5

  1 Why do you like Ed Sheeran?
  2 Whose pencil case it that?
  3 How does your mum get to work?
  4 When do you usually do your homework?
  5 How often do you download music?

  A It's Peter's.
  B About once a week.
  C Because he's a good singer.
  D By car.
  E At six o'clock.

8 Complete the questions with the question words below. Use each question word only once. ➦ 2.5

  How many What What time Where Which Who

  1 _____ do you usually have lunch?
  2 _____ do you live?
  3 _____ do you usually have for dinner?
  4 _____ DVDs and CDs have you got?
  5 _____ do you prefer, curry or pasta?
  6 _____ is your favourite singer?

9 SPEAKING Work in pairs. Ask and answer the questions in exercise 8.

  What time do you usually have lunch? At 12.30.

2G *should*

10 Complete the sentences with *should* or *shouldn't*. ➦ 2.6, 2.7

  1 You _____ listen to this song. It's great!
  2 We _____ walk home. This part of town isn't safe.
  3 Your brother _____ wear that hat. It looks really bad.
  4 I _____ invite my neighbour. He's really nice.
  5 You _____ eat that sandwich. It's about a week old.
  6 Your parents _____ buy a new laptop. This one is really slow!

2H Imperatives

11 Complete the imperatives with the verbs below. Use the affirmative or negative. ➦ 2.8

  not be not eat meet not open put share stop
  not swim

  1 _____ all the cake! _____ it with your brother!
  2 _____ talking!
  3 'Let's see a film tomorrow evening.' 'OK. _____ me at the cinema at six. _____ late!'
  4 _____ your hand up if you know the answer.
  5 _____ in that river. It's dangerous.
  6 It's cold outside. Please _____ the window.

Grammar Reference

have to

2.1

Affirmative	Negative
I / You / We / They have to go home.	I / You / We / They don't have to go home.
He / She / It has to go home.	He / She / It doesn't have to go home.

Interrogative	Short answers
Do I / you / we / they have to get up?	Yes, I / you / we / they do. No, I / you / we / they don't.
Does he / she / it have to get up?	Yes, he / she / it does. No, he / she / it doesn't.

We do not normally use a short form of *have to*.
I have to phone my dad.
NOT ~~I've to phone my dad.~~ ✗

2.2 We use *have to* to say that something is necessary or compulsory.
She has to be home before midnight.

We use *don't have to* to say that something is not necessary (but it isn't against the rules).
They don't have to start work at 9 a.m. Some people start at 10 a.m.

Adverbs of frequency

2.3 We use adverbs of frequency to say how often we do something.

0%	▶	▶	▶	▶	100%
never	hardly ever	sometimes	often	usually	always

2.4 The normal position for an adverb of frequency is:
immediately after the verb *be*.
She's never late for school.
She isn't always happy to see me.

immediately before most other verbs.
We often play football on Saturdays.
She never listens to me.

Question words

2.5 Examples of question words:
how   how many   how often   what   what time   when   where   which   who   whose   why
We use question words to ask for information. The question word comes at the beginning of the question.
Where do you live?
When do you go to bed?

How many, what, which and *whose* are sometimes followed by a noun:
How many pencils have you got?
What subjects do you do at school?
Which students passed the exam?
Whose dictionary is this?

If the question includes a preposition, it usually goes at the end.
What music do you listen to?
Who do you live with?

should

2.6

Affirmative	Negative
I / He / She / It / You / We / They should go to bed.	I / He / She / It / You / We / They shouldn't laugh.

Interrogative	Short answers
Should I / he / she / it / you / we / they tell him?	Yes, I should. / No, I shouldn't. Yes, she should. / No, she shouldn't. Yes, they should. / No, they shouldn't.

2.7 We use *should* to give advice or say that something is a good (or bad) idea.
You should talk to your teacher. (advice)
I should practise the guitar more. (It's a good idea.)
He shouldn't eat chocolate in bed. (It's a bad idea.)

Imperatives

2.8 We use imperatives to give commands and instructions. We often use them in announcements.
We form the affirmative imperative with the infinitive without *to*.
Visit our website for more information.
Phone me this evening.

We form the negative imperative with *don't* and the infinitive without *to*.
Don't forget your mum's birthday!
Don't sit down! The cat's on the chair.

3B Present continuous

1 Write the *-ing* forms of these verbs. ➡ 3.2

1 sing *singing*
2 take _____
3 rain _____
4 wait _____
5 have _____
6 chat _____
7 wear _____
8 do _____

2 Complete the sentences. Use the affirmative of *be* and an *-ing* form from exercise 1. ➡ 3.1, 3.2, 3.3

1 My parents *are waiting* for the bus.
2 We can't play tennis outside. It _____ .
3 My cousins _____ their homework at the moment.
4 I can't hear the TV. My parents _____ to their friends.
5 Can I phone you in five minutes? I _____ dinner.
6 Smile! Grandma _____ a photo of you.
7 What's that noise? My sister _____ in the shower!
8 I _____ a coat – but I still feel cold.

3 Correct the information in these sentences. Replace the underlined verbs with the verbs in brackets. Follow the example. ➡ 3.1, 3.2, 3.3

1 Jack and Sarah are <u>skateboarding</u>. (skate)
   Jack and Sarah aren't skateboarding. They're skating.
2 Those dogs are <u>fighting</u>. (play)
3 The bus is <u>arriving</u>. (leave)
4 My uncle is <u>playing</u> football. (watch)
5 My aunt is <u>doing aerobics</u>. (dance)
6 I'm <u>playing a game</u> on my phone. (write an email)

4 Complete the phone conversation. Use the interrogative form of the present continuous and short answers.
➡ 3.1, 3.2, 3.3

Alice   Hi, Edward. Where are you?
Edward   I'm at home. What (you / do) ¹_____?
Alice   Not much. I'm at a café in town.
Edward   (you / have) ²_____ lunch?
Alice   No, ³_____. Just a drink. I'm waiting for Freddie and Julia.
Edward   Really? (they / plan) ⁴_____ to meet you at the café?
Alice   Yes, ⁵_____.
Edward   That's strange. Because they're here with me!
Alice   At your house? What (they / do) ⁶_____ there?
Edward   We're playing computer games.
Alice   Which game (you / play) ⁷_____?
Edward   *Prophets of Doom 3.*
Alice   I love that game! (you / have) ⁸_____ fun?
Edward   Yes, we ⁹_____. You should come and play.
Alice   OK! Thanks! See you soon!

5 SPEAKING Ask and answer in pairs using the present continuous. Choose from the prompts below. ➡ 3.1, 3.2, 3.3

1 wear – trainers / boots / a T-shirt / socks / a dark top
2 sit – near the door / near the window / near the board
3 use – a pen / a pencil / your phone / a tablet
Are you wearing trainers?   Yes, I am. / No, I'm not.

3D Contrast: present simple and present continuous

6 Complete one sentence in each pair with the present simple and one with the present continuous. Use the verb in brackets. ➡ 3.4

1 (have)
   a _____ you _____ a good time?
   b _____ you _____ a shower every day?
2 (not wear)
   a Today I _____ jeans.
   b Wendy _____ jeans to school.
3 (stop)
   a This bus always _____ in the town centre.
   b Look. I think the rain _____.

7 Complete the conversation with the verbs below. Use the present simple and the present continuous. ➡ 3.4, 3.5

do   not joke   like   look for   think   want   wear

Alison   What ¹_____ you _____?
Jake   I ²_____ a jacket and a tie. They're here in my wardrobe, but I can't see them.
Alison   But you never ³_____ smart clothes. Why ⁴_____ you _____ to wear a jacket and tie?
Jake   It's my cousin's wedding this afternoon.
Alison   Really!?
Jake   Yes. I ⁵_____! Ah, here they are. ⁶_____ you _____ them?
Alison   Yes, I do. I ⁷_____ they're really nice!

3G Present continuous for future arrangements

8 Complete the conversation with the verbs in brackets. Use the present continuous. ➡ 3.6

Tom   What ¹_____ you _____ (do) this weekend?
Joanna   Nothing much. What about you?
Tom   I ²_____ (go) to Mark's house on Friday. Do you want to join us?
Joanna   I ³_____ (visit) my grandparents on Friday. What about Saturday morning?
   I ⁴_____ (not do) anything then.
Tom   I ⁵_____ (meet) Catherine and Emma. We ⁶_____ (have) breakfast in a café. Why don't you come along?
Joanna   Thanks. I'd love to. What time?
Tom   We ⁷_____ (meet) at the station at nine.
Joanna   OK. See you there.

3 Grammar Reference

Present continuous

3.1

Affirmative

I'm	walking.
You're	
He's / She's / It's	
We're	
You're	
They're	

Negative

I'm not	walking.
You aren't	
He / She / It isn't	
We aren't	
You aren't	
They aren't	

Interrogative

Am I	walking?
Are you	
Is he / she / it	
Are we	
Are you	
Are they	

Short answers

Yes, I am. / No, I'm not.
Yes, you are. / No, you aren't.
Yes, he / she / it is. / No, he / she / it isn't.
Yes, we are. / No, we aren't.
Yes, they are. / No, they aren't.

We form the present continuous with the correct form of be + the -ing form of the main verb:

drink → She is drinking.
work → They aren't working.
listen → Are you listening?

3.2 Spelling: -ing forms

Most verbs
work + -ing → working

Final -e
smile -e + -ing → smiling

Short vowel + consonant
run double consonant + -ing → running

3.3 We use the present continuous:
for something that is happening now.
My dad is upstairs. He's talking on the phone.
for something that is happening around this time.
No crisps, thanks. I'm trying to eat healthy food.

Contrast: present simple and present continuous

3.4 We use the present simple and present continuous differently. The main uses for each tense are:

Present simple
- We use the present simple to talk about regular actions or events.
  I always go to bed at ten o'clock.
- We use the present simple to talk about a general fact or something that is always true.
  Doctors earn a lot of money.
  Tigers live in India.

Present continuous
- We use the present continuous to describe an action or event happening at this moment.
  Sally is wearing a beautiful blue dress.
  Oh no! It's raining.
- We use the present continuous to describe an action or event happening around this time.
  I'm learning French at evening classes.

3.5 There are some verbs we don't use in the present continuous – or any continuous tense. These include:
believe, hate, know, like, love, mean, need, prefer, understand, want
I'm not dancing because I don't like (NOT I'm not liking) this music.

Present continuous for future arrangements

3.6 We can use the present continuous to talk about arrangements in the future. We often include a future time reference: *this evening, tomorrow afternoon, next Sunday*, etc.
Harry is going ice skating on Friday evening.
We're meeting at six o'clock tomorrow evening.

Sometimes there isn't a time expression when it's clear we are talking about the future.
'What are you doing this evening?' 'I'm doing my homework.'
What time are you having dinner?

4 Grammar Builder

4A Countable and uncountable nouns

1 Are the underlined nouns in these sentences countable or uncountable? Write C or U. ➡ 4.1

1 Do you like <u>cakes</u>? *C*
2 I usually have <u>cereal</u> for breakfast. _____
3 Do you want <u>butter</u>? _____
4 My parents don't drink <u>coffee</u>. _____
5 Please don't put <u>mushrooms</u> on my pizza. _____
6 I always share my <u>crisps</u> with my friends. _____

4B *there is / there are*

2 Write sentences with *there's* or *there are* (1–6) and *there isn't* or *there aren't* (7–12). ➡4.2, 4.3

1 *There's* a melon on the table.
2 _____ five children in that family.
3 _____ some yoghurt in the fridge.
4 _____ always an apple in my packed lunch.
5 _____ some people in the playground.
6 _____ a sandwich in my bag.
7 *There isn't* any bread in this shop.
8 _____ any girls in my football team.
9 _____ an airport in my town.
10 _____ three good hotels in the town centre.
11 _____ any crisps in this packet.
12 _____ any water in that river.

3 Write questions to ask your partner about his or her bedroom. Use *Is there a ... ?* or *Are there any ... ?* ➡4.2, 4.4

1 *Is there a TV?*
2 _____ books?
3 _____ table?
4 _____ CDs?
5 _____ plants or flowers?
6 _____ computer?
7 _____ guitar?
8 _____ photos?

4 SPEAKING Work in pairs. Ask and answer the questions in exercise 3. ➡4.2, 4.3, 4.4

Is there a TV in your bedroom?
Yes, there is. / No, there isn't.

5 SPEAKING Work in pairs. Your partner thinks of a favourite dish. Ask about the ingredients and try to guess the dish. Use the words below and your own ideas. ➡4.2, 4.3, 4.4

beef butter carrots cheese chicken eggs fish mushrooms olives onion rice tomatoes

Is there any beef in it?
Yes, there is. / No, there isn't.
Are there any carrots in it?
Yes, there are. / No, there aren't.

4B *some* and *any*

6 Complete the dialogue with *some*, *any*, *a* and *an*. ➡ 4.5

Freya Have we got [1] _____ homework for tonight?
Blake Yes, we have. We have to write [2] _____ essay.
Freya Oh, OK. Can I borrow [3] _____ pen?
Blake Yes, there are [4] _____ pens in my bag.
Freya Thanks. Yuk! What's this?
Blake It's [5] _____ sandwich. Are you hungry?
Freya Yes, I am. But I don't want that sandwich.
Blake OK, don't worry. We can make [6] _____ fresh sandwiches.
Freya Great! Can I have [7] _____ cheese and cucumber sandwich, please?
Blake Sorry. There isn't [8] _____ cucumber. But there's [9] _____ cheese. And there are [10] _____ olives too.
Freya I don't want [11] _____ olives in my sandwich.
Blake Not in your sandwich – on the side!

4D *How much / How many; much / many / a lot of, a few / a little*

7 Correct the mistakes in these sentences. ➡ 4.6, 4.7, 4.8

1 How much desks are there in the classroom? ✗
   How many desks are there in the classroom? ✓
2 There is much cheese in the fridge. ✗
3 We've got lot of dictionaries in our classroom. ✗
4 Have you got a few butter? ✗
5 How many flour is there in the cupboard? ✗
6 There are a little pens on the desk. ✗
7 How much cakes are there on the table? ✗
8 We've got many milk. ✗

8 Circle the correct words to complete the sentences. ➡ 4.8

1 We've got **a little / a few** prawns and **a little / a few** rice.
2 Can I have **a little / a few** salt on my pasta, please?
3 There are only **a little / a few** books in my schoolbag.
4 There are only **a little / a few** minutes until the end of the lesson.
5 Put **a little / a few** honey and **a little / a few** fruit on your pancake.
6 Oh dear! We've only got **a little / a few** biscuits left.

9 Write questions with *how much* and *how many* and the words below. ➡ 4.6

1 teachers / there in your school?
   How many teachers are there in your school?
2 homework / you usually get at the weekend?
3 English lessons / you have every week?
4 money / you spend on clothes every month?
5 CDs / you got at home?
6 food / you eat at lunch time?

10 SPEAKING Work in pairs. Ask and answer the questions in exercise 9. Answer with *a lot, a little* or *a few*. ➡ 4.6, 4.7, 4.8

How many CDs have you got at home? About fifty.

Grammar Reference

Countable and uncountable nouns

4.1 Countable nouns are things that you can count. They have a singular and a plural form.

an egg   two eggs

Uncountable nouns are things that you can't count, you can only weigh or measure. They only have a singular form and take a singular verb.

I like tea.   This cheese is delicious.

Some nouns can be countable or uncountable, depending on how we're using them.
(countable) *We need four large <u>lettuces</u>.*
(uncountable) *Do you want more <u>lettuce</u>?*
(countable) *Can I have <u>a coffee</u>, please?* (= cup of coffee)
(uncountable) *I don't drink <u>coffee</u>.*

4.2 *there is / there are*

	Singular	**Plural**
Affirmative	**There's** a pizza. **There's** some milk.	There are some prawns.
Negative	**There isn't** a pizza.	**There aren't** any prawns.
Interrogative	**Is there** a pizza?	**Are there** any prawns?
Short answers	Yes, **there is**. / No, **there isn't**.	Yes, **there are**. / No, **there aren't**.

4.3 We usually use the short form of *there is*: *there's*. However, we use the full form in affirmative short answers.
Is there a TV?   Yes. there is. (NOT ~~Yes, there's.~~)
There are does not have a short form.

4.4 We use *Is there a ... ?* to ask about singular countable nouns.
Is there a TV in the class room?

We use *Is there any ... ?* to ask about uncountable nouns.
Is there any water in the fridge?

We use *Are there any ... ?* to ask about plural nouns.
Are there any pens on the desk?

We use *There isn't a ...* with singular countable nouns.
There isn't a notice board in our classroom.

We use *There isn't any ...* with uncountable nouns.
There isn't any tea in my cup.

We use *There aren't any ...* with plural nouns.
There aren't any books in my schoolbag.

some and *any*

4.5 We usually use *some* in affirmative sentences. We use it with plural countable nouns and uncountable nouns.
There are some crisps in the bowl.
There's some butter on the table.

We usually use *any* in negative sentences and questions. We use it with plural countable nouns and uncountable nouns.
He doesn't want any milk.   We haven't got any sandwiches.
Are there any apples?   Is there any coffee?

We don't use *some* or *any* with singular countable nouns. We use *a* or *an*.
Do you want a snack?

How much / How many

4.6 We use *How many ... ?* with plural countable nouns. The answer is often a number.
How many tomatoes do you need? Three.

We use *How much ... ?* with uncountable nouns. The answer is often a quantity.
How much sugar have we got?   Two kilos. / A lot. / Not much. / A little.

much / many / a lot of

4.7 We use *a lot of* in affirmative sentences.
There's a lot of rice.   There are a lot of bananas.

We use *a lot of, much* and *many* in negative sentences. We use *much* with uncountable nouns, and *many* with countable nouns.
There's isn't much rice.
There's isn't a lot of rice.
There aren't many bananas.
There aren't a lot of bananas.

a little and *a few*

4.8 We use *a little* with uncountable nouns.
We've only got a little butter.

We use *a few* with countable nouns.
There are only a few students in the classroom.

Grammar Builder

5B Comparatives

1 Write the comparative forms of these adjectives.
➡ 5.1, 5.2, 5.3

1 early	5 wet	9 large
2 quick	6 popular	10 exciting
3 excited	7 kind	11 polluted
4 sunny	8 expensive	12 warm

2 Complete the facts with the comparative form of the correct adjective from each pair. ➡ 5.1, 5.2, 5.3

1 Vegetables are _____ for your health than cakes. (good / bad)
2 The Pacific Ocean is _____ than the Indian Ocean. (big / small)
3 Dolphins are usually _____ than sharks. (friendly / unfriendly)
4 The Pyramids in Egypt are _____ than the Eiffel Tower in Paris. (old / modern)
5 Daniel Radcliffe is _____ than Tom Hanks. (old / young)
6 Travelling by plane is _____ than travelling by car. (safe / dangerous)
7 From the UK, Singapore is _____ than Berlin. (far / near)
8 In Australia, rugby is _____ than football. (popular / unpopular)

3 Look at the information about these two celebrities and write sentences using the comparative form of the adjectives. Remember to include *than*. ➡5.1, 5.3, 5.4

	Joey B	Carly J
Age	19	24
Height	1.86 m	1.72 m
Money	$2.8 million	$6 million
Number of fans	6 million	5 million
Work (days per year)	320 days	210 days

1 young	5 hard-working
2 tall	6 old
3 rich	7 short
4 popular	

1 *Joey is younger than Carly.*

4 Write sentences about famous people using the comparative form of these adjectives. Give your own opinions. ➡5.1, 5.3, 5.4

1 creative	5 nice
2 famous	6 attractive
3 rich	7 unusual
4 funny	8 intelligent

1 *I think Adele is more creative than Taylor Swift.*

5D Superlatives

5 Complete the sentences with the superlative form of the adjective in brackets. ➡ 5.5, 5.6, 5.7, 5.8

1 The library is _____ (quiet) room in the school.
2 June is often _____ (sunny) month of the year.
3 Today is _____ (hot) day of the year.
4 Delhi is the _____ (polluted) city in the world.
5 *The Walking Dead* is _____ (scary) show on TV.
6 These are _____ (expensive) trainers in the shop.
7 New Zealand is _____ (far) country from the UK.
8 Walking is _____ (slow) form of transport.

6 Write your opinions. Use superlative adjectives.
➡ 5.5, 5.6, 5.7, 5.8

1 talented actor in the world
  I think _____ is the most talented actor in the world.
2 beautiful actress in the world
3 bad singer in my country
4 good day of the week
5 easy subject at school

7 **SPEAKING** Work in pairs. Take turns to read your sentences from exercise 6. Say if you agree or disagree.
➡ 5.5, 5.6, 5.7, 5.8

I think Matt Damon is the most talented actor in the world. I agree. / I disagree. I think Robert Pattinson is the most talented.

8 Use the table to make true sentences. ➡ 5.5, 5.6, 5.7, 5.8

1 Mercury	is the	big	city in Germany.
2 Everest	are the	dangerous	mountain in the world.
3 Platinum		high	metal in the world.
4 Berlin		expensive	river in the world.
5 The Amazon		near	planet to the Sun.
6 Mosquitoes		wide	animals in the world.

1 *Mercury is the nearest planet to the Sun.*

9 Write the words in the correct order to make questions.
➡ 5.5, 5.6, 5.7, 5.8

1 the / in the world? / football club / What's / best
2 comedian / the / most / Who's / in the world? / famous
3 the / What's / programme / on TV? / funniest
4 the / Who's / in America? / actor / best-looking
5 the / pop group / worst / in the world? / What's
6 sport / in the world? / the / What's / exciting / most

10 **SPEAKING** Work in pairs. Ask and answer the questions in exercise 9. ➡ 5.5, 5.6, 5.7, 5.8

What's the best football club in the world?

5

Grammar Reference

Comparatives

5.1 Short adjectives: spelling rules

We add -er to short adjectives to make the comparative form.

small → smaller

If the adjective ends in -e, we add -r.

safe → safer

If the adjective ends in a vowel and a consonant, we double the consonant and add -er.

big → bigger

If the adjective ends in -y, we change the -y into -ier.

funny → funnier

5.2 Irregular adjectives

Some adjectives have irregular comparative forms.

good → better
bad → worse
far → further

5.3 Long adjectives

We use *more* for most long adjectives (adjectives with more than one syllable).

comfortable → more comfortable

Most two-syllable adjectives ending in -y behave like short adjectives.

friendly → friendlier

5.4 *than*

We use *than* when we compare two things.

Mexico City is more polluted than London.
We are older than him.

We usually use the object pronoun after *than*. The subject pronoun sounds very formal.

She's taller than me. ✓
NOT *She's taller than I.* ✗
But *She's taller than I am.* ✓

Superlatives

5.5 Short adjectives: spelling rules

We use *the* and add -est to short adjectives to make the superlative form.

new → the newest

If the adjective ends in -e, we add -st.

wide → the widest

If the adjective ends in a vowel and a consonant, we double the consonant and add -est.

big → the biggest

If the adjective ends in -y, we change the -y into -iest.

easy → the easiest

5.6 Irregular adjectives

Some adjectives have irregular superlative forms.

good → the best
bad → the worst
far → the furthest

5.7 Long adjectives

We use *the most* for most long adjectives (adjectives with more than one syllable).

comfortable → the most comfortable

5.8 After a superlative, we often use *of* with a noun.

The shortest day of the year …
My favourite day of the week …

But we use *in* with the name of a place or a group.

The longest river in the world …
The shortest boy in the class …

Grammar Builder

6B Past simple (affirmative): regular

1 Write the past simple forms of these verbs. ➡ 6.1, 6.2

1 arrive _____
2 plan _____
3 work _____
4 stop _____
5 wait _____
6 travel _____
7 live _____
8 watch _____
9 marry _____
10 move _____

2 Complete the sentences with the past simple forms from exercise 1. Use each verb once. ➡ 6.1, 6.2

1 We _____ around Spain for three weeks last summer.
2 My aunt and uncle _____ in Canada before they _____ to the UK.
3 The taxi _____ because the light was red.
4 Thanks for the present. It _____ yesterday.
5 I _____ nearly an hour for my bus.
6 We _____ a party for my dad's fiftieth birthday.
7 My grandfather _____ for the BBC.
8 My cousin _____ an American in Las Vegas, and we _____ the wedding on the internet.

3 Complete the text with the past simple form of the correct verb from each pair. ➡ 6.1, 6.2

My great-grandfather ¹_____ (live / move) to England in 1947. He ²_____ (carry / marry) my great-grandmother in 1950 and they ³_____ (start / stop) a family the next year. They ⁴_____ (arrive / live) in a small house in London. My great-grandfather ⁵_____ (want / work) for London Transport for twenty years, but he ⁶_____ (walk / want) to be a photographer. So in 1958, he ⁷_____ (chat / stop) working and ⁸_____ (travel / wait) the world with his young family. They ⁹_____ (interrupt / visit) more than a hundred different countries. Years later, he ¹⁰_____ (describe / like) his journey in a book. The photos are amazing!

4 Complete the sentences with true information about yourself. Use the past simple affirmative of the verbs in brackets and a past time expression. ➡ 6.1, 6.2, 6.3

1 I (arrive) at school _____.
  I arrived at school three hours ago.
2 We (visit) relatives _____.
3 I (work) very hard _____.
4 I (start) at this school _____.
5 I (watch) a great programme on TV _____.
6 It (rain) a lot _____.

6D Past simple: *be* and *can*

5 Complete the sentences. Use *was, were, wasn't* and *weren't*. ➡ 6.4

1 Kate and Liam _____ at school yesterday because they were ill.
2 We _____ at a football match yesterday. It was really exciting.
3 You _____ at home last night. Where were you?
4 On my last birthday, I _____ sixteen.
5 The weather _____ really bad last week – cold, windy and rainy.
6 My uncle _____ a doctor. He was a vet.
7 Today is Sunday. Yesterday _____ Saturday.
8 Louis was at school, but he _____ in the classroom.

6 Complete the sentences about the people. Use *was, were, wasn't, and weren't*. ➡ 6.4

1 John wasn't in bed at ten o'clock. ✗
2 Harry _____ at home last night. ✓
3 Sue and Simon _____ at school yesterday. ✗
4 Martin _____ in town at three o'clock yesterday afternoon. ✓
5 Rachel _____ at the supermarket at midday on Saturday. ✓
6 Tom and Emma _____ in the school canteen at breaktime. ✗
7 Danny _____ at the doctor's yesterday morning. ✗
8 Miranda _____ at a pop concert on Saturday evening. ✓

7 SPEAKING Ask and answer questions about the people in exercise 6. ➡ 6.4

Was John in bed at ten o'clock?
No, he wasn't.

8 Complete the sentences. Use *could* or *couldn't*. ➡ 6.5

1 Mario _____ read and write when he was two! He was a very clever boy!
2 It was very noisy in the classroom, so I _____ hear the teacher.
3 Joe _____ phone you because his phone was broken.
4 Kate _____ eat her dinner because she wasn't hungry.
5 My great-grandmother _____ speak German. She was from Berlin.
6 I was very tired, but I _____ sleep.
7 I _____ find my pencil case. I looked everywhere!
8 I heard the lorry coming down the road, but I _____ see it.

Grammar Reference

Past simple (affirmative): regular

6.1 The affirmative form of the past simple is the same for all persons.

Affirmative
I walked home.
You walked home.
He / She / It walked home.
We walked home.
You walked home.
They walked home.

6.2 Spelling: past simple form (affirmative) of regular verbs

- Most verbs:
  work + -ed → worked
- Verbs ending in -e:
  live + -d → lived
- Verbs ending in a consonant and -y
  carry -y + -ied → carried
- Verbs ending in a short vowel and a consonant
  chat + t + -ed → chatted

6.3 We use the past simple for an action or event at a definite point in the past. We often use it with past time expressions: *a few minutes ago, last month, last night, last week, ten years ago, three hours ago, two months ago, yesterday, yesterday morning,* etc.
We usually put the time expressions at the beginning or end of the sentence.
We visited our cousins this morning.
Yesterday, I cycled to school.

Past simple: *be* and *can*

6.4 The past simple of *be* is *was* or *were*.
wasn't = was not
weren't = were not

Affirmative	Negative
I was at home.	I wasn't at home.
You were at home.	You weren't at home.
He / She / It was at home.	He / She / It wasn't at home.
We were at home.	We weren't at home.
You were at home.	You weren't at home.
They were at home.	They weren't at home.

Questions	Short answers
Was I at home?	Yes, I / he / she / it was.
Were you at home?	No, I / he / she / it wasn't.
Was he / she / it at home?	Yes, we / you / they were.
Were we at home?	No, we / you / they weren't.
Were you at home?	
Were they at home?	

6.5 The past simple of *can* is *could*. The forms of *could* are the same for all persons.
couldn't = could not
We use the infinitive without *to* after *could*, not an infinitive with *to*.
I could see everything.
NOT ~~I could to see everything.~~ ✗

Affirmative	Negative
I could swim.	I couldn't swim.
You could swim.	You couldn't swim.
He / She / It could swim.	He / She / It couldn't swim.
We could swim.	We couldn't swim.
You could swim.	You couldn't swim.
They could swim.	They couldn't swim.

Questions	Short answers
Could I swim?	Yes, I / you / he / she / it / we / they could.
Could you swim?	
Could he / she / it swim?	No, I / you / he / she / it / we / they couldn't.
Could we swim?	
Could you swim?	
Could they swim?	

Grammar Builder

7B Past simple (affirmative): irregular

1 Write the past simple forms of all the verbs. Then circle the eight irregular verbs. ➡ 7.1, 7.2

1 get _____
2 make _____
3 enjoy _____
4 buy _____
5 play _____
6 draw _____
7 teach _____
8 take _____
9 like _____
10 have _____
11 work _____
12 build _____

2 Complete the sentences with the eight irregular past simple forms from exercise 1. ➡ 7.1, 7.2

1 You _____ some great photos on holiday.
2 She _____ my present for £2 in a charity shop.
3 The ancient Greeks _____ some amazing temples.
4 We _____ lunch in a Chinese restaurant in London.
5 I _____ 45% in my science exam.
6 He _____ friends with a boy from Turkey.
7 My mum _____ in Greece for a year.
8 I _____ a face on the window with my finger.

3 Rewrite the sentences with the past simple. Use the time expression and new information in brackets. ➡ 7.1, 7.2

1 Lessons begin at 9:00. (yesterday – 8:30)
   Yesterday, lessons began at 8:30.
2 She goes to secondary school. (last year – primary)
3 I see Luke on the bus to school. (this morning – Luke's sister)
4 She catches the train to work at 6:45. (last Monday – 5:45)
5 He reads the newspaper at breakfast. (yesterday morning – a magazine)
6 They bring sandwiches to school. (last week – salad)
7 She does her homework in her bedroom. (last night – kitchen)
8 My mum comes home early from work. (yesterday – late)

4 Complete the email with the past simple form of the verbs in brackets. ➡ 7.1, 7.2, 7.3

Hi Damian,

How are you? I hope your weekend **1** _____ (be) better than mine!

I **2** _____ (fight) with my brother on Saturday. He **3** _____ (find) his trainers in my bedroom and he **4** _____ (get) really angry with me. I **5** _____ (think) that they **6** _____ (be) my trainers. They look very similar. And then, on Sunday, my phone **7** _____ (fall) on the pavement and it **8** _____ (break). What a disaster! But I **9** _____ (speak) to my dad and he thinks he can repair it.

See you soon!

Freddie

7D Past simple (negative and interrogative)

5 Choose the correct verb and write negative sentences. ➡ 7.4, 7.5

buy   clean   ~~finish~~   forget   have   study   take   win

1 I *didn't finish* my homework before dinner.
2 Mum _____ the house last weekend.
3 Last weekend Kate _____ dinner at home.
4 We _____ the football match.
5 Liam and Sarah _____ maths at university.
6 My brother _____ my birthday.
7 Zoe _____ a new MP3 player.
8 Fran _____ any photos.

6 Make the sentences negative. ➡ 7.4, 7.5

1 I went to school yesterday.
   I didn't go to school yesterday.
2 I saw you at the party.
3 Joe and Elli came to the cinema with us.
4 Cathy spent a year in France.
5 The lesson began on time.
6 Tom wrote his name on his Workbook.

7 Write the words in the correct order to make questions about yesterday. ➡ 7.4, 7.6, 7.7

1 did / to bed? / What time / you / go
2 in the morning ? / it / Did / rain
3 do / did / Where / your homework? / you
4 phone calls / make?/ How many / did / you
5 you / Who / did / sit / in class?/ next to
6 What / after school? / you / did / do
7 did / get up? / you / What time
8 get / did / you / When / home / school? / from

8 **SPEAKING** Work in pairs. Ask and answer the questions in exercise 7 about yesterday. Answer in full sentences. ➡ 7.4, 7.6, 7.7

What time did you go to bed yesterday?
I went to bed at eleven o'clock.

9 Write questions to match the answers. Start with the word in brackets. ➡ 7.4, 7.6, 7.7

1 I went to London last Saturday. (Where?)
   Where did you go last Saturday?
2 I went shopping in Oxford Street. (What?)
3 I went by train. (How?)
4 I spent about six hours there. (How long?)
5 I got back at about midnight. (What time?)

10 Correct the mistakes in these sentences. ➡ 7.4, 7.5, 7.6, 7.7

1 Joe taked some photos. ✗
2 What time they arrive at school? ✗
3 Did Andy had a good weekend? ✗
4 Pam not tidied her room. ✗
5 They didn't travelled to France by plane. ✗
6 'Did you download the app?' 'Yes, I downloaded.' ✗

Grammar Reference

Past simple (affirmative): irregular

7.1 Some verbs have irregular past simple (affirmative) forms. There are no spelling rules for these forms; you need to learn them as vocabulary. See the list of common irregular verbs below. There is a fuller list on page 143.

go – went I went shopping yesterday.
find – found I found £10 on the ground.

Irregular verbs		
be	was / were	/wɒz/ /wə(r)/
become	became	/bɪˈkeɪm/
begin	began	/bɪˈɡæn/
break	broke	/brəʊk/
bring	brought	/brɔːt/
build	built	/bɪlt/
buy	bought	/bɔːt/
catch	caught	/kɔːt/
come	came	/keɪm/
do	did	/dɪd/
draw	drew	/druː/
eat	ate	/eɪt/
fall	fell	/fel/
fight	fought	/fɔːt/
find	found	/faʊnd/
get	got	/ɡɒt/
give	gave	/ɡeɪv/
go	went	/went/
have	had	/həd/
make	made	/meɪd/
meet	met	/met/
read	read	/red/
see	saw	/sɔː/
send	sent	/sent/
speak	spoke	/spəʊk/
take	took	/tʊk/
teach	taught	/tɔːt/
think	thought	/θɔːt/
throw	threw	/θruː/

The affirmative form of the past simple is the same for all persons, singular and plural (*I, you, he, we,* etc.).

…ook her phone to school.
…took some great photos.
…e Olympics took place last year.

…gular verbs behave in the same way as regular verbs in …gative sentences and questions. (See Grammar Builder 7D.)

Remember that the past simple of *be* is *was / were.* It …aves differently from other verbs. (See Grammar …lder 6D.)

Past simple (negative and interrogative)

7.4

Negative	Questions
I didn't go.	Did I go?
He / She / It didn't go.	Did he / she / it go?
We / You / They didn't go.	Did we / you / they go?
Full form	**Short answers**
didn't = did not	Yes, I did. / No, I didn't.

The forms are the same for all persons, singular and plural (*I, you, he, she, it, we, they*).

7.5 In negative sentences, for regular *and* irregular verbs, we use:
I, you, he, she, it, we, they + **didn't** + infinitive without *to*
We DO NOT use the past simple form of the main verb:
I didn't watch TV. ✓
NOT I didn't watched TV. ✗

7.6 In questions, for regular *and* irregular verbs, we use:
did + *I, you, he, she, it, we, they* + infinitive without *to*
We DO NOT use the past simple form of the main verb.
Did he go to school? ✓
NOT Did he went to school? ✗

Time expressions usually go at the end of the question.
Did you go to the cinema last weekend?
Did she have breakfast this morning?

7.7 We can put a question word before *did* to ask for information.
What did you do last weekend?
When did you buy that jacket?

8

Grammar Builder

8B *going to*

1 Complete the sentences with the correct form of *be*: *am*, *is* or *are* (or short forms *'m*, *'s*, *'re*). ➡ **8.1**

1 I'm going to do karate next weekend.
2 My parents _____ going to visit Canada.
3 We _____ going to have dinner at home.
4 My sister and I _____ going to do our homework together.
5 Lucas _____ going to buy a new bike.
6 I _____ going to play video games all evening.
7 She _____ going to make lunch for us.
8 They _____ going to start school tomorrow.

2 Rewrite the sentences in exercise 1 in the negative. ➡ **8.1**

1 I'm not going to do karate next weekend.

3 Look at the prompts. Write two sentences with *going to*, one affirmative and one negative. ➡ **8.1, 8.2**

1 I / get a new bike / tomorrow ✗ / next weekend ✓
  I'm not going to get a new bike tomorrow. I'm going to get a new bike next weekend.
2 we / take an exam / in a few days ✗ / this afternoon ✓
3 I / write a letter ✗ / tonight / send an email ✓
4 they / move house / tomorrow ✗ / next week ✓
5 she / go running ✗ / this evening / do aerobics ✓
6 I / start university / next month ✗ / next year ✓

4 Look at the prompts. Write questions with *going to*. ➡ **8.1, 8.2**

1 you / use a computer next weekend?
  Are you going to use a computer next weekend?
2 your best friend visit you / tonight?
3 you / travel abroad next summer?
4 your friends / start university next year?
5 you / take any exams next year?
6 you and your classmates / have maths tomorrow?

5 **SPEAKING** Work in pairs. Ask and answer the questions from exercise 4. ➡ **8.1, 8.2**

Are you going to use a computer next weekend?
Yes, I am. / No, I'm not.

8D *will*

6 Write the words in the correct order to make sentences. ➡ **8.3, 8.4, 8.5**

1 at home / be / Josh / this weekend. / won't
2 you / 'll / this evening. / I / phone
3 next / Our / won't / easy. / be / maths exam
4 will / 47 / be / My dad / 14 October. / on
5 and / I hope that / famous. / I / be / 'll / rich
6 today. / need / You / an umbrella / won't

7 Complete the predictions about the year 2040 with your opinions. Use *will* or *won't* and the verbs below. ➡ **8.3, 8.4, 8.6**

be   disappear   discover   live   speak   travel

1 Scientists _____ a cure for cancer.
2 People _____ to the Moon again.
3 Everyone in the world _____ English.
4 Climate change _____ a very serious problem.
5 Most people _____ past the age of 100.
6 Books _____ .

8 Write questions about your partner's future. Use *Do you think … ?* ➡ **8.3, 8.4, 8.5**

1 you / watch / TV this evening?
  Do you think you'll watch TV this evening?
2 you and your friends / go out on Friday evening?
3 you / pass all your exams?
4 your country's team / win the next World Cup?
5 you / study English at university?
6 you / wear jeans to school tomorrow?

9 **SPEAKING** Work in pairs. Ask and answer the questions in exercise 8. ➡ **8.3, 8.4, 8.5, 8.6**

Do you think you'll watch TV this evening?
Yes, I do. / No, I don't.

8G *too* + adjective

10 Complete the sentences with *too* and the adjectives below. ➡ **8.7**

difficult   early   heavy   hot   scary   short

1 Liam can't reach the shelf. He's _____.
2 I'm not going to bed now. It's _____!
3 I can't carry these bags. They're _____.
4 I hate horror films. They're _____.
5 I can't do this exercise. It's _____.
6 Don't drink the coffee yet if it's _____.

going to

8.1 We form the *going to* future with the present simple of *be* + *going to* + the infinitive without *to*.

Affirmative	
I'm / You're / He's / She's / It's	going to work.
We're / You're / They're	

Negative	
I'm not / You aren't	going to work.
He / She / It isn't	
We / You / They aren't	

Interrogative	
Am I	going to work?
Are you	
Is he / she / it	
Are we / you / they	

Short answers	
Yes, I am.	No, I'm not.
Yes, he / she / it is.	No, he / she / it isn't.
Yes, we / you / they are.	No, we / you / they aren't.

We use affirmative short forms of *be* after most pronouns: *I, you, he, she, it, we, they, that* and *there*.

We use the short form of *is* ('s) after question words: *what, who, where*, etc.

In informal English, we often use the short form 's after names and other nouns too.
Jack's going to arrive soon. His dinner's ready.

However, we don't use the short form 're after plural nouns.
My friends are going to help. (NOT ~~My friends're going to help.~~ ✗)

In the negative, we only use full forms in formal language.

8.2 We use *going to* to talk about plans for the future.
I'm going to have a holiday abroad next year.
She isn't going to play basketball at the weekend.
Are you going to visit friends on Saturday?
Yes, I am. / No, I'm not.

will

8.3 We form the *will* future with *will* + the infinitive without *to*. The form is the same for all persons.

Affirmative	
I'll / You'll / He'll / She'll / It'll	go to the party.
We'll / You'll / They'll	
Full form I / He / She / It / We / You / They	will go to the party.

Negative	
I / You / He / She / It	won't go to the party.
We / You / They	
Full form I / He / She / It / We / You / They	will not go to the party.

Interrogative	
Will I / he / she / it	go to the party?
Will we / you / they	

Short answers	
Yes, I / he / she / it / we / you / they will.	
No, I / he / she / it / we / you / they won't.	

8.4 We usually use the short form of *will* after pronouns (*I, you, he*, etc.) and *there*.
I'll buy you an ice cream.

We do not use the short form in short answers.
Yes, I will. ✓
NOT ~~Yes, I'll.~~ ✗

We usually use the full form of *will* after names and nouns.
My dad will cook dinner this evening.
The concert will finish at eleven o'clock.

8.5 We use *will* to talk about the future.
Dad will get home at six o'clock.
Kate is ill. She won't be at school tomorrow.
Will there be a full moon tonight? Yes, there will. / No, there won't.

8.6 We use *will* to make predictions.
Jake works very hard. He'll pass all his exams.
Will you live in this town all your life?

We often use *I think* and *I don't think* with *will* to make and ask about predictions.
I think it'll snow tomorrow.
I don't think it'll snow tomorrow.

We do not use *won't* with *I think* and *I don't think*.
NOT ~~I think it won't snow tomorrow.~~ ✗

When we use *Do you think ... ?* to ask for predictions, we reply with *Yes, I do. / No, I don't.*
Do you think it'll rain tomorrow? Yes, I do. / No, I don't.

too + adjective

8.7 We use *too* + adjective to describe a problem with something. We put *too* before the adjective.
These jeans are too short. (They need to be longer.)

9 Grammar Builder

9B Present perfect (affirmative)

1 Complete the sentences with the present perfect of the verbs below. ➡ 9.1, 9.2, 9.3

chat live marry start stop travel visit work

1 We _____ a long way to get here.
2 Sit down! The film _____ .
3 I don't know Rita, but I _____ to her online.
4 Let's go outside now. The rain _____ .
5 This project is excellent. You _____ very hard on it.
6 My next-door neighbour _____ his Italian girlfriend.
7 My cousins _____ in five different countries.
8 We _____ all the museums and art galleries in New York!

2 Rewrite the sentences with the present perfect affirmative. Choose the correct verb. ➡ 9.1, 9.2, 9.4

1 I **take** / **write** 500 words of my history essay.
2 We **eat** / **give** two pizzas each. I feel so full!
3 My friend **speak** / **tell** Henry about the surprise party.
4 I **give** / **forget** my old bike to my younger sister.
5 Lucy **be** / **come** ill and needs to rest.
6 Thanks! You **make** / **meet** a sandwich for me!

3 Look at the prompts. Write sentences in the present perfect affirmative. Some of the verbs are regular and some are irregular. ➡ 9.1, 9.2, 9.3, 9.4

1 we / meet / all of our teachers for next year
  We've met all of our teachers for next year.
2 Ed Sheeran / reply / to my tweet!
3 you / forget / your coat
4 our train / stop / between two stations
5 my teacher / email / my parents
6 my friends / plan / a great trip
7 we / see / the latest Bond film
8 you / take / a lot of photos

4 Rewrite the sentences with the present perfect affirmative. Use *just* instead of the underlined time expression. ➡ 9.1, 9.2, 9.3, 9.4, 9.5

1 They moved house <u>yesterday</u>.
  They've just moved house.
2 My friends arrived <u>a few minutes ago</u>.
3 We saw that film <u>very recently</u>.
4 They did their homework <u>a short while ago</u>.
5 I told Tara about the party <u>this morning</u>.
6 My mum bought a new computer <u>last weekend</u>.
7 I tidied my bedroom <u>earlier today</u>.

9D Present perfect (negative and interrogative)

5 Make the sentences negative. ➡ 9.6

1 I've seen that film.
2 Jo has forgotten Molly's phone number.
3 James and Emily have learnt Spanish.
4 We have had breakfast.
5 You have finished your project.
6 It has stopped raining.
7 The cat has caught a mouse.

6 Write questions and short answers. Use the present perfect interrogative. ➡ 9.6

1 Fran / meet anyone famous? ✗
  Has Fran met anyone famous?   No, she hasn't.
2 you / hear the weather forecast for tomorrow? ✗
3 Evie / write any emails today? ✗
4 Ruby and Zack / answer any questions in class today? ✓
5 we / buy our tickets for the concert on Saturday? ✗
6 Chloe / post a photo of me on her Facebook page? ✓
7 Aisha and Muhammad / reply to your email? ✗
8 you / find your keys? ✓

7 Write responses with *already*. Use the present perfect affirmative. ➡ 9.7

1 Please phone Mandy.
  I've already phoned her.
2 Are you going to do your homework?
3 Do you want to watch this DVD?
4 You should apologise to Ben.
5 Why don't you buy a new phone?
6 Please do the washing up.

8 Emma and Oscar are visiting London. Look at the things that they have and have not done. Write sentences with the present perfect affirmative and negative. Use *yet* with the negative sentences. ➡ 9.6, 9.7, 9.8

Things to do in London
1 visit the Madame Tussauds museum ✗
  They haven't visited the Madame Tussauds museum yet.
2 take a boat trip on the Thames ✓
  They've taken a boat trip on the Thames.
3 see the paintings in the National Gallery ✗
4 walk along Oxford Street ✗
5 have a meal in Chinatown ✓
6 buy tickets for a musical ✓
7 take a ride on the London Eye ✓
8 visit Buckingham Palace ✗

9 SPEAKING Work in pairs. Ask and answer questions about the things Emma and Oscar have done. Use the present perfect interrogative with *yet*. ➡ 9.6, 9.8

Have they visited the Madame Tussauds museum yet?
No, they haven't.

Present perfect (affirmative)

9.1 We form the present perfect with the auxiliary verb *have* and the past participle.

Affirmative
I've arrived.
You've arrived.
He / She / It's arrived.
We've arrived.
You've arrived.
They've arrived.

Full forms
I've = I have
she's = she has

9.2 We use the present perfect to talk about past events that have a result in the present, for example, recent events and news.

Oh no! I've forgotten my keys! They aren't in my bag.

9.3 The past participle of regular verbs is the same as the past simple.

worked   stopped   lived   carried

9.4 There aren't any rules for the past participles of irregular verbs. Sometimes they are the same as the past simple form, sometimes they are different.

make – made - made

break – broke - broken

For a list of irregular verbs see on page 143.

9.5 *just*

We use *just* with the present perfect affirmative to talk about very recent events.

I'm not hungry. I've just had breakfast.

Present perfect (negative and interrogative)

9.6 We form the negative with *haven't* or *hasn't* and the past participle. We form the interrogative with *have* or *has* + subject + past participle.

Negative
I haven't finished.
He / She / It hasn't finished.
We haven't finished.
You haven't finished.
They haven't finished.

Full forms
haven't = have not
hasn't = has not

Interrogative
Have I finished … ?
Has he / she / it finished … ?
Have we finished … ?
Have you finished … ?
Have they finished … ?

Short answers
Yes, I have. / No, I haven't.
Yes, she has. / No, she hasn't.

9.7 *already*

We use *already* with the present perfect affirmative to say that something has happened earlier than expected.

'Please tidy your room.' 'I've already tidied it.'

We've already booked our summer holiday for next year.

9.8 *yet*

We use *yet* with the present perfect interrogative to ask if something expected has happened.

It's late. Have you done your homework yet?

We use *yet* with the present perfect negative to say that something expected hasn't happened.

Tom's exam is next week, but he hasn't started his revision yet.

Extra Speaking Tasks

Unit 2

SPEAKING Work in pairs. Student B: Look at the timetable below. Student A: Look at the timetable on page 19. Imagine this is your timetable for Monday and Tuesday. Ask and answer questions about the missing lessons.

	Monday	Tuesday
8.20		Geography
9.05	French	
09.50–10.30 BREAK		
10.30		English
11.15	Biology	
12.05–1.00 LUNCH		
1.00		I.C.T.
1.50	Physics	

> What do we have at five past nine on Monday?

> French.

Unit 4

SPEAKING Work in pairs. Student B: Look at the picture below. Student A: Look at the picture on page 42. Find three differences between the pictures. Ask and answer using *Is there … ? / Are there … ?*

> Is there any cereal?

> No, there isn't.

> Are there … ?

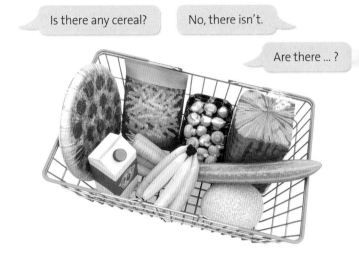

Unit 6

Work in pairs. Choose one photo each. Decide what vocabulary from exercises 2, 4 and 7 on page 70 you need to describe it.

SPEAKING Describe one of the photos to your partner. Use words and phrases from lesson 6G and follow the advice in the Strategy box.

Unit 9

SPEAKING Work in pairs. Student B: Look at the two photos below. Student A: Look at the photos on page 104. Compare and contrast the photos. Say which living room you prefer and why.

Irregular verbs

Base form	Past simple	Past participle
be	was/were	been
become	became	become
begin	began	begun
bend	bent	bent
bite	bit	bitten
blow	blew	blown
break	broke	broken
bring	brought	brought
build	built	built
burn	burned / burnt	burned / burnt
buy	bought	bought

Base form	Past simple	Past participle
can	could	been able to
catch	caught	caught
choose	chose	chosen
come	came	come
cost	cost	cost
cut	cut	cut

Base form	Past simple	Past participle
do	did	done
draw	drew	drawn
drink	drank	drunk
drive	drove	driven

Base form	Past simple	Past participle
eat	ate	eaten

Base form	Past simple	Past participle
fall	fell	fallen
feel	felt	felt
fight	fought	fought
find	found	found
fly	flew	flown
forget	forgot	forgotten

Base form	Past simple	Past participle
get	got	got
give	gave	given
go	went	gone
grow	grew	grown

Base form	Past simple	Past participle
hang	hung	hung
have	had	had
hear	heard	heard
hide	hid	hidden
hit	hit	hit

Base form	Past simple	Past participle
keep	kept	kept
know	knew	known

Base form	Past simple	Past participle
lay	laid	laid
lead	led	led
learn	learned / learnt	learned / learnt
leave	left	left

Base form	Past simple	Past participle
lend	lent	lent
lose	lost	lost

Base form	Past simple	Past participle
make	made	made
mean	meant	meant
meet	met	met

Base form	Past simple	Past participle
overcome	overcame	overcome

Base form	Past simple	Past participle
pay	paid	paid
put	put	put

Base form	Past simple	Past participle
read	read	read
ride	rode	ridden
ring	rang	rung
run	ran	run

Base form	Past simple	Past participle
say	said	said
see	saw	seen
sell	sold	sold
send	sent	sent
set	set	set
shake	shook	shaken
shine	shone	shone
shoot	shot	shot
show	showed	shown/-ed
shut	shut	shut
sing	sang	sung
sink	sank	sunk
sit	sat	sat
sleep	slept	slept
smell	smelled / smelt	smelled / smelt
speak	spoke	spoken
spell	spelled / spelt	spelled / spelt
spend	spent	spent
spill	spilled / spilt	spilled / spilt
stand	stood	stood
steal	stole	stolen
swim	swam	swum

Base form	Past simple	Past participle
take	took	taken
teach	taught	taught
tell	told	told
think	thought	thought
throw	threw	thrown

Base form	Past simple	Past participle
understand	understood	understood

Base form	Past simple	Past participle
wake	woke	woken
wear	wore	worn
win	won	won
write	wrote	written

OXFORD
UNIVERSITY PRESS

Great Clarendon Street, Oxford, OX2 6DP, United Kingdom

Oxford University Press is a department of the University of Oxford.
It furthers the University's objective of excellence in research, scholarship,
and education by publishing worldwide. Oxford is a registered trade
mark of Oxford University Press in the UK and in certain other countries

© Oxford University Press 2017

The moral rights of the author have been asserted

First published in 2017

2021

11

ISBN: 978 0 19 456183 9

Printed in China

This book is printed on paper from certified and well-managed sources

ACKNOWLEDGEMENTS

Back cover photograph: Oxford University Press building/David Fisher
*The authors and publisher are grateful to those who have given permission to reproduce
the following extracts and adaptations of copyright material*: pp.13, 33, 45 and 79
Definitions from the *Oxford Essential Dictionary, new edition*. © Oxford University
Press 2012. Reproduced by permission.

Sources: p.37 "Teen and Tween Beauty and Personal Care Consumer
– US", August 2013. p.45 "A framework for implementing the set of
recommendations on the marketing of foods and non-alcoholic beverages to
children", © World Health Organization 2012. p.56 "Worldwide Cost of Living
Report 2015" by Economist Intelligence Unit. p.56 NOAA National Centers for
Environmental Information. p.110 "Taking Stock With Teens – Spring 2015"
by Piper Jaffray.

*The publishers would like to thank the following for the permission to reproduce
photographs*: 123RF pp.5 (couple with phone/Edyta Pawlowska), 8 (woman/
Cathy Yeulet), 8 (man/goodluz), 17 (school girl/Hongqi Zhang), 17 (school boy/
Hongqi Zhang), 22 (students/Edyta Pawlowska), 23 (student/Cathy Yeulet),
36 (straightening hair/citalliance), 39 (bracelet/tempusfugit), 40 (sausage and
mash/Robyn Mackenzie), 40 (sausages and mash/Robyn Mackenzie),
41 (mushrooms/Alexandar Iotzov), 45 (pizza/serezniy), 53 (Sultan Ahmed
mosque/jackmalipan), 53 (Marina Bay Sands Hotel, Singapore/ximagination),
56 (airplane/pzaxe), 56 (train/Tomas Anderson), 58 (Botanic Garden, Brazil/
Christophe Schmid), 63 (butterfly wing/colette2), 63 (tree frog/Sascha
Burkard), 63 (snake/pat138241), 63 (chimpanzee/Sergei Uriadnikov), 63 (hippo/
Navin Moungsiri), 67 (rainforest/Carlos Edgar Soares Neto), 71 (hikers/Galyna
Andrushko), 75 (USB stick/Gunnar Pippel), 83 (smartphone/neyro2008),
83 (payment machine/natulrich), 84 (yoga pose/Dmitriy Shironosov),
85 (Olympic torch/Michael Spring), 85 (FIFA World Cup trophy/bagwold),
86 (judo/tykhyi), 92 (sport icons/pradono kusumo), 93 (Cristian Cofine/
sportgraphic), 112 (Chrysler building/Ricahrd Semik), 134 (boy reading/
joingate); Air Rarotonga Ltd pp.102 (Palmerston Island); Alamy Stock Photo
pp.6 (busking/Keith Morris), 9 (Prince William/newsphoto), 10 (The Big Bang
Theory cast/AF Archive), 18 (cereal/Itani), 18 (sleeping/Charles Bowman),
18 (lunch/Image Source), 18 (teen boy/Hero Images Inc.), 18 (school drop off/
MBI/Stockbroker), 18 (leaving school/redsnapper), 24 (kids swimming/
Megapress), 27 (school performance/Bob Daemmrich), 30 (girls/Splish Splosh),
52 (fire station/Leslie Othen), 52 (buses/Travel Pictures), 53 (fountain/Paul
Carstairs), 54 (snowy New York/Tim Cordell), 55 (Oxford Street/
incamerastock), 58 (garbage city/Haytham Pictures), 61 (market cross,
Beverley/geogphotos), 64 (Kalahari/Dennis Cox), 70 (meditating/Steffen binke),
87 (climbers/National Geographic Image Collection), 92 (teen boy/OJO Images
Ltd), 96 (living room/Andreas von Einsiedel), 100 (mother & son/MBI),
102 (Palmerston Island/Cindy Hopkins), 103 (snorkelling/Cindy Hopkins),
104 (watching TV/Anthony Hatley), 105 (apartment/Andreas von Einsiedel),
109 (student/robjudgesstudying), 109 (Keble College/Jochen Tack), 109 (dining
hall/Alistair Berg), 109 (degree ceremony/robjudges degree ceremony),
114 (William Herschel/World History Archive), 142 (Lake Brunner/Harriet
Cummings); Big Up Productions pp.87 (El Capitan climber/Aurora Photos);
Christoph Otto pp.25 (girl on zipwire); Corbis pp.14 (couple with tablet/Bruno
Gori), 81 (Sean O'Brien/Joe Stevens/Retna Ltd.); Epic Challenges pp.57 (Race
the Tube); Getty Images pp.4 (greeting/zerocreatives/Westend61), 9 (Malia &
Sasha Obama/Saul Loeb/AFP), 9 (Jon Voight & Angelina Jolie/Jeff Vespa/
WireImage), 13 (Beckham family/Stuart C. Wilson), 15 (siblings fighting/JGI/
Jamie Grill), 16 (man/Mike Harrington), 16 (teens with pizza/Image Source),
25 (rope bridge to school/Sijori Images/Barcroft India), 37 (fitness drink/Sava
Alexandru), 37 (boy with weights/Caiaimage/Tom Merton), 37 (applying lip
gloss/Ed Bock), 43 (food waste/Peter Dazeley), 46 (underwater restaurant/
George Steinmetz), 49 (teen slumber party/Sharie Kennedy), 55 (Brecon
Beacons/FLPA/Allen Lloyd), 59 (Oil Rocks/Reza), 64 (Sahara Desert/Peter
Adams), 70 (camping/Hero Images), 71 (kayaker/Thomas Barwick),
74 (computer/Ryan McVay), 76 (Jin Hai 1 homemade airplane/ChinaFotoPress),
81 (Sean O'Brien/Victor Decolongon), 84 (Tommy Sugiarton/Adek Berry/AFP),
84 (karate/JGI/Tom Grill/Blend Images), 85 (LeBron James/Jonathan Daniel),
85 (Jordan Spieth/Sam Greenwood), 88 (Ellie Simmonds/Tom Dulat), 89 (Mount
Fuji/Whitworth Images), 90 (Alana Nichols/Jamie McDonald), 94 (jump/Giulio
Bisio), 99 (dorm room/Blend Images/Hill Street Studios), 104 (boys/Ronnie
Kaufman), 104 (girl in bedroom/Hero Images), 104 (gaming/Hero Images),
108 (Royal Family/Mario Testino/Art Partner), 108 (Duchess of Cambridge/
Chris Jackson), 110 (woman with purse/JGI/Jamie Grill/Blend Images),
114 (illustration of Sir Isaac Newton/Dorling Kindersley), 115 (Cristiano
Ronaldo/Helios de la Rubia), 142 (playing guitar/Nick Dolding), 142 (family/
ONOKY-Eric Audras); Haute Route pp.91 (Christian Haettich); Mark Bassett
pp.42 (What the World Eats); Oxford University Press pp.6 (swimmer/l i g h t p
o e t), 6 (break-dancer/Comstock), 6 (basketball/Monkey Business Images),
8 (senior woman/Johner Images), 8 (senior woman/Olliver Eltinger), 8 (young
woman/Todd Fong Photography), 8 (teen girl/KidStock), 8 (teen boy/Mark
Bassett), 8 (happy girl/Goodluz), 8 (smiling girl/Glowimages), 16 (young girl/
Tetra Images), 16 (boy/Max Topchii), 26 (teens/Mark Bassett), 27 (judo/Score by
Aflo), 36 (taking selfie/Black Rock Digital), 39 (wallet/photovs), 39 (sunglasses/
Mark Mason), 39 (headphones/Alexander Demyanenko), 41 (bread/Joe Gough),
41 (lemons/Valentyn Volkov), 41 (potatoes/Deep OV), 41 (meat/Brian Kinney),
41 (salmon steak/Nataliia Pyzhova), 41 (pineapple/Mark Mason), 44 (cooking/
Mark Bassett), 45 (chips/D. Hurst), 45 (burger/rvlsoft), 45 (food/Elena
Schweitzer), 48 (waitress/Dex Image), 52 (gym/Lucky Business), 56 (tram/
Steppenwolf), 56 (students/Comstock), 62 (Humpback whale/Ocean), 62 (tiger/
Corbis/Digital Stock), 62 (brown bear/Imagebroker), 62 (eagle/Photodisc),
63 (wolf in snow/Corbis/Digital Stock), 63 (crocodile/Photodisc), 63 (tarantula/
Eleonora Ghioldi), 63 (squirrel monkey/l i g h t p o e t), 68 (komodo dragon/
Anna Kucherova), 71 (abseiling/Jakub Cejpek), 74 (headset/graficart.net),
74 (USB stik/Christophe Testi), 85 (EU flag/EyeWire), 111 (fish and chips/
numb), 111 (roast dinner/Joe Gough), 111 (strawberies/EMWestwood
Photography), 111 (chef/wavebreakmedia), 112 (Central Park/Corbis),
112 (Statue of Liberty/Matej Hudovernik), 112 (gallery/UpperCut), 122 (family/
Chris King); Press Association Images pp.21 (school voting/Bebeto Matthews/
AP Photo), 35 (clothes factory/Mario Lopez/AP), 81 (Meghan Trainor & Sean
O'Brien/John Angelillo/Landov), 87 (free climbing, El Capitan/Bay Area News
Group/ABACA), 90 (Alana Nichols/Jonathan Hayward/The Canadian Press); Rex
Shutterstock pp.20 (rehearsing/Paul Grover), 24 (mountain footpath/HAP/
Quirky China News), 46 (Zauo Izakaya restaurant/Sutton-Hibbert), 47 (dinner
in the sky/dinnerinthesky.com/Solent/Rex Features), 50 (Heston Blumenthal/
Eddie Mulholland), 90 (Mike Newman/Magic Car Pics), 101 (bedsit/
Photofusion), 115 (Jade Boho-Sayo/Paul Knight/JMP); Science Photo Library
p.69 (giant squid/Christian Darkin); Shutterstock pp.6 (horse riding/Ahturner),
7 (studying/Andresr), 8 (man/Nadino), 8 (smiling man/Liquorice Legs), 8 (young
woman/arek_malang), 8 (woman/BestPhotoStudio), 8 (paper tree/Deyan
Georgiev), 9 (family/wavebreakmedia), 9 (Jay-Z/FeatureFlash), 12 (arguing/
Monkey Business Images), 18 (alarm clock/Mindscape studio), 18 (family meal/
Monkey Business Images), 18 (blue abstract background/flowerstock), 27 (cat
faces/LindsayC), 28 (father & son/VGstockstudio), 30 (teenagers/William
Perugini), 31 (friends/Soloviova Liudmyla), 32 (concert/Nikola Spasenoski),
33 (fashion model/crystalfoto), 33 (young man/new vave), 33 (catwalk model/
FashionStock.com), 33 (model/crystalfoto), 34 (shopping/antoniodiaz),
37 (abstract orange background/Ozerina Anna), 38 (smiling teen/dgmata),
40 (Greek starter/KArl Allgaeuer), 40 (sandwich/Envyligh), 40 (salmon/Joerg
Beuge), 40 (fruit salad/Hannamariah), 40 (spaghetti/Olha K), 41 (spaghetti/
Ninell), 45 (cola/M. Unal Ozmen), 46 (abstract cutlery/Ramona Kaulitzki),
51 (soup/GoBOb), 51 (salad/Pinkyone), 51 (chicken curry/India Picture),
51 (Japanese pizza/napat uthaichai), 51 (baklava/gorkem demir), 51 (sorbet/
iprachenko), 51 (honey cake/Vlaislav Nosik), 52 (shopping centre/Ozgur
Guvenc), 52 (Natural History Museum/Bikeworldtravel), 54 (Venice Beach/
telesniuk), 56 (cruise ship/Ruth Peterkin), 58 (compass/James Weston), 59 (bus/
Marcio Jose Bastos Silva), 63 (various textures/Ursa Major), 63 (reef shark/
Shane Gross), 63 (lion paws/Claudia Otte), 64 (brown paper/Elena Kazanskaya),
65 (bear at campsite/Mat Hayward), 66 (safari/Matej Kastelic), 68 (okapi/
MarcISchauer), 68 (zebra skin/Kilroy79), 69 (gorilla/erwinf), 73 (metro train/
Koraysa), 73 (Ibirapuera Park/Filipe Frazao), 74 (laptop/You can more),
74 (router/Thailand Travel and Stock), 74 (tablet/tatajantra), 74 (charger/
Thailand Travel and Stock), 74 (printer/Bohbeh), 75 (laptop/ifong), 77 (stressed
woman/Syda Productions), 78 (filming with phone/antb), 79 (computer class/
wavebreakmedia), 81 (blue background/Toria), 82 (phone selling/Adam
Gregor), 83 (door security/lovemelovemypic), 85 (handball/Dziurek), 85
(Olympic flag/lazyllama), 93 (swimmers/Pavel1964), 93 (runner/Maridav),
96 (bedroom/m6photo), 96 (lounge/Iriana Shiyan), 96 (dining room/
ShortPhotos), 98 (Brandenburg gate/photo.ua), 107 (office space/
bikeriderlondon), 107 (family living room/Monkey Business Images),
109 (Merton College/Andrei Nekrassov), 110 (shopper/www.BillionPhotos.
com), 111 (sausages & mash/Joe Gough), 112 (Times Square/Marco Rubino),
113 (Grand Prismatic Spring/Lorcel), 113 (brown bear/Eduard Kyslynskyy),
113 (geyser, Yellowstone/Delpixel), 115 (man on laptop/g-stockstudio), 115 (girl
selfie/Yulia Mayorova), 116 (), 142 (camping/Gergely Zsolnai); The Hammock
Café pp.47 (restaurant interior); Warren Smith pp.11 (Radford family).

Commissioned Illustrations: Andy Parker pp.7, 25, 42, 44, 69, 97, 118 (emoticons
and jewellery), pp.121 (sports equipment); Kate Rochester/Pickled Ink pp.60;
Martin Sanders/Beehive Illustration pp.19, 63, 70; Ben Scruton/Meiklejohn
pp.20; Paul Williams/Sylvie Poggio Artists pp.77, 79.